Africa's Quest for Economic Development
Uganda's Experience

I0094481

Jossy R. Bibangambah

Fountain Publishers

Fountain Publishers Ltd
P. O. Box 488
Kampala, Uganda

ISBN 9970 02 248 2

Cataloguing-in-Publication Data

Bibangambah, Jossy R.
Africa's quest for economic development: the Uganda experience/Jossy R. Bibangambah, – Kampala: Fountain Publishers, 2001.
204p. 21 cm
Includes bibliographical references and index.
ISBN 9970-02-248-2.

1. Structural adjustment (Economic policy) – Uganda.
2. Agricultural price supports – Uganda. I. Title.
   338.1'096761-DC 21

Dedication

This book is dedicated to:

My father Eliphaz Bibangambah and my uncle Eric Katabarwa – Abagahe for investing in my education.

My mother Faith Bibangambah for her role in a noble partnership.

My friend Elidad Ruterane for unforgettable sympathy.

Professors H.V. Thimm and V.F. Amann for their contribution to my perseverance.

Professor Gideon Sherurah for being a real genius.

Ntare School and Makerere's Northcote Hall for times to remember.

Contents

List of Tables		iii
List of Figures		iv
Abbreviations		v
Acknowledgements		viii
Preface		ix

1. Introduction — 1
- Government intervention and control in African economies — 2
- A Synopsis of the markets versus state debate — 7

2. Government Intervention in Agricultural Commodity Markets — 10
- Agricultural marketing boards — 10
- How marketing boards deviate from the free market system — 19
- Marketing boards in Uganda — 20
- Evaluation of marketing boards — 21
- Agricultural marketing boards under the World Bank/IMF structural adjustment — 23
- The emergence and development of agricultural marketing co-operatives — 24
- International commodity agreements — 28
- Overall evaluation of the developmental effect or impact of government intervation in product markets — 37

3. Government Intervention in Agricultural Market Prices — 43
- Effects of inappropriate pricing policies — 47

4. Government Intervention in Factor Markets — 63
- Government intervention in credit markets — 75
- Government intervention in foreign exchange markets — 92
- Government control over land — 93
- The effects of a state dominated development strategy — 105

5. A Synthesis of the Economic Crisis in Uganda 1971-1990 — 111

6. Response to Poor Economic Performance — 118
- The early 1980s (1981 - 1984) — 119
- The transitional period (1985 - 1986) — 120

The recovery programmes 1987 (onwards)   121
The impact of the reform process   128

7. Responses to Medium and Long-term Challenges   **135**
Responses to food insecurity   136
Responses to agricultural backwardness   149
Responses to mass poverty   159
Constraints on rural financial services   175
Responses to environmental degradation   183
Responses to long-term challenges   185
Conclusion   185

8. Lessons for the Future   **187**

Bibliography   193
Index   201

List of Tables

Table 3.1:   Price Structure   45
Table 3.2:   Allocation of Robusta Coffee Earnings   47
Table 3.3:   Production of Export Crops   48
Table 3.4:   Average Producer Price for Coffee   50
Table 3.5:   Production of Main Crops   52
Table 3.6:   Agricultural Cost of Production   55
Table 3.7:   Average Processing Cost   56
Table 3:8:   Cost of production and prices of export crops   58
Table 3.9:   Cost of production and prices of food crops   58
Table 3.10:   Export Realisation and Producer Prices at the 1988
               Official Exchange Rate   59
Table 3.11:   Export parity price at different exchange rates   60
Table 3.12:   Export Realisation and Producer Prices at Exchange
               rate   60
Table 4.1:   Estimated value of inputs imported into Uganda,
               1981-1990   67
Table 4.2:   Value of Agricultural Inputs imported by various
               agencies   69
Table 4.3:   Relationship between sectoral GDP and commercial
               band credit   76
Table 4.4:   Aids Commitments to Uganda   83
Table 4.5:   Allocation of land in Buganda under the 1900 Agreement
               (in sq. miles)   93
Table 6.1:   Coffee sector participants   123
Table 6.2:   Export Market Share (%)   125
Table 6:3:   Major exporters of coffee in the wake of liberalisation   125
Table 6:4:   Key Indicators of Economic Trends in Uganda
               1987 and 1996   130
Table 6:5:   Problems of Production and Percentage or Respondents 131
Table 7:1:   Funds earmarked for the PEAP   171

List of Figures

Figure 2:1:   Agricultural marketing channels in Uganda before
              market liberation pre 1990   11
Figure 3:1:   Production of cotton and coffee   49
Figure 3:2:   Percentage of output in relation to 1971   53
Figure 4:1:   Agricultural inputs flows in Uganda before
              liberalisation   68
Figure 4:2:   Established government channels for distribution of
              agricultural inputs   70
Figure 4:3:   Main channels for agricultural inputs distribution under
              SWRARP   72
Figure 4:4:   Flow of agricultural finance   78
Figure 4:5:   Conceptual Model Linking Title and Tenure Security
              with Agricultural Performance   96
Figure 5:1:   Uganda economic crisis 1970-1983   114
Figure 6:1:   The post-liberalisation coffee marketing structure   124
Figure 6.2:   Food crops marketing channels   127
Figure 7:1:   Principal determinants of the Nutritional Status at the
              Household level   138
Figure 7:2:   Relations in the generation of poverty   159

Acronyms and Abbreviations

ACFODE	Action for Development
ADP	Agricultural Development Project
APC	Agricultural Policy Committee
ARP	Agricultural Rehabilitation Project
ASAC	Agricultural Sector Adjustment Credit
BAT	British American Tobacco
BCGA	British Cotton Growing Association
BOU	Bank of Uganda
CAAS	Co-operative Agriculture and Agribusiness Support
CBOs	Community Based Organisations
CCS	Cooperative Credit Schemes
CDRN	Community Development Resource Network
CMB	Coffee Marketing Board
CMBL	Coffee Marketing Board Limited
DANIDA	Danish International Development Agency
DAO	District Agricultural Officer
DCU	District Co-operative Union
DFD	Development Finance Department
DFID	Department for International Development (of UK)
EASh.	East African Shilling
ECPP	Emergency Cotton Production Programme
EDF	European Development Fund
EEC	European Economic Community
EPADU	Export Policy Analysis and Development Unit
EPRC	Economic Policy Research Centre
ERP	Economic Research Programme
FAO	Food and Agricultural Organisation
FIDA	International Federation of Women Lawyers
FINCA	Foundation for International Community Assistance
GDP	Gross Domestic Product
GFP	Group Farm Project
GOU	Government of Uganda
HIPC	Highly Indebted Poor Country
HYV	High Yield Variety Rice Seed
ICO	International Coffee Organisation
IDA	International Development Association
IFAD	International Fund for Agricultural Development
IGADD	Inter Governmental Authority on Drought and Development

IFPRI	International Food Policy Research
IMF	International Monetary Fund
ITCRAF	International Investment Term Credit Refinance Fund
LMB	Lint Marketing Board
MAAIF	Ministry of Agriculture, Animal Industry and Fisheries
MFED	Ministry of Finance and Economic Development
NARO	National Agricultural Research Organisation
NEWFIS	National Early Warning and Food Information System
NGO	Non-Governmental Organisation
NEAP	National Environmental Action Plan
NEMA	National Environmental Management Authority
NAWOU	National Association of Women Organisation in Uganda
NICU	The National Inputs Co-ordination Unit
NRM	National Resistance Movement
NTC	National Tobacco Corporation
NPART	Non Performing Assets
OPEC	Organisation of Petroleum Exporting Countries
PAP	Poverty Alleviation Project
PAPSCA	Programme for Alleviation of Poverty and the Social Cost of Adjustment
PCS	Primary Co-operative Society
PEAP	Poverty Eradication Action Plan
PMB	Produce Marketing Board
PRESTO	Private Enterprise Support Training Organisation
RFI	Rural Financial Institutions
RFS	Rural Farmers Scheme
RPE	Rehabilitation of Produce Enterprises
SAF	Structural Adjustment Facility
SCC	Swedish Co-operative Centre
SDR	Special Drawing Rights
SIDA	Swedish International Development Authority
SWRARP	South Western Regional Development Rehabilitation Project
UCA	Uganda Co-operative Alliance
UCB	Uganda Commercial Bank
UCCU	Uganda Co-operative Central Union
UCDA	Uganda Coffee Development Authority
UDB	Uganda Development Bank
UGAFODE	Uganda Agency for Development
UNBS	Uganda National Bureau of Standards

UNCTD	United Nations Conference on Trade and Development
UNDP	United Nations Development Programme
UNEX	Union Export Services
UPE	Universal Primary Education
UPPAP	Uganda Participatory Poverty Assessment Project
URDTP	Uganda Rural Development and Training Programme
USAID	United States Agency for International Development
UShs.	Uganda Shilling (Currency)
USP	Uganda Seed Project
UTA	Uganda Tea Authority
UWESO	Uganda Women's Effort to Save Orphans
VEDCO	Volunteer Efforts for Development Concerns

Acknowledgements

Like all authors, I owe a debt of appreciation and gratitude to several people. My former professors, my colleagues and my students have all had influence on my development and, directly or indirectly, on the writing of this book.

I owe a debt of gratitude to Professor H. Thimm of the University of Giessen, Professor A. Webber of the University of Kiel, both in Germany, Drs M. Rukandema and A. Odero-Ogwel of FAO, Dr J. Opio-Odongo, my colleague and friend since our high school days, for their friendship and encouragement in the 1980s when research and academic work seemed impossible under Uganda's abnormal economic circumstances. My perseverance is due to the proper initiation I received from Professors D.G.R. Belshaw and I. Livingstone now at the School of Development Studies, University of East Anglia, the late Prof. J. J. Oloya formerly head of the Department of Rural Economy (now Agricultural Economics), Makerere University, Dr E. Clayton, now retired from the University of London and Dr V. F. Amann presently with USAID.

I owe gratitude to my very able research assistants and secretaries. I particularly owe special recognition to Miria Tiberondwa (now Mrs Miria Antipa), Mrs Vicky Ameda and Ms Connie Atia-Echodu who word-processed several drafts of the manuscript.

In a more special way I am very grateful to Mr B. E. Jansson of the Federation of Swedish Farmers for his friendship and encouragement.

Finally, it would be unforgivable if I forgot the support of my late brother, Dr Andrew Kagina Bibangambah, my children and my wife, Jane.

Jossy R. Bibangambah
Kampala, Uganda,
December 2000

Preface

This book is a product of policy research. It focuses on two distinguishable periods in the development of Africa. The first period (1890 - 1990) - the era of state intervention or state control – was characterised by state action or institutions (i.e. rules and organisations) established to exercise state control. Besides state control, this period was also characterised by policy measures and institutions that were intended to reduce the impact of external changes (i.e. changes in the world economic environment) on the domestic economy. The best known of these measures were agricultural marketing boards, agricultural price-fixing, foreign exchange controls, imports control and international commodity agreements. These policy measures stressed the vulnerability of developing economies to external instabilities and dangers arising from unlimited openness to the world economy.

The second period (1991 todate) - the era of liberalisation and privatisation - is characterised by outward orientation, economic openness (both commercial and financial), free prices, and divestiture of public enterprises. This orientation is based on the philosophy that productivity, competitiveness and efficiency are the key determinants of economic success. In this era, emphasis has shifted from state ownership and control to the private sector as the engine of growth. It is thus an era whose economic policies are based on the philosophy that a dynamic economy must mainly rely on the private sector, on markets and on the price incentive system for most economic decisions and activities.

Work on the first part of this book, which focuses on market intervention, started in 1984 as part of a USAID Agricultural Policy Analysis Project (APAP) with ABT Associates as the principal contractor. I am very grateful to Professor Luther Tweeten of Ohio State University and Professor Dean F. Schreiner of Oklahoma State University, the principal consultants on the APAP, for their comments. The second part that focuses on economic liberalisation (of the free market school or structural adjustment of the IMF/World Bank) is a product of research undertaken in the 1990s to analyse Uganda's experience with economic reforms.

The book is organised in eight chapters. Chapter One briefly explores what prompted the adoption of the 'Control Model' or the statist approach in the first era (1890-1990) of the search for Africa's development. The history of agricultural market intervention and restrictive pricing policies in former British colonial Africa is associated with the development of export agriculture and the establishment of state monopolies in the form of statutory marketing organisations. The description of these policies and the review of international commodity agreements or schemes are the subject of Chapter Two.

The discussion on price intervention, which forms Chapter Three, takes us through the principles of pricing, pricing methodologies and the agricultural crisis that resulted from inappropriate pricing policies. Besides intervention in markets for agricultural products, i.e. industrial crops largely destined for export and food crops destined for both domestic consumption and for export, governments intervened in markets for factors of production by influencing the performance of these markets and hence the allocation of economic resources. This intervention took the form of procurement (by import) and distribution of farm inputs, or subsidisation of farm inputs such as seeds, fertilisers and tractor hire services. Through their control over property rights, African governments also influenced the land market. Governments also intervened in money and foreign exchange markets through interest rate and foreign exchange policies. This intervention in factor markets is the subject of Chapter Four.

Inappropriate policy interventions and other forms of economic mismanagement, especially in 1970s and 1980s, and externally induced problems in the years after 1970 led to an economic crisis that characterised Uganda's economic environment up-to 1990. An integrated or synthesised presentation of the causes of the crisis constitutes Chapter Five of the book.

Chapters Six and Seven are concerned with targeted priority challenges and new policy-orientations designed to propel Uganda's transition to social and material well-being. Chapter Eight is the conclusion, written in the form of lessons for the future.

1

Introduction

After the Second World War, the nations of the world appeared to be divided into three groups. One comprised the advanced industrial economies whose inhabitants enjoyed a relatively high level of per capita consumption (in terms of goods and services purchased). Another comprised still largely agricultural economies industrialising rapidly under socialist institutions. The last was a group of various colonial, neo-colonial and ex-colonial regimes with low levels of living characterised by low per capita incomes, low consumption levels and limited freedom to choose between variables that satisfy human wants.

In an effort to promote economic development - defined here as graduation from poverty and vulnerability to well-being and security – in a situation of international inequality caused by the failure of the evolution of human society to proceed at the same rate in different regions of the world and greatly compounded by the scientific, technological and industrial revolution that started in western Europe but failed to immediately and quickly spread in Latin America, Asia, Africa and the Caribbean governments in Africa, both governments in colonial and post-independence eras (1890-1990) chose to influence the process of historical change towards certain desired goals rather than complying with the principles of *laissez faire* and free trade. But instead of remaining promoters, post-independence governments changed into indisciplined controllers and prebendaries.

This book submits that the adopted approach – the 'Control Model' – to policy strategy and management led to policy-failures which, together with externally induced problems, are responsible for Africa's perpetual failure to establish and maintain capacity for sustainable development.

This book also holds that, just as in the case of Europe where a new era characterised by a scientific and technological revolution came into being after a crisis period, the so-called Dark Ages, policy strategists and managers have, in the last quarter of the twentieth century, begun launching new policy-orientations designed to propel Africa's transition to social and material well-being. This concurs with the prediction of a group of intellectuals that convened at Kericho, Kenya, in 1987, trying to foresee the Africa of 2057. In their analysis, the period between 1957 and 1980 was euphoric and optimistic; from 1980s to the end of this century is a time for trouble under the impositions of the international financial institutions; the subsequent period, until 2015, will be marked by readjustments on the political and economic front, that will

1

reinvigorate and motivate Africans; the following era will be one of consolidation, growth and prosperity[1].

The analyses, assessments and inferences presented in this book will benefit policymakers, researchers and students of development concerned with formulating, or reflecting on a future development agenda for Africa, with knowledge of what policy strategies have been tried before, and their effectiveness (or ineffectiveness) during the five centuries in which peoples in some other parts of the world have experienced unprecedented prosperity, while those of Africa continue to be victims of deprivation.

Government intervention and control in African economies

Control is an element of the management process and the final link in the functional chain of management - checking up on activities to ensure that they are going as planned or required by those in authority. At the sector or economy level, government control is synonymous not only with regulation but also with government planning.

Government controls originated from historical developments and views that have evolved regarding human behaviour and how society should, be organised. In Africa these developments include: first, colonisation by European powers, second, the colonial administrators' view of the nature of Africans, third, universal faith in the view that organisation is the most decisive factor in the success of any mission.

With respect to the first origin of state control and intervention, a reviewer of African development management has had this to say:

> State institutions in Africa were established by the colonial conquerors. With only minor modifications these represented extensions or replications of institutions found in the colonising country itself. The administrators of these institutions were all members of a guardian class: a group that upheld the social logic of the metropolitan system in the colonies.[2]

This is held to be so in spite of a long history of empires in West and Central Africa and kingdoms of eastern and southern Africa. Goran Hyden's explanation of this apparent paradox is that pre-colonial Africa was dominated by a peasant mode of production in which there was no imperative for the development of structural dependencies, as the productive and reproductive needs of the peasants could be met without the support of other classes. In turn, there was no imperative for development of public institutions through adherence to formal rules. The overall effect was that relations between those who ruled and those who derived their livelihood from the land – the overwhelming majority of the population – were not firmly rooted in the production system. This means that the African state, whether in the form of an imperial power or kingdom, did not have any effective control on society's productive activities whose organisation, we have said, is the key determinant of economic advancement.

The second origin of government controls relates to the expatriates' negative view of the African worker which was basically as negative as the one that Douglas McGregor[3] has labelled Theory X. Under this theory, the assumptions held are that:

i) Employees inherently dislike work and, whenever possible, will attempt to avoid it.

ii) Since employees dislike work, they must be coerced, controlled or threatened with punishment to achieve desired goals.

iii) Employees will shirk responsibilities and seek formal direction whenever possible.

iv) Most workers place security above all other factors associated with work, and will display little ambition.

Similarly, the African worker was held to be lazy, lacking the Protestant ethics of hard work, but adept at finding excuses for absenteeism. This negative view of the African worker was responsible for the backward - bending labour supply curve hypothesis claimed to represent labour market behaviour in colonial Africa. It stipulated that the labour supply curve was backward – bending for higher labour incomes, rather than being positively sloped throughout its length. It was maintained that in a pre-industrial society workers prefer leisure to additional wage incomes once they have achieved their customary real standards of living. In such a situation, an increase in the wage rate would call forth less and not more labour effort. This hypothesis was used to justify low wage levels for African workers and like McGregor's Theory X it emphasised the use of coercion.

The third origin of state intervention – also called regulation or economic planning or national economic management – is the incapability of the *laissez -faire* system to simultaneously ensure growth, stability, welfare and equity. This weakness has convinced many people to believe that the swiftest way to economic development is the organisation of the complete resources of a state, and that it is the responsibility of the state to find ways of increasing a country's productive powers as well as obtaining the necessary capital for investment.

When African countries gained formal independence; political leaders embraced intervention and regulatory programmes in order to satisfy popular expectations and ensure rapid economic development. Post-independence governments also saw the state as the only institution that could counter the entrenched powerful foreign private enterprises which dominated the post-colonial economies. As Goran Hyden has put it, post-independence African leaders had faith in the possibility of the rational control of the economic environment and planning. This faith was a driving force, not only in the drawing up of five-year national development plans, but also the publication of the Lagos plan of action for the economic development of Africa to the year 2000. It is this faith, therefore, that made the expansion of state responsibility and regulation in the service of developmentalist objectives the central element of African governmental politics during the first two decades of independence.

The concept and patterns of intervention

According to Argyris, to intervene is to enter into an ongoing system of relationship, to come between or among persons, groups or objects for the purpose of helping them.[4] He adds that the reasons for intervention may range from helping the clients make their own decisions about the kind of help they need to coercing clients to do what the intervener wishes them to do. It is the second part of Argyris' definition that is pertinent to government intervention in African economies.

Three main patterns of government intervention can be identified. The first pattern takes the form of macro-economic management. This is necessitated by the fact that economy-wide markets for labour, credit, and foreign exchange do not always adjust rapidly enough to balance supply and demand as conditions change. Characteristic macro-economic imbalances in modern economies require government interventions such as monetary management, fiscal policy, exchange rate adjustments, and incomes policies.

The second pattern of intervention is in the form of initiatives in the production process. These initiatives may take the form of state industrial and commercial enterprises, agricultural extension services, ancillary services such as c edit and input supply schemes managed by government or parastatal bodies, and agricultural research.

The third form of intervention relates to the involvement of government in the marketing and pricing of products. Government intervention in marketing takes the form of either facilitative or restrictive policies. A government may want to facilitate marketing by encouraging the development of markets for certain industries or products to stimulate the production of certain goods, or to promote particular producers[5], consumers or traders. Facilitative policies may also be employed in order to increase a country's share of the world market.

Governments intervene in various sectors of the economy partly in the hope of accelerating the rate of income growth. Investment programmes such as research and development of new technologies, and the provision of the infrastructure (roads, schools, health facilities) are examples of public sector interventions essential for increased economic activity. In general, these sectors are unlikely to attract private investment. Apart from the fact that private investors may be unable to capture the full benefit from investment in public goods, the capital requirements of such investment in terms of financial resources mobilisation tend to be prohibitive. For most of these investments, the public sector has the potential to recover the costs of intervention through user fees (as in the case of electricity and water) or through taxation.

One area that is particularly recommended for intervention is agricultural research.[6] The view that agricultural research, if left to market forces in accordance with the 'Induced innovation model'[7], will deliver a stream of innovations that respond to factor prices and endowments in an economically efficient manner, has been challenged. Markets of this type tend to be highly imperfect and specific interventions have to be made to ensure that at least some of the needs of the poorer groups are addressed by public sector research and extension.[8]

The correction of market failures (or imperfections) represents a second rationale for government intervention. If market imperfections are present, the prices of goods or services will not reflect their true scarcity values because the private sector is unable to develop the institutions necessary for efficient market functioning. Market power is a good example of a market failure: private sector suppliers (or consumers) are able to influence prices because their numbers are small (i.e. they are monopolists/oligopolists or monopsonists/oligopsonists) and because buyers (or sellers) have no other market outlets. These conditions often prevail in factor and commodity markets especially in Africa or for commodities from Africa. Rural credit markets are another example of market failure. They might be hampered by lack of information on alternative lending and borrowing opportunities in other regions or, by the absence of formal lending institutions that can mobilise savings. This has been the case in Uganda where, until recently, rural banks or formal credit institutions in rural areas did not exist.

Another type of market failure arises because of externalities – costs or benefits from production activities that are not fully reflected in market incentives as in the case of soil erosion, environmental pollution, overutilisation of land resources, etc. Under such circumstances, taxes, subsidies or regulatory controls are justified so that user costs (or returns) will reflect fully the effects of the externality. The value of an externality is often difficult to quantify and, in most cases, subjective judgements must be made as to whether externality effects are significant. These measurement problems, combined with the administrative costs of tax and subsidy policies, cause legislative regulations to be widespread policy responses to externalities.[9]

The third set of reasons for government intervention in developing countries is the promotion of non-efficiency objectives. Income distribution concerns are often at the top of the list of these objectives. Food is the most basic of necessities, and low food prices are considered an important determinant of the level of welfare of poor consumers. Food riots associated with food price increases are also common in developing countries. The countries of North and West Africa are particularly prone to these riots. Thus, behind food prices there are both welfare as well as political objectives. Staple food prices influence producer income levels and the manipulation of producer prices may generate a more equitable distribution of income in the economy. Income distribution policies will also reflect the influences of rent-seekers-agricultural suppliers, food consumers, and industrialists who view changes in agricultural prices as ways to increase profitability in production or to increase purchasing power in consumption. Government policies can provide market power to target groups through direct regulation of prices such as tariffs or subsidies on imports, or governments can benefit target groups through policies such as the designation of monopoly suppliers or buyers of particular agricultural products, or the allocation of import and export licenses.

Price stabilisation is a second common non-efficiency justification for intervention. Dependence on weather causes agricultural production to exhibit a relatively large degree of random variation. When combined with inelastic demand, supply variations can cause market prices to fluctuate substantially from one production cycle to the next. To avoid such fluctuations in domestic market prices, many governments establish a set of policies, ranging from trade controls to storage schemes, price fixing, and rationing.

Concern over the appropriate role of agriculture in the national economy provides a third set of non-efficiency rationales for government intervention. Food security, self-reliance and price stability of staple food supplies are commonly held objectives of agricultural policy. For food-importing countries, the attainment of these objectives requires intervention to increase domestic production. This intervention might involve changes in producer prices of outputs and inputs, investment in infrastructure for production or marketing activities or quantitative restrictions on the production of alternative crops. Agriculture also contributes to government revenue and the maintenance of fiscal balance in the public sector. As income taxes are a relatively unimportant source of revenue in most developing countries, and as the administrative costs of income monitoring and tax collection are often prohibitive, the agricultural sector, because of its large size, is usually forced to play a prominent role in tax revenues generation.

A Synopsis of the markets versus state debate

There is a consensus among economists, policy-makers and development institutions that one set of policy interventions - investment in education, health and sanitary facilities, and transport infrastructure - has had a broad positive impact on general economic development. There is also a consensus that government intervention is necessary with respect to protection of the environment, food security, land reform and political reform. But no consensus has emerged on the appropriate use of market and price controls, exchange rates, taxes and subsidies. The disagreement is between those who advocate government regulation and control and those who advocate a market-oriented economy with a market oriented trading system. The advocates of state control argue that the market doctrine, in its pure form, ignores the 'decisive role which must be played by the state in regulating the relationship between inherently antagonistic private actors', especially in Africa where the development of an effective private African trading class was long inhibited by the monopoly powers and economic dominance of expatriates. Those who advocate a market-oriented trading system argue that market controls inhibit or dampen markets' economic function of price discovery and the role of prices as signals to both producers and consumers.

Our summation of the debate is that there are three parallel views, namely the:

i)   pro-market view (or government failure view) which states that government intervention in markets creates a rigid centralised and bureaucratic system that has great difficulty operating businesses efficiently.

ii) pro-state view (or market failure view) which contends that continued poverty, income inequalities, food shortages, hunger, low productivity and lack of economic structural transformation are evidence that markets have failed to produce the desired economic growth in Africa. It also argues that the revolutions from above in Germany and Japan in 1800s and South Korea and Taiwan since 1945 entailed broad state involvement in industrialisation.

iii) the new view which calls for open competitive markets but with more distinct roles defined for the private sector and for the government. Under this view, it is argued that private enterprise and capitalist economic development require capable, not passive government - government that can 'fashion' a sanctuary within which the profit motive and price mechanism can work; that the state has both an enabling role as in the provision of infrastructure,[10] restraining or protective role as in curbing the excesses of private sector in such matters as pollution, in product safety, and a regulatory role as in prevention of unfair banking practices, anti-monopoly laws, and government-established quality standards. It is also argued that even Adam Smith who is regarded as the greatest champion of the laissez-faire economic policies did not hold that the best economic policy is always to have no policy at all. It is pointed out that Smith credited the public sector with critical roles for supporting commerce - that 'commerce and manufactures can seldom flourish long in any state which does not enjoy a regular administration of justice, in which people do not feel themselves secure in possession of their property, in which the faith of contracts is not supported by the law'. Here, Smith highlighted three public goods - basic law and order, the right to property and the enforcement of contracts[11]. It is further pointed out that even Milton Friedman a renowned member of the 'Chicago School' acknowledges that the state is needed to prevent coercion from within or without.[12] With respect to agriculture, D. Gale Johnson[13], an advocate of increased reliance on market forces, has conceded that government action is a needed component in this sector, particularly in order to provide public goods, correct for non-optimal markets, develop rural infrastructure, support agricultural research, provide market information and develop appropriate economic institutions.

In Africa the evolution of agricultural policies[13], especially marketing and pricing policies, represents the best manifestation of the use of state controls or interventionist policies. For this reason, our analysis from now onwards will focus on agriculture.

Notes

1.   C. Achebe et al (1990), *Beyond Hunger in Africa: Conventional Wisdom and a Vision for Africa in 2057*, Nairobi: Heinemann.
2.   G. Hyden, (1983), *No Shortcuts to Progress: African Development Planning in Perspective*, London: Heineman.
3.   D. McGregor, (1970), *The Human side of Enterprise*, New York: McGraw Hill.
4.   C. Argyris, (1970), *Intervention Theory and Method: A behavioral Science View*, Addison -Wesley Publishing Company.
5.   The infant industry argument is a very familiar case.
6.   S. Biggs and J. Farrington (1991), *Agricultural Research and the Rural Poor: A review of Social Science Analysis,* International Development Research Centre (IDRC).
7.   Y. Hayami and V.W. Ruttan (1972) 'Strategies for Agricultural Development', *Food Research Institute Studies*, No 11; Y. Hayami and V.W. Ruttan (1985), *Agricultural Development: An International Perspective,* (revised edition) Baltimore: Johns Hopkins University Press.

8.   S. Biggs, and J. Farrington, op.cit. See also, S.M. Essang, 'On the relevance of Growth Models to Rural Development', in: J.R. Bibangambah and Barri Wanji (eds) (1978), *Contemporary Problems and Issues in Rural Development*, Nkanga edition No.10 Makerere Institute of Social Research, Kampala.

9.   E.A. Monke and S.R. Pearson, (1989) *The Policy Analysis Matrix for Agricultural Development*, Cornell University Press.

10.   Infrastructure in its broadest sense includes: educational, technological, financial, physical, environmental and social infrastructure of the economy.

11.   P. Werhane, (1991), *Adam Smith and his Legacy for Modern Capitalism*, Oxford: University Press. See also A. Goldsmith (1995) 'The State, the Market and Economic Development: A second look at Adam Smith in Theory and Practice' *Development and Change, Vol. 26, No. 4.*

12.   M. Friedman and R. Friedman, (1980) *Free to Choose*, Harcourt Brace.

13.   Proceedings of the XX11 International Conference of Agricultural Economists, Harare, Zimbabwe 22-29 August 1994.

14.   Policy implies a purposeful course of action by any particular social actor in respect to certain issues in order to advance towards perceived objectives. Thus policies are formal or informal positions, actions, rules and regulations geared to affect the actions of determined groups of people in a particular way or geared to establish a determined pattern of behaviour in a target group.

2

Government Intervention in Agricultural Commodity Markets

Both during the colonial and the post-independence periods (prior to 1990), the state in Uganda, as elsewhere in Africa, intervened in agricultural marketing and pricing via monopolies granted to parastatal marketing boards; via export taxes; control of wholesale and retail prices to processors and consumers; via control of imports and exports through licensing; and regulated exchange rates. The justification for this intervention included the need to:

- create orderly marketing - a convenient description which is often a vehicle for an assortment of policy objectives - which generally aims at securing an adequate share of the market so as to facilitate the manipulation of prices (and hence production) as an element of national or regional planning, including in some cases the levying of agricultural produce cesses (or the payment of subsidies) and even the collection of loans;
- provide better incentives and increase farmer incomes;
- guarantee the supply of food and establish and maintain national or regional reserves;
- secure for the state a greater share of the profits which it is assumed are being made by private traders; and
- facilitate import-substitution, the promotion of exports or the achievement of added value through processing, agro-allied industry, etc.[1]

The marketing channels for Uganda's main agricultural products prior to the 1990s economic reforms are shown in Fig 2.1

Agricultural marketing boards

Agricultural marketing boards were public bodies set up by government, and were delegated exclusive legal powers to buy, handle, process and sell primary or processed agricultural products. Unlike direct government departments, they enjoyed considerable autonomy in management and procedure, and they included representatives of the producers and other stakeholders. They were distinguished from co-operatives chiefly by their public sector status and their power to enforce compliance with their rules.

10

Figure 2.1: **Agricultural marketing channels in Uganda before market liberalisation (Pre 1990)**

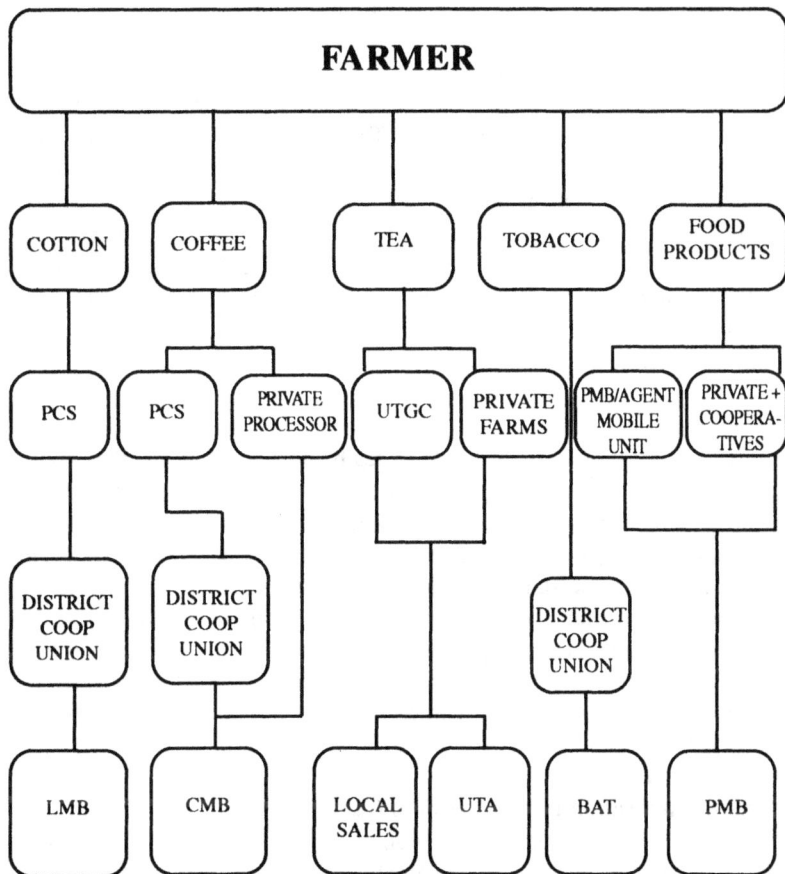

```
                        FARMER

   COTTON    COFFEE      TEA    TOBACCO     FOOD
                                          PRODUCTS

                PRIVATE          PRIVATE  PMB/AGENT  PRIVATE +
   PCS    PCS  PROCESSOR  UTGC    FARMS    MOBILE   COOPERA-
                                           UNIT      TIVES

  DISTRICT  DISTRICT              DISTRICT
   COOP      COOP                  COOP
   UNION     UNION                 UNION

   LMB      CMB      LOCAL   UTA    BAT      PMB
                     SALES
```

KEY:

BAT	=	British American Tobacco (Private monopsony)
CMB	=	Coffee Marketing Board
LMB	=	Lint Marketing Board
PCS	=	Primary Co-operative Society
PMB	=	Produce Marketing Board
UTA	=	Uganda Tea Authority
UTGC	=	Uganda Tea Growers Cooperation

In an FAO handbook[2], J.C. Abbot categorised marketing boards into six common types showing progressively greater responsibility, administrative requirements, marketing skills and application of capital:

a) Advisory and promotion board

The main duties of this type of board were to carry out market research and sales promotion for specific commodities. This might include pilot programmes to develop new uses and outlets for the commodity. Such a board advised on product varieties, packing methods and grade standards. It could conduct quality analyses and arbitrate in disputes. The board does not own marketing installations or equipment, nor does it engage in trade. It does not maintain any direct control over volume of sales or prices. The existing pattern of marketing enterprises and channels remain unchanged. Its legal powers are usually confined to a levy on sales to finance the board's operations.

b) Regulatory board

Examples of this type were the sisal and tea boards in Kenya and the export control offices in certain francophone African countries. They developed and applied uniform quality standards and packing procedures for export produce. Enforcement was by licensing and inspection, either by the board or by other government agencies working in collaboration with the board. Some regulatory boards also set up laboratories for quality analyses. They may provide installations for grading, storage, packing and processing as well as sales. They may also operate facilities such as central auction markets. The existing marketing structure remains but can be modified by the board's regulatory policy. It may become obligatory to use the facilities provided by the board.

c) Price stabilisation boards (without trading)

These boards negotiated prices with large-scale processors, wholesale buyers and distributors, on behalf of a large number of producers and/or consumers. This has been the case for tea and dairy produce in Kenya and pyrethrum in Tanzania. Such boards may also guarantee prices for a given volume of output, any additional output being allowed to find its own market. Programmes associated with price guarantees are likely to involve the registration and inspection of individual producers and traders, as well as the supplementation of prices obtained for specific quantities sold. The programmes are most easily applied where the producers concerned are specialised and relatively few in number. The existing marketing structure continues, with a tendency to crystallise if the sales quotas are allocated to individual traders and processors on the basis of the volume they have handled in previous years.

d) Price stabilisation boards (by trading alongside other enterprises)

Boards for this purpose had their own storage and marketing installations. They had the financial means to buy, and hold in store, substantial stocks. Usually they operated in competition with pre-existing marketing enterprises. They would buy from farmers through licensed agents or field stations opened by the board and then sell to existing wholesalers and retailers, sometimes with special measures to control retail prices, e.g. 'fair price' shops. A monopoly of imports and/or exports was needed. Judicious buying, storing and selling by an official body was expected to reduce seasonal price extremes and provide a floor price to farmers. Most Asian, Latin American and African countries, where the basic food was a seasonal grain, set up a board, corporation or institute to stabilise supplies and prices.

e) Monopoly export marketing board

This board would be made sole buyer and seller of specified products which were primarily produced for export. Its operations would include selling produce to domestic enterprises for processing into products for export. Independent firms formerly engaged in the export trade were replaced by the board, in principle. They might, however, continue as agents for the board in domestic buying, processing and overseas selling. Domestic purchases would also be made through co-operatives and stations operated directly by the board. Export sales were made locally by the board or through selling agents on major international markets. The board might own or hire marketing installations and processing facilities. Its price stabilisation policy was normally based on fixed producer prices backed by reserve funds. This type of board was originally developed in anglophone West African countries. It was subsequently used widely in African countries, mainly in order to gain greater control over sources of foreign exchange and government revenue. Examples are the boards that were responsible for exporting citrus in Morocco, groundnuts in Senegal, cocoa in Cameroon and, coffee and cotton in Uganda.

f) Board with monopoly of trading and processing in specified areas or market channels within a country

This type of organisation was used to implement a policy of uniform and stable prices throughout a country. Prices would be fixed for both producers and retailers. Independent wholesale buyers and processors would be employed as agents of the board or would be replaced by board depots. In some cases, monopolies in specified areas would be allowed on condition that the board provided marketing and processing facilities which were not being supplied by existing enterprises. An example of this is the Kenya Meat Commission.

H.L. Van der Laan and W.T.M Van Haaren[3] have used a classification different from that of FAO. They have distinguished, on the one hand, grain marketing boards (GMBs) trading in millet, maize, sorghum, teff, or rice, and on the other, raw materials marketing boards (RMBs) trading in cocoa, coffee, cotton, tea, groundnuts or palm kernels. However, the two authors recognise that in some countries (e.g. Madagascar and Malawi) some marketing boards have handled both grains and raw materials. Accordingly, therefore, in their listing of selected African marketing boards by broad categories and crops, they divided their sample into three groups: (i) grain marketing boards (ii) raw material marketing boards (iii) combinations of GMB and RMB as shown below:

Selected African marketing boards by board categories and crops, 1980-1989

Grain Marketing Boards:
Millet, sorghum and/or teff

Agricultural Marketing Corporation	AMC	Ethiopia
Office des Products Agricoles du Mali	OPAM	Mali
Office des Produits Vivriers du Niger	OPVN	Niger
Commissariat a la Securite Alimentaire	CSA	Senegal

Maize

National Cereals and Produce Board	NCPB	Kenya
National Milling Corporation	NMC	Tanzania
Produce Marketing Board	PMB	Uganda
National Agricultural Marketing Board	NAMBOARD	Zambia
Grain Marketing Board	GMB	Zimbabwe

Rice

Office du Niger	ON	Mali
Riz du Niger	RINI	Niger
Caisse de Perequation et de Stabilization des Prix	CPSP	Senegal

Miscellaneous

Nigerian Grains Board*-	–	Nigeria
Agricultural Development Corporation	ADC	Somalia

Raw Materials Marketing Boards:
Cocoa and/or coffee

Office National de Commercialisation des Produits de Base	ONCPB	Cameroon
Ethiopian Coffee Marketing Corporation	ECMC	Ethiopia
Ghana Cocoa Marketing Board	GCMB	Ghana
Caisse de Stabilization	CAISTAB	Ivory Coast
Nigeria Cocoa Board*	–	Nigeria
Coffee Marketing Board	CMB	Uganda

Cotton

Societe Cotonniere du Tchad	COTONTCHAD	Chad
Cotton Board of Kenya	CBK	Kenya
Compagnie Malienne pour le Development des Textiles	CMDT	Mali
Nigerian Cotton Board*	–	Nigeria
Tanzania Cotton Marketing Board	TCMB	Tanzania
Lint Marketing Board	LMB	Uganda

Tea

Kenya Tea Development Authority	KTDA	Kenya
Uganda Tea Growers Corporation	UTGC	Uganda

Groundnuts

Gambia Produce Marketing Board	GPMB	Gambia
Societe Nigeriene de Commercialisation de l'Arachide et du Niebe	SONARA	Niger
Nigerian Groundnut Board*	–	Nigeria
Office National de Cooperation et d'Assistance pour le Development	ONCAD	Senegal
Societe National de Commercialisation des Oleagineux du Senegal	SONACOS	Senegal

Palm produce

Nigerian Palm Produce Board*	–	Nigeria

Rubber

Nigerian Rubber Board*	–	Nigeria

GMBs + RMBs:

Societe d'Interet National des		
Produits Agricoles	SINPA	Madagascar
Tranombarotra Roso	ROSO	Madagascar
Societe Malgache de la Collecte		
et de la Distribution	SOMACODIS	Madagascar
Agricultural Development and		
Marketing Corporation	ADMARC	Malawi

* No longer in existence

Historically, the establishment of marketing boards - also called statutory marketing schemes or crop authorities - was associated with periods of crisis or emergency and, hence the tendency for some analysts to regard them as emergency measures to meet exceptional and temporary conditions. In Australia, United Kingdom, Canada and New Zealand they were introduced in the depression years of the 1920s and 1930s after the breakdown of voluntary attempts to maintain prices under the weight of excess supplies.

In developing countries they were introduced during World War II when normal marketing channels were disrupted. In 1942, for example, responsibility for the purchase and sale of all the cocoa, palm oil, and oil seed exportable surplus in the British West African territories was assigned to the West African Produce Control Board – the predecessor of the post-independence Nigerian and Ghana marketing boards – as a wartime arrangement for the orderly marketing of West African produce and the protection of supplies of industrial raw materials to the UK.

Similarly, the marketing boards in East Africa (i.e. Uganda, Kenya, and Tanganyika) had their origin in the British Emergency Powers (Defence) Act of 1940 which was extended to the colonies in the form of defence regulations empowering the colonial governments to intervene in the organisation and management of agricultural exports marketing. Accordingly, each colonial government had to become an active participant in export trade using statutory centralised marketing organisation and, henceforth, private firms handling export trade became agents of statutory organisations and monopoly sellers to the British government. In the case of Uganda, the 1942 Defence (Control of Coffee) Regulations made the Director of Agriculture also the Controller of Coffee assisted by the Coffee Control Committee (appointed by him). The regulations stipulated that no person, other than the controller, was empowered to fix prices to producers at buying posts, prices for unprocessed coffee delivered to any licensed curing works and prices f.o.b. Uganda or Mombasa for processed coffee. He could also make forward sale or sell coffee in bulk for government or military orders and call for returns of coffee stocks. For cotton, there was a bulk purchase agreement between Uganda and Britain which committed the British Ministry of Supply to purchase over 50 percent (instead of the pre-war 2.6 per cent) of Uganda cotton.

The food crop marketing boards in East and Central Africa were partly inspired by the British colonial administration's desire to give preferential price treatment to large-scale European farmers, and partly by a belief that controlled marketing would somehow ensure a steady flow of basic foodstuffs while, at the same time, protecting Africans from exploitation by unscrupulous Asian middlemen.

Besides their historical origin, which most analysts maintain was to enable the United Kingdom to secure cheap bulk supplies of food and raw materials as part of the British war effort, three explanations have been offered for the establishment of marketing boards in Africa. One is that of price and income stabilisation. For instance, it has been argued, in connection with Uganda, that inflationary pressures generated by shortages of consumer goods during and immediately after World War II had to be checked by some form of price control, and that there was need to operate price assistance funds to reduce the price uncertainty facing peasant producers with low risk-bearing capacity. Concern about variability or instability of earnings or incomes as well as inflationary consumer prices is a valid one. The second explanation is that there was need to bring 'order and efficiency into the marketing process by regulating quality, packing standards, market procedures and setting up the necessary marketing and processing facilities'. In a pre-capitalist economy where previously there had been no imperative to adhere to formal marketing procedures, an institution to promote the satisfaction of marketing utilities of form, time, and place was necessary. The third explanation is exploitation by middlemen. It has been argued that export trade at that time was controlled by a few large firms who could easily exert oligopolistic or oligopsonistic influence on the economy. It is accepted that the state has a restraining or protective role against the excesses of the private sector.

Whatever merits of these reasons or explanations, they did not constitute the sole or even main responsibility of the boards. It is observed that African marketing boards, unlike the American price support programmes, became tax collection agencies for the government and important means of accumulating funds to finance general development.

Fundamentally, however, marketing boards were not a mere emergency arrangement. Nor did they necessarily aim at safeguarding the standard of living of farmers (especially under a governance style characterised by prebendalism). They represented a deliberate state intention to participate in and control the marketing sector of the economy. They were one of the instruments of the ideology behind state monopolies. The fact that all of them owed their existence to some enabling legislation that gave authority to the marketing board to impose controls or regulations on the marketing of the prescribed commodity, clearly supports this point.

The critics (neoclassical economists) of agricultural marketing boards especially of the raw material export marketing type have argued that while those funds were worthwhile or useful, the resources accumulated in stabilization funds were never invested in African agriculture or in projects immediately connected with the growers' direct needs. Instead, the funds were used on general government projects such as the industrial infrastructure to attract foreign capitalists. They thus constituted another form of taxation.[4] It is therefore reasonable to argue that the extractive policies of the marketing boards had the following effects on the agricultural sector.

Firstly, they hindered the sector to invest and expand its productive capacity and, hence, they perpetuated rural poverty. Secondly, through influencing existing as well as potential producers, they discouraged potential expansion in production. Thirdly, they contributed to structural distortions in African economies, especially the growth of the informal sector. Fourthly, they kept the peasant farmers' purchasing power or capacity low and, hence, they facilitated increased inequality in income distribution. It is emphasised that under a system of price incentives, the farmers might have increased their output more than they did under administered prices. The point was stressed as early as 1954 by Prof. Peter Bauer that, '... the prolonged payment of producer prices far below commercial values cannot fail to affect the ability and incentive to expand production, and maintain, improve and extend production'.[5]

Among the African academics concerned with economic development policy, the main proponents of state control were what Robert Bates called 'class analytic theorists'. They hold that the 'pro-market position of neoclassical economics' (with its emphasis on market efficiency) 'evades problems of power and domination and of the structural link between the state and markets ... and of the prevalence of exploitative relations in agriculture ...'[6]

With respect to marketing boards, the controversy between the pro-market view and the 'structuralist view' is a controversy not only about the 'real purpose' of the marketing boards but also about the rationale for state intervention. It, therefore, has something to do with contrasting an economistic approach with a political economy approach that takes into account political organisation and survival.[7] Since the controversy between the pro-market and the structuralist views is central to the agricultural policy debate, their comparative features are summarised below for purposes of clarification.

General features of the structuralist versus the neoclassical view in explaining the development crisis in developing countries

Structuralist view	Pro-market view
* class-based distribution of income-	marginal-productivity-based distribution.
* oligopolistic markets.	free markets.
* unequal exchange-based world trade system.	comparative advantage and competition-based world trade system.
* low supply elasticities incentives.	immediate responses to price.
* poor performance due to external dominance.	poor performance due to internal weakness.
* limited involvement in world trade due to structural rigidities.	limited involvement in world trade due to subsistence production

How marketing boards deviate from the free market system

Marketing channels dominated by marketing boards usually exhibit two deviations from a free market system i.e. monopoly and price interventions. A marketing board's monopoly is statutory and enforceable by the state to varying degrees. Thus the monopolies in exports of raw materials were real ones, while those of grain marketing were rather fictitious, or at best partial, because a parallel market for grain tended to develop, in which private enterprise competed with the GMB. The case of the Produce Marketing Board in Uganda is a good example. Private traders always traded along the PMB even in those crops gazetted as 'controlled'.

Secondly, the monopolies have been double monopolies in the sense that they combined a buying and a selling monopoly. In Uganda, processed coffee could only be bought by the Coffee Marketing Board, which was also the only agency that could export or sell abroad. It would, therefore, be impossible to abolish the buying monopoly without also ending the selling monopoly.

Thirdly, marketing board monopoly is not to be equated with the exclusion of private enterprise as many marketing boards have interacted or even co-operated with private enterprise (including agricultural co-operatives) in the marketing channel, on the basis of licenses or contracts. A common arrangement was that co-operatives and licensed buying agents acted as auxiliaries of the marketing board with regard to buying, storing, processing and transporting.

Price intervention was usually by means of 'administered producer prices'. A "producer price system" was, in theory, set up to protect producers against price and income fluctuations. For exports the producer price system was against fluctuations of the world market price. It was a cornerstone of RMB operations. Conversely, the RMB was also indispensable for the producer price system because the marketing board acted as a buyer of last resort, thus guaranteeing an outlet to the farmers for sales at the official price.

In the marketing channel of a GMB there was price intervention at two stages: the producer price regulated the collection stage, and the consumer price did the same for the distribution stage. The former was supposed to assist the producers, while the latter protected the consumers. Having obligations towards producers as well as consumers – often conflicting obligations - made the task of a GMB difficult.

Marketing boards in Uganda

From the perspective of marketing systems, between 1948 and 1990 agricultural marketing was controlled by government through statutory marketing schemes.[8] The first marketing boards to be established in Uganda were the Lint Marketing Board (LMB), and the Coffee Marketing Board (CMB) which were respectively responsible for marketing cotton and coffee exports. Although these two boards were given virtual monopoly in marketing those crops, the private sector (especially the co-operatives) was not excluded from all sections of the marketing chain. Ugandan producers having created co-operative groups, not only challenged the monopoly enjoyed by the two boards but also demanded to participate in the marketing of these crops. By 1968, co-operatives had acquired a monopoly power over the domestic market for cotton and a considerable share of the market for coffee.

The two boards, in collaboration with co-operatives, controlled the whole institution of agricultural marketing until 1990. The commanding place of these boards and the co-operatives over the marketing system was favoured by the central government, because they provided a convenient and workable institutional mechanism for the collection of agricultural revenue. The institutional arrangement was endorsed by international financing and donor agencies which believed that boards and co-operatives were easier to work with because they were controllable.

The LMB and CMB were followed by the Uganda Tea Growers Corporation with a monopoly on the collection and processing of greenleaf tea of smallholder farmers and small estates. The Uganda Tea Authority had a monopoly for tea exports, and the Dairy Corporation for milk processing.

In the same period, the government established the Produce Marketing Board (PMB) in 1968 to promote the commercialisation of the food sector by providing ready market channels for food produce, and to regulate the marketing of food crops. Its purposes were officially stated as : 'stabilizing the prices of food crops by buying when prices are low, storing the surplus and releasing stock when the prices are high'. Furthermore, the PMB was exclusively responsible for the procurement and export of maize, beans, simsim, soyabeans and groundnuts. It was also expected to maintain a food reserve. Although it was granted monopsony power in the 1970s, it did not take advantage of this privilege. It never took an active part in the market place either as a buyer or as a seller. It tended to buy what was on offer and sell in response to requests, from various government institutions. Besides the lack of facilities to buy effectively in rural areas, it also lacked competitive power. Being state controlled, it could only offer prices determined by the official exchange rate in contrast to those of its competitors which were determined by the domestic prices or the official exchange rate.

Generally, the presence of the PMB in the market place did not present a strong disruptive force to orderly and efficient marketing. This is in strong contrast to the marketing roles of CMB and LMB. Despite the existence of the PMB in the era of statutory marketing boards, the food crops marketing system appeared to have performed well. The imperfections and deficiencies in the market were primarily the result of poor roads, inadequate lorries to transport produce, and occasional government interference with the movement of produce within and across districts.

Evaluation of marketing boards

Marketing boards have been a major instrument of state intervention in agricultural commodity markets. Supporters of state intervention base their arguments on market imperfections or market failures and underdeveloped institutions such as inadequate information about markets and products, while critics point to distortions of incentives for growth, innovation and structural change.

The supporters of marketing boards emphasise the advantages that marketing boards have over direct government services, and local private enterprises, in obtaining working capital for investment in marketing facilities and assisting in the stabilisation of supplies and prices. With respect to Africa, in the 1940s and 1950s, marketing boards were necessary in order to:

- operate price assistance funds to reduce the price uncertainty facing peasant producers with low risk-bearing capacity (by having a stabilisation fund the governments protected the producers against the risk of a low world market price);
- operate some form of price control to check inflationary pressures generated by shortages of consumer goods during and immediately after World War II;
- check the monopolistic or monopsonistic influence that was likely to result from the situation whereby export trade, at the time, was controlled by a few large foreign firms;
- serve as the most viable means of taxing the agricultural surplus in subsistence economies given the lack of administrative capacity to impose other taxes;
- serve as a reliable channel through which financial arrangement for agricultural marketing operations could be made;
- act as keepers of food security reserve stock to protect consumers;[9]
- facilitate the maintenance or raising of export quality;[10] and
- serve as a major instrument in the policy of governments to keep the cost of living low.[11]

The use of marketing boards to minimise variability, instability and vulnerability during the transition from a subsistence to a market economy was inevitable. What is objectionable about marketing boards are the usual cost inefficiencies (caused by overstaffing, lack of cost consciousness and prebendalism) in government parastatals or the public sector. Marketing boards also became heavily associated with taxation and other restrictionist policies that governments imposed on agriculture. As we have already stated above, these policies have had adverse effects on the agricultural/rural sector. A more detailed analysis of the effects of taxation and restrictionist policies will be presented in Chapter Three.

Agricultural marketing boards under the World Bank/IMF structural adjustment

Agricultural marketing boards and international commodity agreements are components of the 1950-1970 development strategy, which suggested that countries could benefit from policies that would reduce the impact of external changes on the domestic economy, either by delaying them - thus providing more time for producers' response - or by counteracting them. Thus, they were a component of an earlier version of 'adjustment policies' in the form of government actions (or intervention) to mediate external changes.

During the 1980s, 'adjustment' came to refer to a particular way of responding to external changes, namely by facilitating their transmission through the domestic economy. Thus, adjustment came to imply trade liberalisation and diminishing government intervention in markets. According to this new approach, policy changes are necessary not just to accommodate external shocks but also to reform ill-advised or inappropriate policy measures of the past.

The possible fates likely to befall marketing boards under structural adjustment (or the liberalisation approach to adjustment) have included the following:

i)   liquidation.
ii) reduction to a monitoring or regulatory institution.
iii) restructuring in various forms and degrees.
iv) no change imposed.
v)   rehabilitation.

Any of the five solutions listed above may be the final outcome of structural adjustment policies, but some may also be transient.

The effect of structural adjustment on marketing boards in Uganda has, so far, taken the forms indicated below:

Marketing board	Action taken	
CMB	i)	Organisation restructured.
	ii)	Buying and selling monopoly abolished.
	iii)	Producer price system initially maintained but later abandoned.
	iv)	Board assets undergoing divestiture.
LMB	i)	Initially rehabilitated.
	ii)	Buying and selling monopoly abolished.
	iii)	Producer price system initially maintained but later abandoned.
	iv)	Now undergoing divestiture.
UTGC	i)	Organisation is temporarily retained without change.
	ii)	Producer price system maintained.

PMB	i)	Board organisation restructured.
	ii)	Board's export monopoly abolished
	iii)	Under receivership by Ministry of Justice.

As the first part of this book was intended to focus on the pre-reform period and related policies, programmes and activities, details of the post-reform agricultural marketing structures will be presented in Chapters Six and Seven.

What needs to be stated here by way of concluding the discussion is that, with structural adjustment, marketing boards are no longer apex organisations in the marketing system, and no longer have the monopoly of exporting produce. The overall effect has been the change from single-channelled marketing for the principal export crops to a multiple-channelled marketing system with direct vertical intergration of actors involved in the processing and export marketing levels. The liberalisation of markets has freed both producer and consumer prices.

The emergence and development of agricultural marketing co-operatives

A co-operative is, by definition, an association of persons who voluntarily join together to achieve common social, economic and educational aims through the formation of a democratically controlled business organisation. Devised at Rochdale, Britain, in 1844 and modified by the International Co-operative Alliance, the main principles of co-operatives are:

i)   voluntary and open membership;
ii) distribution of dividends to members;
iii) limited interest on share capital;
iv) education of members;
v)   co-operation among co-operators; and
vi) democratic control.

Historically, there have been two main modes of co-operatives. One mode called agricultural producer cooperatives takes the form of farm enterprises in which the labour of a group of farm households is pooled under an output or net revenue-sharing arrangement. This is to say that members engage in agricultural production on a joint basis. Under this arrangement, no employment relationship exists among the co-operators and decision making is in principle participatory as opposed to hierarchial or authority-based. This mode of co-operatives is represented by what used to be collective farms in the former Soviet Union and Eastern Europe, and similar institutions in Vietnam, North Korea, and the People's Republic of China. Uganda's group farms of the 1960s and Tanzania's *Ujamaa* villages of the 1960s to 1980s were of this mode of agricultural producer co-operatives. Producer co-operatives that conform to our definition can be called into question on the grounds that they were created and controlled by the state and party machineries, which left little latitude for inter-decision-making, and which sometimes employed coercion as an internal control device.

The other mode of co-operatives is the marketing and input-supply co-operatives whose members do not engage in agricultural production as such on a joint basis. Africa's main co-operatives (dealing mostly in agricultural raw material exports) and input supply co-operatives (including credit co-operatives) are of this mode.

In his book, *On Being Human*, Ashley Montague says:

> Man is born for co-operation, not for competition or conflict. This is a basic discovery of modern science. It confirms a discovery made two thousand years ago by one Jesus of Nazareth. In a word: it is the principle of love which embraces all mankind. It is the principle of humanity, of one world, one brotherhood of peoples.[12]

It is possible that co-operative philosophy of today follows Montague's lead and that co-operative business in Africa, like everywhere else in the world, represents the institutionalisation of the principle and impulse of mutual aid in the day-to-day economic activities of man. However, it is important to recognise that pioneering co-operative business organisations in Africa, particularly in Uganda, were not simply born out 'of love that embraces all mankind'. They were a response to a challenge. The challenge was that of exploitation of man by man.[13]

The challenge was in form of an unequal division of labour, oligopolistic or oligopsonistic control by alien groups, unequitable distribution of benefits from development of export agriculture, and inequitable distribution of benefits accruing from the value added along the marketing chain.[14]

It should be noted that the unequal division of labour – the challenge that gave birth to cooperatives – was still in existence until September 1990, though not along racial or colour lines. The peasants were still the main producers of export crops, and they were still restricted to primary production and primary marketing as it was in the beginning. It was monopolistic or monopsonistic control over the pricing and marketing of export crops, except that the control was no longer alien. The alien oligopolistic or oligosponistic firms had been replaced with monopolistic or monopsonistic parastatal organisations and exploitation had continued and even intensified.

On achieving independence in 1962, government was pressurised to grant the control of the marketing of agricultural crops to the co-operative movement. In response, the government set up a commission of inquiry into the operations of the coffee and cotton industries in Uganda. The commission recommended free and fair competition between the private sector and the co-operative movement. The government, however, rejected the recommendations and instead gave marketing boards full monopoly powers to market and export agricultural crops. The co-operative movement was entrusted with the internal cotton and coffee procurement and processing. Thus, although the majority of co-operatives were involved in agricultural marketing, they were merely collection agents. The real job of marketing was performed by state monopolies - the state marketing organisations.

We have stressed that in Uganda the birth of co-operatives was a popular initiative and, therefore, an endogenous process rather than a creation of government but, once they were in existence, government initially promoted the ongoing system. However, subsequently, it became a controller (through statutes, registrars/commissioners and ministries of co-operatives) thus transforming co-operatives from autonomous and democratic enterprises into economic and social policy instruments[15]. Once co-operatives were transformed into instruments of government policy, the state did not conform to the subsidiarity principle i.e. limit itself to giving a necessary boost if and where necessary. On the contrary, it intervened massively in the management of co-operatives and, by so doing, perverted the basic co-operative idea which stresses self-help, self-determination and self-responsibility. Co-operative self-help means that people in the same or similar situation join forces, raise the necessary resources for joint co-operative undertakings and they are prepared to give mutual support. This is done to overcome the disadvantages that would arise from competition between individual members. Self-determination means that the members organise the internal conditions of their co-operative society and thereby protect it from external influences. This means that internally a co-operative is not subject to any third party's order (e.g. the government or other authorities). The members decide on organs of their co-operative society (general meeting, board of directors) which have executive function as well as on the economic activities and priorities of their enterprise. The one man, one vote principle holds true here. Self-responsibility means that the members are responsible for the foundation and the up-keep of the co-operative enterprise and (with limited liability) answerable to third parties.

When government shifted from promoting to controlling cooperatives, ownership was separated from control. As a result, the co-operative movement was co-opted into the political power play in the post-independence period. Accordingly, the interests of the rank and file member growers were subordinated to those of the political class. The up-shot of this development was that co-operatives lost the capacity to promote the original goals of the members and failed to live to the above-mentioned principles of the co-operative movement. This failure of the Ugandan co-operatives has been vividly described in the following words:

> Most cannot raise crop finance and rely on parastatals or government programmes. Some have large outstanding debts, especially on ginnery and cotton rehabilitation... But there is now no incentive for district unions to change. Major changes such as staff reduction, selling assets, closing ginneries, etc would create concern in political circles, probably exceeding the ability of boards and management to resist. Alternative offers would likely be made to have skills and motivation to make needed changes. Changes will be precipitated by an outside event, such as competition by a private company competitor or foreclosure by a creditor[16].

For the co-operatives, the economic reforms of the 1980s and 1990s (structural adjustment) have brought about three important changes.

i) Emphasis on decontrol of markets and prices reinforced the co-operatives' own efforts to win autonomy from government. Once a degree of autonomy was achieved, co-operatives could not again expect to enjoy protective monopoly as was the case in cotton ginning in the immediate post-independence years.

ii) Entry into export marketing in 1990 helped to break the state monopoly in exporting coffee and cotton - thus enabling producers to have direct access to the world market.

iii) Co-operatives involved in domestic and export marketing have been compelled to rethink their strategies (i.e. restructure or adjust) if they have to be competitive and remain in the market.[17] They have been compelled to learn to be cost-driven and hence reduce their marketing costs. They have also been compelled to be market-driven and hence learn to satisfy marketing utilities of form, place and time. Finally, they have been compelled to learn that if a co-operative cannot survive as a business, then its effectiveness in serving members interests is endangered.

International commodity agreements

Intervention in commodity markets through the negotiation of International Commodity Agreements (ICAs) became one of the main instruments of the so-called New International Economic Order (NIEO) of the 1970s, but had earlier come into existence in response to the experiences of the 1930s. The ICAs were basically 'export arrangements' negotiated by countries producing primary exports in an attempt to stabilise export prices (i.e. reduce period to period export price variation) and earnings of the producing countries.[18]

Four categories of primary exports that have been subject of commodity agreements (or international markets intervention) are:

a)   temperate zone foodstuffs (wheat and other cereals, dairy products, meat etc).

b)   agricultural raw materials (cotton, wool, natural rubber, timber etc;

c)   metals and other minerals; and

d)   tropical foods and beverages.

In the post-war period, commodity market control under the auspices of the United Nations started in 1954 with the International Sugar Agreement (ISA) and the International Tin Agreement (ITA). Subsequent agreements were the International Coffee Agreement (ICoA, 1962), the International Cocoa Agreement (ICCA, 1972) and the International Rubber Agreement (INRA, 1980). The main concern was the possibility of very low prices, as experienced in the 1930s, attributable to what was called 'a burdensome surplus of supply over demand'.[19] The principal instrument envisaged in the sugar and tin agreements was supply management administered through export quotas, although the ITA also employed a small buffer stock.

The International Coffee Agreement was modelled on the ISA and operated entirely through supply control by means of export quotas. However, it was motivated less by any concern for price stabilisation than by the hope that it might raise prices and hence the export revenues of the coffee producers. It was a price-supporting agreement. The concern of primary producers in developing countries was the price level rather than the variability or 'predictability in the real export earnings' as expressed in UNCTAD I, 1964.

The following instruments or arrangements have been tried:

Type of arrangement or instrument	Commodity
Agreements with buffer stocks	tin
	cocoa
	sugar
	rubber
	wheat
Pure quota agreements	coffee
Producer-consumer forums[20]	jute
	sisal
	cotton
	meat
	manganese ores
	copper
'Other measures' [21]	tropical timber
No arrangement	vegetable oils and fats
	bauxite
	iron ore
	phosphates

Source: Detlef Radke, in *Economics,* Vol. 19, 1979.

The International Coffee Agreement (ICoA) initially came into force, for a five-year period, on 1 October 1963. It is the only one of the five commodity control agreements successfully negotiated in the post-war period in which participating countries have played the role of almost total exporters or importers. It is also the only one in which the participating developed countries have been solely in a position of importers and consumers. In the case of the other four agreements, – the cocoa, wheat, sugar and tin, – the developed countries have or had important positions as either producers or providers of financial services.

The erratic production levels that have characterised the industry since its earliest days, and the dependence of many poor countries on coffee as a source of foreign exchange and therefore development funds, made it imperative for the governments of these countries to attempt to influence or even control world coffee prices. As early as 1906, state governments in Brazil had started buying stocks to prevent the price declines that exceptionally good crops would have precipitated. This function was assumed by the central government in

Brazil in 1921. Between 1921 and 1944, Brazil burned a total of 78 million bags of coffee[22] in an apparent attempt to function as the dominant country in a price-leadership contest. However, as Brazil was reducing supply, other countries in Central America and Africa were expanding production. The net result was that prices fluctuated as widely as ever, and Brazil suffered a progressive decline in her share of the market. It became increasingly obvious that supply control could only be achieved through international cooperation. Prior to 1961, the cooperation of the importing countries seemed impossible to achieve for while Britain, France, Italy and the Netherlands were in favour, the United States (which consumes some 50 per cent of world exports) was not. This situation changed dramatically in March 1961 when President Kennedy announced the formation of 'Alliance for Progress', and detailed a 10-point plan for underdeveloped areas. Point five in this plan ran as follows:

> ... The United States is ready to cooperate in serious, case by case examination of commodity market problems. Frequently violent changes in commodity prices seriously injure the economies of many Latin nations ... draining their resources and stultifying growth. Together we must find practical methods of bringing an end to this pattern.[23]

Armed with this commitment from the world's largest consumer, on 22 May 1962 the UN Secretary General formally invited all member states to participate in a conference to ... 'discuss measures to meet the special difficulties which exist or are expected to arise concerning coffee'.[24] The first five-year agreement went into effect on 1 October 1963. A second five-year agreement was approved in 1968, and expired on 30 September 1973. The third was from 1974 to 1979, the fourth from 1983 to 1989. The fifth and latest International Coffee Agreement came into effect in October 1994, five years after coffee market control had lapsed with the expiration of the fourth agreement in 1989.

The purpose of the international coffee agreements was to stabilise the world coffee markets through self imposed export quotas and new efforts to increase consumption. The specific objectives, stated in the first five year agreement of 1963, were to:

• maintain price stability by fixing quotas for export to traditional markets and allowing sales in non-quota markets;
• bring the level of coffee production in equilibrium with demand;
• promote consumption of coffee through advertising, public relations, consumer education in Europe, North America and Japan.

The distribution of exports among the producer members was regulated by the protocol to the 1962 agreement. These quotas were to be shipped to all importing members who usually made up more than 95 per cent of total shipments. 'Annex B' coffees were shipped to developing markets (primarily Japan) that warranted special treatment. 'Annex A' distribution was based on total exports of about 55.2 million bags, but the agreement stipulated that all member nations meet in August of each year to agree on the total requirements for the next coffee year (1 October - 30 September). This annual quota was then distributed pro rata according to 'Annex A'.

In addition, the Council was given the power to adjust annual and quarterly quotas in relation to price movements of the principal types of coffee. If the composite price rose to certain levels, additional quotas were distributed among all exporters as per 'Annex A'. Conversely, if the composite price fell through specified levels the total quota was reduced. This selective system concentrated on the four specified groups, Columbia mild Arabicas, Other mild Arabicas, unwashed Arabicas, and Robustas, a price range being negotiated for each group. If the indicator moved above or below that range, the quota for that group was adjusted accordingly, without changes to other types.

Before the start of each quota, the International Coffee Organisation (ICO) issued coffee-stamps to each producer country up to a certain per cent of its quota allocation in accordance with the terms of the agreements. The importer nations undertook to only allow entry of shipments (except for certain minor exceptions) accompanied by such stamps. The stamps were deposited by the ICO in the central banks of producer countries and were then distributed by a government agency, typically responsible for the new problems of storage, financing and stamp control.

The operation of this agreement brought stability to coffee markets and prices. It encouraged expansion in production. Under the agreement, Uganda's exports in the 1960s and 1970s averaged approximately three million bags i.e. 180,000 tons annually. However, the agreement maintained export prices artificially high by holding coffee, encouraging more plantings, preventing necessary adjustments and production improvement , measures which resulted in large coffee surpluses over the years. Consequently, producing countries, including Uganda, consistently exceeded the quotas set under the ICO.

The ICoA was both the most important and the most controversial of the international commodity agreements which remained in operation for over thirty years [26]. The agreement was important because more developing countries are dependent on coffee exports than on any other single non-oil primary commodity. It was controversial because, since it operated entirely through export controls, it laid itself open to the charge of being an internationally sanctioned cartel whose objectives were primarily raising rather than stabilising coffee prices. It was also seen as distorting the operation of the market.[27]

The last international coffee agreement with effective export controls was the agreement which came into effect in 1983. The third ICA had come into operation during the 1975-1979 price boom. The consuming country members were initially reluctant to see the reintroduction of quotas, but eventually agreed in September 1980 on the understanding that a group of Latin American producers would desist from attempts to raise the price outside the scope of the ICoA.

Helped by frost in Brazil in 1981, the ICO quotas generally managed to achieve stable prices within the target range of 115 to 150 cents per pound from 1981. Drought conditions in Brazil during the 1985-86 coffee year resulted in the suspension of controls in February 1986. The controls were reintroduced the following year as supply recovered and prices fell back again. The ICoA was suspended in July 1989 despite the fact that the ICO composite indicator price (CIP) had not reached any of the trigger levels for quota reduction. The technical reason for the July 1989 suspension of the ICoA quotas was that, with the fourth agreement due to end on 30 September, there was lack of consensus as to the need for an agreement with economic clauses.

The lack of consensus that led to the lapse of the ICA in 1989 is or can be attributed to five broad reasons.[28]

i)   Consumer opposition to what was perceived to be grade distortion between arabic and robusta beans, and to price discrimination between member and non-member consuming countries. Consumer tastes had shifted over time toward the high-quality arabica beans produced by the colombian 'milds' (Columbia, Kenya, Tanzania) and 'other milds' (mainly central American) group of producers, but that the ICO quota allocation tended to limit the availability of high-quality arabicas thereby generating a higher premium for this type of coffee over the prices of robustas (produced in Brazil, Indonesia and Africa) and unwashed arabicas (produced in Brazil). Dramatic evidence for this was provided by the February 1986 suspension of quotas: over the following year, the premium of mild arabicas over robustas fell from 2 percent to just 6 percent (March 1987 compared with March 1986). Member consumer countries were also irritated by the fact that the coffee agreements permitted unlimited exports to non-member consumer countries at free market prices which, particularly in the case of high quality arabicas, were often at a considerable discount (30 - 50 percent) to ICO prices.

ii)   Producer disagreement over the division of benefits of high and stable export prices that the coffee agreements had helped to achieve. The 'other milds' group of producers saw the existing ICoAs as primarily beneficial to Brazil, which produces robustas and the lower quality unwashed arabicas, as well as African robusta producers. The other milds group would only agree to a fifth ICoA if quotas were reallocated in their favour.

They were supported by the United States, but opposed by Brazil, the African robusta producers and the EU. The determination of the 'other milds' producers to hold out for a quota redistribution may have been reinforced by a World Bank study circulating around this time which argued that, although the third and fourth ICoAs significantly mobilized both prices and producer revenues, they typically did not give rise to higher revenues for countries other than Brazil and Columbia.[29]

iii) Opposition in the US Congress to any form of active ICA. The US Congress was not willing to ratify any export control agreement 'with economic clauses' even if the grade and non-member distortions were to be solved.

iv) Incoherence of the Brazilian government policy on coffee during the Collor presidency. Collor became president in April 1990 and immediately abolished the *Instituto Brasileiro do Cafe* (IBC) which most people in Brazil considered to be the principal beneficiary of coffee stabilisation. The coffee exporters tended to favour a free market, while the roasters (Brazil is the second largest coffee consuming country) were at best ambivalent. Thus, for much of 1990-1991, Brazil had no clear coffee policy.

The fifth ICoA came into effect in October 1994 but lacked any market intervention instruments. Initially, Brazil and Columbia suggested the establishment of a floor price beneath which they would commit themselves not to sell, but this rapidly transformed itself into a proposal for withholding stocks. A series of meetings in July-September 1993 gave birth to the Coffee Retention Scheme (CRS), under which producers agreed to withhold 20 percent of their planned exports. The full 20 percent withholding would take place as long as the ICO indicator price remained beneath 75 cents per pound, dropping to 10 percent for prices within the range 75-80 cents per pound. A price above 85 cents per pound would trigger release.[30] The producers also agreed to form a new organisation, known as the Association of Coffee-Producing Countries (ACPC) which took over the management of the CRS.

As a result of the retention scheme, immediately the coffee price rose from a first quarter 1994 average of 65 cents per pound to 73.5 cents per pound in the final quarter, a rise of 12 percent. Furthermore, even disregarding the effects of the withholding arrangement as demand growth picked up, the coffee market was becoming tighter. Accordingly, the upward movement in the coffee price continued, doubling in the first five months of 1994.[31] This caused the release of the with-held stocks in two tranches, the first in May and the second in July 1994. However, it should be noted that although the CRS resulted in coffee price increases, the ACPC has less power than the ICO had under the ICoAs, because the CRS can not be enforced by the governments of coffee consuming countries. Article 30 permits the International Coffee Council to 'examine the possibility of negotiating a new ICA which could contain measures to balance supply and demand for coffee', an indication that the cooperation of the consumer side of the coffee industry is still considered useful in arrangements to effectively intervene in the coffee market.

The available evidence about the performance of the ICAs shows that, in each case, the lapse of the agreement was associated with prices of around 40 percent lower than those in the period preceding the breakdown. In the case of coffee, prices fell by 40 percent in the two years following the suspension of quotas (coffee years 1990-1991) compared with the 1987-1988, the last full year of control, and remained at around that level for four years. This means that, while in operation, the ICAs were price-supporting.

Gilbert[32] shows that during the three-year period immediately following the lapse or collapse of stabilisation, the coefficient of variation of coffee prices fell from 23.6 percent to 10.7 percent implying that coffee moved from a regime of relatively high but volatile prices to one of stable depressed prices. By contrast, the coefficients of variation of cocoa and tin rose respectively from 6.9 percent to 1.3 percent and 8.3 percent to 1.3 percent, meaning that there was a rise in the variability of the cocoa and tin prices. The sugar price remained highly volatile both before and after the lapse of the ISA.

In the case of the Coffee agreement and with respect to African producers, our evaluation of the ICoAs is that they made a positive contribution despite the fact that much of the benefit of high prices may have been lost either to governments (through export taxes) as was the case in Uganda or to third parties, notably export marketing boards (through rent-seeking). Although it has been argued by some analysts, notably George Gwyer[33], that African countries did not derive much, in terms of net gains, from commodity agreements because no single African country is a dominant supplier of a particular commodity, the African growers' estimated loss of 12 billion dollars resulting from the fall of coffee prices following the suspension of the Coffee Agreement in 1989; and the doubling of prices from $ 0.60/kg to $ 1.2/kg as the producers announced a 20 percent retention scheme in October 1993, are clear indications that, while it existed, the ICA served a useful purpose.

In two recent presentations[34], Professor Henk L. M. Kox of the Free University, Amsterdam has submitted that much ecological damage in Third World countries is associated with commodity production for the world market. But, free competition in international commodity markets prevents exporting countries from making the costs of environmental protection a recurrent element in pricing. Using the example of the International Tropical Timber Agreement, Professor Kox has argued that ICAs provide a real possibility and opportunity for integrating environmental protection elements into the international commodity price by including a price mark-up which can be levied in the form of an export tax for environmental preservation and reconstruction in commodity producing countries.

However, the new ICAs or international commodity-related environmental agreements (ICREAs) are not intended to focus on price stabilisation like the old ICAs, but should be created to deal with commodity-specific environmental issues in relation to international trade, in order to foster the use of production technologies that make production more sustainable. They are a means of establishing a direct link between consumption, trade and production. Kox has suggested three types or forms of ICREAs.

i)   A standard-setting ICREA without side-payment. This is an agreement to phase out polluting or resource-wasting production methods. It can either take the form of a producer's cartel or of an international agreement between exporting and importing countries. Trade or other sanctions might be necessary against non-participants.

ii) An ICREA with side-payments: This would be an agreement that governments be assisted with funds to implement policies to make producers switch to environmentally sound techniques. These transfer payments would be made from a fund fed by an import levy charged at border crossing in importing countries (especially developed countries) and maintained by an ICREA secretariat.

iii) A standard-setting ICREA with trade preferences: This is an agreement between exporting and importing countries in which the producing countries agree to diminish environmental degradation by commodity production to specified targets, while importing countries grant signatories some form of preferential trade access to their market.

In earlier decades, intervention in commodity markets was sustained by the belief that the stabilisation of market prices was good for both producers and consumers. Today, in a world in which market liberalisation and competitiveness appear to have taken hold of almost every country, there is less enthusiasm in producers and resentment in consumers for what is seen as 'internationally sanctioned cartels'. There is a shift in emphasis toward using futures markets for risk management. There are active futures markets for each of the commodities which have been subject to international control. However, whatever benefits – increased productive efficiency, increased collateral value of commodity stocks – futures sales may have, they do not amount to revenue stabilisation. Nor do they shift the terms of trade in favour of commodity producers. Thus, the tendency to form producer organisations or to take unilateral action to manage supply, as happened recently with regard to coffee, still remains alive.

An alternative to commodity agreements is concessionary trade agreements, such as the Lome Convention, now renewed four times, between the EU and 71 African, Caribbean, and the Pacific (ACP) countries. This agreement effectively built on the earlier trade agreement between the EEC and francophone African countries (the Yaounde Agreement). The Lome Convention, first signed in 1975, was an attempt by the EEC to compensate developing countries, particularly former colonies, for the loss of bilateral privileges, when the European Economic Community was formed. It was designed to promote trade cooperation, to stabilise export earnings, and to accelerate financial and technical aid. Under the agreement, up to 7 percent of the agricultural exports of the developing country members were to enter the EEC duty free. On the other hand, EEC members' exports to ACP were to be guaranteed most-favoured-nation treatment.

Also, under the same agreement, a stabilisation scheme of a preferential kind was introduced. It involved an export revenue stabilisation scheme known as STABEX, whose aim was to compensate the 71 Lome convention countries for shortfalls in their export earnings in any one year compared with the average value for the preceding four years. Unfortunately, this arrangement, which has governed the trade and aid of the wealthy 15-nation European Union and the ACP group of developing countries since 1975, is to be radically overhauled in favour of free trade. Negotiations have already started and the poor nations are naturally apprehensive because they cannot compete on equal terms with the European Union. The proposal that EU's Generalised System of Preference (GSP) should serve as an alternative for those countries which do not want to negotiate free trade agreements is not considered suitable because the benefits are unlikely to be as good as the preferences provided under the previous arrangement.

Overall evaluation of the impact of government intervation in product markets

Marketing boards and international commodity agreements - the instruments used by African governments to intervene in product markets - were intended to mediate external changes and absorb external shocks.

Variability in export earnings caused by fluctuations in world commodity prices, or by a country's unstable production caused by variable weather, wars or other disruptions, leads to instability in levels of resources available for the functioning of the economy and the welfare of the people. To the extent that these arrangements helped to minimise the tendencies towards instability and decline of commodity prices and the adverse consequences associated with them, they were helpful. Acceptable prices for primary commodities were obtained on the world market.

They facilitated accumulation of substantial investable resources necessary for development. The resources enabled both the colonial and post-independence governments to adopt the strategy of development planning to facilitate economic development in Africa. In the case of Uganda, the colonial administration initiated a number of important development projects such as the extension of the railway from Kampala to Kasese and the building of the hydro electricity dam on river Nile at Jinja. The Jinja hydro-electric scheme was of critical importance in the development strategy of the Uganda government. According to a World Bank report, 'it was expected that the availability of ample energy at a reasonable price would bring about an industrial revolution in Uganda.'[35] Additionally, the colonial administration set up a public corporation - the Uganda Development Corporation (UDC) – to act as a catalyst of economic development. This parastatal was supposed to be a channel for state investments in the economy. It was expected to mobilise investment funds for agricultural modernisation and industrialisation. The rationale for these government initiatives was that private individuals were not in a position to generate sufficient funds for economic development. These initiatives extended state control beyond agricultural policy to industrial production.

Between 1961 and 1971 the post - independence Uganda government progressed from project planning, inherited from the colonial administration, to comprehensive development planning especially with the publication of the Second Five Year Development plan, *Work for Progress* (1966-1971) which, according to D.F. Watt, was 'superior to previous planning documents by virtue of its comprehensiveness.'[36] P.G. Clark, the chief architect of the Second Development Plan, has pointed out that the aim of development planning in Uganda was to accelerate the growth of the gross national product by increasing the rate of investment from 18 percent of GDP in 1966 to 21 percent in 1971.

Uganda's economic performance during the era of marketing boards, international commodity agreements, and development planning may appear modest and below plan expectations but it was positive with relatively rapid rates of growth, and enabled the country to achieve relative prosperity. The growth rate during the first plan period (1961-1966) was 5.8 percent. During the second plan period (1966-1971) the economy grew at the rate of 4.4. percent and monetary output grew at 4.8 percent. Also during the same period there was substantial expansion of education (at both primary, secondary and university level) and health services.[37] Although some critics, notably Landell, declared the first three decades of African independence an economic, political, and social disaster,[38] this positive performance was not unique to Uganda. A publication of the International Monetary Fund and World Bank stated, in 1994, that Africa grew rapidly in the late 1960s and early 1970s, and experienced decline from the mid 1970s.[39] According to an article by the Scandinavian Institute of African Studies, UNICEF classifies the two decades of independence as 'remarkable'. The African economy performed relatively well in aggregate terms during the 1960s and 1970s, especially up to 1973 and then between 1976 and 1978.[40] According to UNICEF:

> indicators like GDP and exports grew at sustainable rates comparable to other developing regions. Manufacturing production increased significantly. There was a sustained expansion of education especially primary education; an important mobilisation of domestic savings and foreign resources; investment rate grew from 14 percent in 1965 to 20 percent in 1980.

The famous Berg report published by the World Bank in 1981 said that in the 1970s the African economic picture was not uniformly bleak. According to the report, there were signs of progress throughout the continent; vastly more Africans were in schools, and most were living longer; roads, ports and new cities had been built and new industries had been developed; and technical as well as managerial positions, formerly occupied by foreigners, were then held by Africans.[41]

Unfortunately for Uganda and most other sub-saharan African countries, these positive developments and growth turned out to be transient and later, in the late 1970s and 1980s, these countries became victims of destruction, externally induced crises[42] and decay. Firstly, there was no real structural transformation of the economy and though agriculture, the predominant sector of African economies, improved, it was not substantially modernised.[43] It is also true that government efforts were not matched by the outcome, or as Tony Killick has put it, there was a vacuum between the theoretical benefits and practical results of development planning.[44] Secondly, under colonialism there had emerged a discriminatory type of division of labour that excluded Africans from the high - growth and capacity-enhancing sectors of the economy (manufacturing and commerce) and an education system that did not emphasise practical skills and technology. Unlike agriculture, the industrial sector in Uganda was mainly controlled by the Europeans - most of them British - and Asians. These two communities not only owned and controlled the major industries in the country but also monopolised commerce, banking, export and import trade as well as large - scale commercial agriculture.

Thus, on the eve of independence, Uganda's industrial and commercial sectors were characterised by the absence of African industrialists and business executives. Even as late as 1972, when a military government expelled non-citizens, the commercial life of Uganda was still dominated by non Africans and therefore, the expulsion of Asians immediately created a technological and a managerial vacuum which significantly contributed to the decay from which we have not yet completely cleared out.[45] This is clear evidence that while the colonial period swept away some of the old traditions, it also undermined the creation of capacity (technological and organisational or managerial) or foundations for sustainable economic growth and long term development. Thirdly, besides the usual indiscipline and incompetence in the implementation of plans, more of the resources ripped or siphoned off commodity producers through export taxes went to the 'controllers' - state and parastatal officials and cronies - in the form of government consumption, war funds, prebends, wastefulness, extravagancies, and embezzlements. The misused resources were not beneficial to commodity producers whose incentives and motivation are the determinants of overall economic growth and, therefore, ought to have been enhanced.

The net result of negative tendencies was loss of opportunity to enhance capacity (productive, infrastructural, technological, organisational) for growth and long term development. Essentially, therefore, marketing boards and international commodity agreements facilitated the extraction of resources from commodity producers in a manner that did not provide for incentives or motivation to the producers. Moreover, the resources were largely put to uses that did not make a positive contribution to the transformation and enhancement of the capacity of the very sector from which the resources had come. These negative effects are empirically demonstrated in the next Chapter.

Notes

1. C.K. Eicher and D.C. Baker, (1982). *Research on Agricultural Development in Sub-Saharan Africa:* A critical survey, MSU International Development Paper No.1 1982; P.T. Bauer, (1952). 'Fluctuations in Incomes of Primary Producers', *Economic Journal*, P.T Bauer, (1954) *West African Trade*, Cambridge University Press.

2. J.C. Abbot, and H.C Creupelandt, (1966). *Agricultural Marketing Boards, Their Establishment and Operation*, Rome: FAO.

3. H.L Van der Laan and W.T.M Van Haaren, (1990). *African Marketing Boards under Structural Adjustment: The Experience of Sub-Saharan Africa During the 1980s*, Working Paper No.13 Leiden: African Studies Centre.

4. J.E. Harring, S. Christy and J.F. Humphrey, (1969). 'Marketing Boards and Price Funds in Uganda 1950-1960,' *Journal of Agricultural Economics* vol.20 No.3. See also D.G.R Belshaw, (1968). 'Price and Marketing Policy for Uganda's Export Crops', *East African Journal of Rural Development Vol. 1*, No 2.

5. P.T. Bauer, *West African Trade* op.cit.

6. T. Mkandawire (1985) 'Agricultural Economics Training and Research in Africa: A perspective from ZIDs', A paper presented at a *Conference on Agricultural Economics Training and Research in Africa*, Harare, Zimbabwe.

7. R.H. Bates, (1981) *Markets and States in Tropical Africa*, University of California Press; R.H. Bates, (1983) *Essays on the Political Economy of Rural Africa*, Cambridge University Press; R.H. Bates, (1990). 'The Political Framework for Agricultural Policy Decision' in C.K. Eicher and John M.Staaz *Agricultural Development in the Third World*, Johns Hopkins University Press.

8.   For a more detailed presentation on marketing boards in Uganda, see, J.R. Bibangambah, (1996). *Marketing of Smallholder crops in Uganda,* Fountain Publishers, Kampala, 1996, (Chapter 2).

9.   This responsibility took two forms: One exemplified by Tanzania's National Milling Corporation was a complete marketing responsibility of collecting, transporting, sorting, milling and distributing grain. The other was that of boards handling food aid, selling it commercially and generating counterpart funds which are then handed over to the Treasury.

10   This point is underscored by complaints about the quality of export crops after the boards have been abolished. The case of cocoa in Nigeria has been cited as a good example.

11.   For the protection of consumers there is general support for ceiling prices backed up by a local grain reserve as well as foreign currency reserves to pay for imports to replenish the reserve stock. However, there is disagreement about whether the instrument of the ceiling price should be used only once in 10 years. It has been argued that grain marketing boards that performed this function did not cause significant distortions in the market because they had very little grip on the marketing channel due to the parallel market, with private traders and co-operatives participating in conjunction with the grain boards at both the collection and processing stages.

12.   A. Montague, *On being Human* noted in J. Voorhist, (1961) American Cooperatives, Happer publishers.

13.   Analysts from outside Africa give a different reason for the emergence of co-operatives in Africa. They say co-operatives were promoted by donors and governments as sources of grassroot participation in the development of commodity markets. If this is true, the co-operative movement in Uganda is an exception; R.E Christian and U.Lele (1989). 'Markets, Marketing Boards and Co-operatives in Africa: Issues in Adjustment Policy,' *MADIA Discussion Paper II,* Washington D.C: the World Bank. See also S.O. Olayide et al, (1974). 'Effects of Marketing Board Pricing Policies on the Nigerian Economy', *Journal of Agricultural Economies* vol 25, F.S. Idachaba, (1973). 'Marketing Board crop Taxation and input subsidies' Second – Best Approach', *Nigerian Journal of Economic and social Studies* vol. 15,; F. Ellis. 'Evolution of Price and Marketing Policy in Tanzania', in C. Harvey (ed), (1988). *Agricultural Pricing Policy in Africa,* Macmillan Publishers.

14.   A.R. Kyamulesire, (1988) *A History of the Uganda Co-operative Movement 1913-1988,* Kampala; J. Opio - Odongo, (1988) 'Uganda's Co-operative Movement at Seventy-Five' UCA Development Paper No.5.

15.   For detailed evidence of this control, see J. Opio-Odongo, (1987) 'Agricultural co-operatives and the Emasculation of Producer-members in Uganda', in P.B. Webe and C.P. Dodge (eds), *Beyond Crisis : Development Issues in Uganda,* 1987; J. Opio -Odongo, 'Uganda Co-operative movement at Seventy-Five', *op. cit* A.R. Kyamulesire, *A History of Uganda Co-operative Movement,* op.cit

16.   J. Katorobo, (1995). 'Reforming the Export Marketing System', in P. Langseth *et al* (eds): *Uganda: Landmarks in Rebuilding a Nation,* Kampala: Fountain Publishers.

17.   J.R. Bibangambah, (1996). *The Marketing of Smallholder Crops in Uganda,* Kampala: Fountain Publishers.

18.   Developed countries' governments have opposed this interpretation on various occasions.

19.   J.W. Rowe, (1965). *Primary Commodities in International Trade,* Cambridge University Press.

20.   These are institutionalised contacts between producers and consumers. Forum can make recommendations in the form of "indicative prices but is not authorised to intervene directly in the market itself.

21.   The expression 'Other measures' refers to the case of those commodities whose problems have not or have been only partially included in the three types of arrangements.

22.   T. Geer, (1971) *An Oligopoly, The World Economy and Stabilisation Schemes,* New York: Dunellan Press.

23. *New York Times*, 14 and 15 March 1961
24. UN EC 243/1 Coffee, 22 May 1962.
25. V. Yorgarson, (1976). 'The International Coffee Agreement: Prospect and Retrospect', *Development and Change* , vol. 7, No. 2.
26. This section greatly benefited from a very up-to-date article by C.L. Gilbert, (1996). 'International Commodity Agreements; An Obituary', *World Development* , vol. 24 No.1.
27. M. Bohman and L. Jarvis, (1990). 'The International Coffee Agreement; Economics of the non-member market' *European Review of Agricultural Economics*, vol 17 No 1.
28. T. Akiyama and P.N. Varangis, (1990). 'The impact of the International Coffee Agreement on Producing countries', *World Bank Economic Review.*
30. In 1995 the support range of 75-85 cents per pound was revised upwards by the Association of coffee producing countries (ACPC) with the effect that from June 1995 implied support range for the 'other milds' arabicas was raised to 165-190 cents per pound.
31. Evaluation of the impact or real effect of the coffee retention scheme is complicated by the fact that the coffee market is always vulnerable to Brazilian weather conditions. The severe frost in 1975 caused the boom prices of 1976/78 and drought conditions in 1985/86 resulted in high prices of 1986. The winter frost and low rainfall in 1994 are held responsible for the major part of the jump in the coffee price during June and July 1994 resulting in an overall five fold increase over the year.
32. C.L. Gilbert, 'International Commodity Agreements' *op.cit.*
33. G.D. Gwyer, (1973). 'East Africa and Three International Commodity Agreements: The lesson of the Experience' in V.F. Amann (ed), *Agricultural Policy Issues in East Africa*, Kampala Makerere University.
34. H.L.M. Kox, (1991). 'Integration of Environmental Externalities in International Commodity Agreements' *World development* vol.19, No.8, H.L.M Kox, (1993) 'International Agreements to deal with Environmental Externalities of Primary Commodity Exports', Paper prepared for the *International Conference on Striking a Green Deal: Europe's Role in Environment and South-North Trade relations*, European Parliament, Brussels.
35. Quoted in J.B. Mugaju, (1990). 'Development Planning versus Economic Performance in Uganda, 1961-1971,'*Transafrican Journal of History* , Vol 19.
36. D.F. Watt, (1966). Work for Progress and the Design of Agricultural Development Policy in Uganda', *The East African Economic Review* , vol. 2, No. 2.
37. Under the Second Plan government planned to create 200,000 more primary school places and to increase university places from 1800 to 3000. The government also planned and built 22 rural hospitals, thus increasing hospital bed capacity by 85 percent. In addition, it was the declared intention of the government to create 100,000 new jobs.
38. P. Landell-Mills, Pierre, (1992). 'Governance, Cultural Change, and Empowerment', *The Journal of Modern African Studies.*
39. C. Jonnes and M.A. Kiguel, (1994). 'Africa's Quest for Prosperity: Has Adjustment Helped?' *Finance & Development* , Vol 31 No 2.
40. C. Lopes, 'Enough is enough!: An alternative diagnosis of the African Crisis', *Discussion paper No 5* , Uppsala: Scandinavian Institute of African Studies.
41. World Bank, (1981). *Accelerated Development in Sub-Saharan Africa*, Washington DC: World Bank.
42. These Crises include the fall in export earnings owing to changes in commodity prices; the accumulation of arrears on debt payments; the oil price crisis; high interest rates; increased cost of imported manufactured goods especially equipment and spares.
43. The authors of the 1998 Uganda Human Development report who refer to 1962-1970 as a 'period of rapid transformation' (p.39) must have a different meaning for the word 'transformation'. Yes, there was socio-economic progress, but not structural transformation. It is true that efforts were directed at transforming the agricultural sector through rigorous research, extension support, and mechanisation through Group Farm and Tractor Hire Serv-

ice Programmes but 'improvement' of small holder agriculture and not 'transformation' was achieved as the mechanisation programmes were not successful. It is also true that progress in agricultural and livestock development was complemented by the promotion of import substitution industries based on processing of agricultural produce (beef, dairy, cotton, tobacco) and the production of basic consumer goods (blankets, textiles, iron sheets, footwear), but the economy remained predominantly agricultural.

44. T. Killick, (1974). Possibilities of Development Planning', IDS/WP No. 165.

45. In Uganda, another legacy of colonialism is the disparities in development between the different regions of the country.

46. W.O. Jones has submitted that 'the question of economic motivation in Africa is of fundamental importance because no other motivation can be substituted for it without great loss in effectiveness', see W.O. Jones, (1960). 'Economic Man in Africa', *Food Research Institute Studies,* Vol 1, No.2.

3

Government Intervention in Agricultural Market Prices

Paul Streeten has pointed out that it is important to distinguish between *laissez-faire*, a policy which permits prices to be determined solely by the free play of market forces, and price-policy which attempts to use prices as instruments of policy, but works through the market.[1] The distinction is consistent with Peter Timmer's definition of price policy as interventions to alter domestic prices relative to border prices.[2] But, as Streeten has indicated, price policy is concerned not only with the level of prices but also with their structure, that is, the relative level of prices for different products that may be substitutes or complements, in consumption or production, their predictability, their effectiveness and their stability. What is particularly important to note is that the existence of price policies suggests the active intervention of government for a purpose or several purposes which are thought to be better achieved by such intervention.

Governments influence agricultural prices both directly, through agricultural sector policies, and indirectly, through industrial protection and macroeconomic policies. Direct policies are defined as sectoral policies that affect the price of the agricultural sector relative to the price level of the nonagricultural sector - the domestic terms of trade. Such policies include agricultural price controls, export taxes or quotas, import subsidies or taxes, and more. Indirect policies are defined as policies originating outside agriculture, such as industrial protection and macroeconomic policies. Indirect interventions depress the prices of agricultural tradables relative to nontradables (through their impact on the real exchange rate) and relative to other tradables (due to industrial protection). These policies affect production incentives by making agriculture less attractive than other sectors of the economy.

The formulation of agricultural price policy is complicated by a multiplicity of often conflicting objectives such as:

i)   promoting maximum food production to achieve self-sufficiency versus keeping prices for food and agricultural raw materials low.
ii) encouraging the production of export commodities versus raising maximum government revenue from export taxes.
iii) domestic food production versus production of export commodities.
iv) devaluation versus avoiding importing inflation.

v)   terms of domestic trade in favour of the agricultural sector versus domestic terms of trade in favour of urban and industrial sector.[3]

The task for policy-makers is to weigh the trade-offs and make an optimal choice. In making optimal choices, the role of price policy analysis is relevant and desirable.

Under a free market system, market prices are determined by the interaction of supply and demand. A market-oriented price policy requires that producer prices and marketing margins should accurately reflect the market value to ensure remunerative prices and full utilisation of the country's comparative advantage in agricultural production.

Given an appropriate market-oriented price system and efficient market organisation, the producer price will reflect the domestic consumer price which in an open economy will be derived from the world market price. Where domestic demand exceeds the domestic production, the market price will reflect what an importer has to pay for imported goods i.e. import parity price. When production exceeds domestic demand, the market price will be equal to what an exporter gets paid for exported goods i.e. export parity price. The basic criterion of efficiency prices is, therefore, that they should be set at border price levels. For export commodities, that means they should be set at FOB prices, evaluated at undistorted exchange rate. For commodities that compete with imports, they should be set at CIF prices and also evaluated at undistorted exchange rates. Thus, the price formula for efficiency prices can be stated as:

Pp	=	Pcd = (Ip - Tc) = Pce = (Ep - Ct) Where
Pp	=	producer price
Pcd	=	consumer price of crops
Ip	=	Import parity price
Tc	=	Cost of transport from point of imports entry
Pce	=	Consumer price of crops mainly for export
Ep	=	Export realisation.
Ct	=	Cost of transport, handling, processing etc.

The most important feature that characterised the prices of agricultural products in Uganda in the period 1890-1990 was the pre-determination and fixing of the reward of each 'actor' or participant along the marketing chain into a price structure. Accordingly, the price structure of the major agricultural products, which happen to be agricultural exports, had five components:

i)   the producer's or farmer's price.
ii)   the primary buyer's margin/commission.

iii) the processor's margin (including handling from the primary buyer and from processing factory to the exporter).
iv) export marketing margin
v) Government export tax.

An example of a pricing structure for coffee and cotton as at July 1990 is given in Table 3.1.

Table 3.1: Price structure

Robusta coffee	Price Structure July 1990
1. Average export price (US $/kg)	0.95
Exchange rate (per US$)	650.00
2. Export realisation (Shs.)	617.50
3. Government tax (%)	42.00
4. Export marketing	116.00
5. Processors' margin	82.00
6. Society commission buying transport	
7. Farmers' price	21.00
	139.00
Total	**358.00**

Arabica coffee

1. Average export price (US$/kg)	1.00
Exchange rate (US$)	650.00
2. Export realisation (Shs)	910.00
3. Government tax (%)	52.40
4. Export marketing	105.00
5. Processors' margin	82.00

6. Society commission	21.00
buying	
transport	
7. Farmers' price	225.0
Total	**433.0**

Lint cotton

1. Average Export Price (US%/kg)	1.5
Exchange rate (per US$)	650.0
2. Export realisation (Shs.)	975.0
3. Government tax (%)	35.79

4. Export marketing	105.0
5. Processor's margin	94.0
6. Society commission	
buying	27.0
transport	
7. Farmer' price	400.0
Total	**626.0**

Source : The former Ministry of Co-operatives and Marketing

Up to 1980, the process of fixing producer prices for export crops was what can be termed the 'residual method'. This method begins from the world market end of the marketing chain making deductions for export duty, marketing costs, then processors' margin and, finally, allocating the residue to farmer who is at the farm end of the marketing chain.

Farmer<—Processor<——Exporter<—G.tax<—Export price

This method did not take into account the farmers' production costs and the reward for management of the farm enterprise. Allocations of the export price to the various 'actors' along the marketing chain are shown in Table 3.2 using Robusta coffee earnings as an example.

Table 3.2 Allocation of Robusta Coffee earnings (in percentages)

Year	Farmers %	Miller %		CMB %	Govt/Tax %	Total %
1973	39	10	Combined	11	0	100
1974	27	7	miller /	8	58	100
1975	32	8	Exporter	10	50	100
1976	19	5		7	59	100
1977	15			6	75	100
1978	28			6	63	100
1980	57			7	29	100
1981	26				32	100
1982	48				20	100
1983	22	42			46	100
1984	24	32			31	100
1985	24	32			56	100
1990	22	45			53	100
1991	47	20			31	100
		25				

Source: Coffee Marketing Board

This residual approach was inappropriate for a number of obvious reasons. Firstly, there was no objective basis for allocation of the product price among the market participants. Secondly, it was mere maximisation with respect to government revenue objective in total disregard of the farmer's income objective. Thirdly, it disregarded the important relationship between cost and revenue. Fourthly, it ignored the concept of incentives and disincentives to farm production.

Effects of inappropriate pricing policies

Adverse effects resulting from low producer prices and a declining farmer's share of the export price manifested themselves in loss of motivation or incentives which loss, in turn, led to:

i)   drastic decline in the production of the major export crops especially coffee, cotton, tea and tobacco.

ii) a particularly marked decline in the productive capacity of the capital-intensive estate sub-sector as shown by the figures on tea.

iii)   an outflow of resources from the agricultural export sector into subsistence
        agriculture and informal trading.

The negative effect on the production of export crops was as shown in Table 3

Table 3.3: Production of export crops ('000 units)

Year	Coffee (mts)	Cotton (Bales)	Tea (mts)	Tobacco (mts)
1961	91.2	N/A	N/A	1.7
1962	117.0	181	N/A	2.0
1963	156.0	358	N/A	2.1
1964	169.0	379	N/A	3.3
1965	150.0	420	N/A	3.1
1966	152.0	445	N/A	2.6
1967	161.0	27	N/A	3.9
1968	165.0	334	N/A	4.5
1969	232.5	N/A	N/A	4.4
1970	201.5	467	N/A	3.9
1971	175.5	412	18.0	4.4
1972	183.7	411	23.0	5.0
1973	215.7	422	22.0	3.9
1974	198.6	270	22.0	3.2
1975	198.5	170	18.4	4.0
1976	137.9	134	15.4	3.7
1977	155.9	75	15.2	2.5
1978	121.2	110	11.0	1.4
1979	103.1	41	1.8	0.8
1980	135.2	33	1.3	0.4
1981	97.0	22	1.7	0.1
1982	157.4	28	2.6	0.6
1983	138.7	54	3.1	1.6
1984	166.6	66	5.2	2.0
1985	157.0	88	5.6	1.5
1986	138.7	24	3.2	0.9
1987	155.0	16	3.5	1.3
1988	133.0	11.3	3.3	2.5
1989	131.7	14	4.7	3.8
1990	128.7	23	6.7	3.3

Table 3.3 continued

1991	147.4	44	8.9	5.1
1992	110.3	40	9.5	6.7
1993	144.6	43	12.3	5.2
1994	194.3	20.8	13.4	6.5
1995	168.8	30.2	10.7	3.5
1996	278.7	52.7	14.6	3.1

Sources: Various issues of Uganda Background to the Budget

The consequent decline in is depicted graphically for coffee and cotton production in Figure 3:1.

Figure 3.1: Production of cotton and coffee

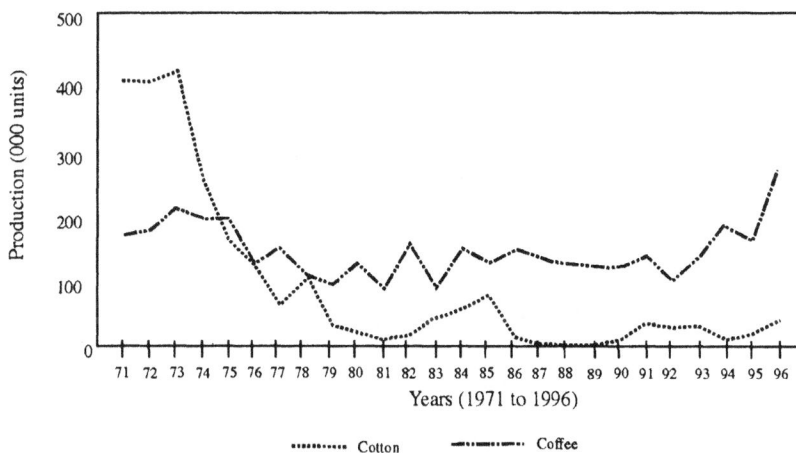

Production (000 units)

Years (1971 to 1996)

••••••••••• Cotton   —••—••—•• Coffee

These negative developments marked the emergence of an agricultural production crisis characterised by a drastic and continuous decline in output and a structural distortion of the relative importance of the various segments of the agricultural sector. The most critical element of the crisis was the drastic decline or collapse of the agricultural export sector, a direct result of the outflow or resources 'flight' into subsistence agriculture and informal activities. The crisis went beyond agricultural production and caused:

a)   an overwhelming and increasing dependence upon coffee for Uganda's foreign exchange earnings as cotton abdicated and tea deserted.

b)   smuggling of large quantities of primary produce, especially coffee across Uganda's international borders. It is estimated that coffee smuggling was running at 25-35 percent of the total crop during the crisis period.

c)   a heavy debt burden on many co-operative marketing organisations through rising costs and falling throughputs of primary products.

d)   extreme difficulties in getting purchased agricultural inputs.

e)   intensified problems of low income and absolute poverty in some of the remote districts.

Comparative producer price figures of Kenya, Uganda and Tanzania for the period 1974 to 1979 are shown in Table 3.4.

Table 3.4: Average producer price for coffee: Uganda, Kenya and Tanzania, 1974-79

1974		1975		1976
Producer prices	Uganda	16.23	16.23	16.23
(Cts/Us)	Kenya	62.9	59.7	121.3
	Tanzania	33.8	31.8	59.3
Producer price	Uganda	2.50	2.56	2.20
National currency	Kenya	9.82	9.40	22.30
Sh/kg	Tanzania	4.80	4.00	8.40
Producer prices:	Uganda	1.00	1.00	1.00
in constant terms	Kenya	12.12	9.90	21.0
(Shs/kg July 75=100)	Tanzania	7.00	4.37	8.20
Proportion of	Uganda	51.13	49.15	23.51
export	Kenya	92.4	93.6	92.1
value	Tanzania	66.7	60.9	49.5

Table 3.4 continued

		1977	1978	1979
Producer prices	Uganda	22.8	22.8	45.5
(US Cts/US)	Kenya	218.6	149.6	N/A
	Tanzania	101.0	76.5	N/A
Producer price:	Uganda	3.50	3.50	7.00
(national currency	Kenya	40.1	26.06	N/A
Shs/Kg	Tanzania	14.90	11.00	N/A
Producer prices:	Uganda	1.4	1.4	2.8
in constant terms	Kenya	36.6	20.04	N/A
(Shs/Kg July	Tanzania	13.20	28.90	N/A
75=100)				
Proportion of	Uganda	18.77	28.48	50.76
export value	Kenya	92.1	87.7	N/A
	Tanzania	45.3	49.9	N/A

Source: The Rehabilitation of the Economy of Uganda: a Report by the Commonwealth Secretariat 1979.

The figures show that very much higher prices, around three times the Uganda's prices, were obtainable in Kenya and Tanzania. This is because tax deductions in the two countries were small. The higher prices and greater profitability in Kenya and Tanzania were some of the causes of the smuggling of Uganda coffee into those countries.

The decline in the production of the traditional exports – cotton, coffee, tea, tobacco - was accompanied by shifts of resources towards food crops such as bananas, beans, groundnuts, etc which were not subject to statutory price controls. The shifts in resource allocation in accordance with the shift in relative profitability is clearly demonstrated by contrasting the trend for the uncontrolled crops - bananas, beans, etc – with that of the traditional export crops, e.g. coffee, as shown in Table 3.5 and Figure 3.2.

Table 3.5: Production of main crops ('000 MTs)

	Bananas	Beans	Coffee	Tea	Tobacco	Cotton
1971	7734.2	221.8	175.5	18.0	4.4	411.9
1972	9261.9	236.8	183.7	23.0	4.1	410.29
1973	9293.2	170.4	215.7	22.0	3.9	428.5
1974	8880.0	169.3	198.6	22.0	3.8	270.06
1975	9107.0	325.8	198.5	18.4	4.7	172.6
1976	8138.0	337.1	137.9	15.4	3.7	133.0
1977	8531.0	252.5	155.9	15.2	2.5	73.31
1978	8855.0	291.1	121.2	11.0	1.4	110.33
1979	6090.0	182.0	103.1	1.8	0.8	41.05
1980	5699.0	133.0	135.2	1.3	0.4	33.15
1981	5900.0	240.0	97.0	1.7	0.1	22.13
1982	6596.0	300.0	166.6	2.6	0.6	27.71
1983	6647.0	314.0	97.6	3.1	1.7	54.00
1984	6641.0	265.0	157.4	5.2	2.0	66.00
1985	6655.0	267.0	138.7	5.8	1.6	88.00
1986	6565.0	267.0	155.0	3.3	0.9	24.00
1987	7039.0	299.0	143.0	3.5	1.2	16.00
1988	7293.0	338.0	133.0	3.5	2.6	11.30
1989	7469.0	389.0	131.7	4.7	3.5	14.00
1990	7842.0	396.0	128.7	6.7	3.3	23.00
1991	8080.0	383.0	147.4	8.9	5.1	44.00
1992	7806.0	402.0	110.3	9.5	6.7	40.00
1993	8222.0	428.0	144.6	12.3	5.2	43.00
1994	9000.0	378.0	194.3	13.5	6.5	20.80
1995	9519.0	378.0	168.8	10.7	3.5	30.02
1996	9303.0	451.0	278.7	14.6	3.1	52.07

Source: 1. Ten-Year Development Plan 1981-90 (for figures of 1971/79).
             2. Background to the Budget for Years (1989-1995).

Figure 3.2: Percentage of output in relation to 1971

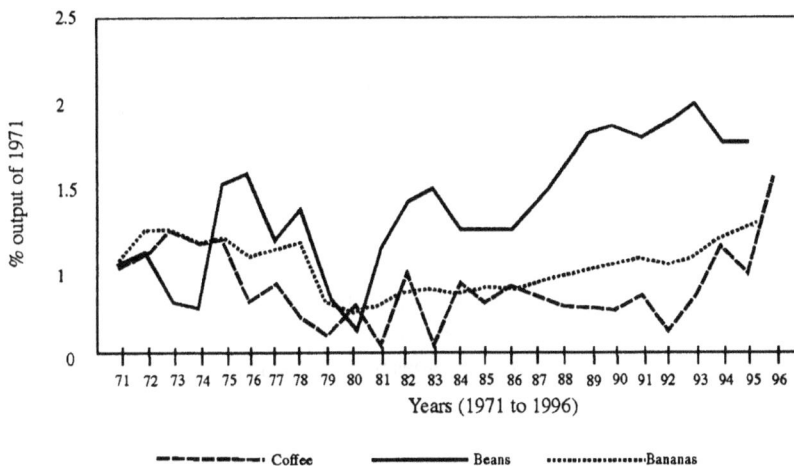

Years (1971 to 1996)

- - - - - - - Coffee   ——————— Beans   ·················Bananas

The collapse of the agricultural export which – main source of government revenue – led to a fiscal crisis, i.e. extreme shortage of revenue or resources for the provision of social services, the maintenance of the infrastructure and the enhancement of physical, technological and economic capacity through investment. This crisis curtailed the development effort and hence hindered the progress in the quest for prosperity.

Besides the collapse of the agricultural export sector, the other critical consequence of inappropriate pricing policies was the emergence and growth of the informal sector. The phenomenon called 'informalisation', which is libertarian in its aspirations, can be interpreted in two ways: first, it can be seen as a response to economic repression in the form of controls, regulations and procedures; second, it can be viewed as a response to economic decline. In both instances, the emphasis is survival and hence it is an aspect of short-term crisis management. This being the case, informalisation cannot be a basis for long term sustainable development.

To restore incentives and prevent further deterioration, especially of the agricultural export sector, a more objective way of determining producer prices and an organisational structure for agricultural price management (i.e. the Agricultural Policy Committee and the Agricultural Secretariat) were introduced in 1981. The basic objective of these measures was to create positive incentives for the production of export crops. The 'appropriate' or 'incentive' support producer price was:

i)   the price which yields revenue from the sale of the product that exceeds the cost of producing that product.

ii) the price which yields a profit margin adequate to support the producer's family and induce him to adopt new techniques of production to increase productivity and production.

iii) the price which yields profit that exceeds the levels of profits to be earned from the production of other competing commodities.[5]

The pricing methodology that was chosen is the cost of production approach, also known as the cost plus method[6]. According to this method, the producer price is determined on the basis of the cost of production and the profit margin. The cost of production normally includes both operating or variable, and fixed costs.

The operating costs include the cost of material inputs such as seeds, fertilizers, chemicals, etc, and the cost of labour. The fixed costs include overhead expenses such as depreciation and maintenance costs of the farm machinery, equipment and farm buildings, the wage cost of permanent staff, interest on production loans, transport and marketing costs, and the return on capital employed. The profit margin is added to the costs estimate as reward for the management input and entrepreneurial function which also includes an incentive component to induce producers to adopt new techniques of production.

Accordingly, the appropriate incentive support producer price is the price which yields a return from the sale of the product that exceeds its production costs and provides adequate margin to induce the investor to adopt new techniques to increase production. From the farmer's point of view, the cost-price relationship is relevant because an increase in the price of a commodity does not provide incentives, unless the price fixed covers the cost of production and provides an adequate profit margin.

The computation of the producer price on the basis of the costs of production is illustrated in Table 3.6.

Table 3.6: Agricultural cost of production

		Cotton	Coffee (AR)	Coffee (R)	Maize	Beans	Soya beans	G. nuts	Simsim
A.	Labour input (man-days)								
	Land preparation	40	2	2	40	30	40	40	10
	Planting	10	120	140	10	5	5	10	4
	Weeding/thining	80	30	30	75	50	50	80	50
	Pruning		30	30					
	Pesticide application	10			5	5	5	5	5
	Fertilizer appplicaiton								
	Mulching								
	Harvesting	60	60	60	20	10	10	40	20
	Pulping/podding		10	10		10	10	10	10
	drying		10	45	5	10	10	10	10
	Marketing	10	30		10				
	Total man-days	**210**	**292**	**317**	**165**	**120**	**130**	**195**	**109**
B.	Materials								
	Seed				25	70	30	100	15
	Fertilizer								
	Amm. sulphate								
	SSP								
	CAN								
	NPK								
	Pesticide	5	5	7.5	2	2		2	2
	Average yield								
C.	Cost of production per ha								
	Seed	0	0	0	6250	7700	4800	40000	4050
	Labour	147000	204400	221900	115500	84000	91000	136500	76300
	Fertilizer								
	Amm. sulphate	0	0	0	0	0	0	0	0
	SSP	0	0	0	0	0	0	0	0
	CAN	0	0	0	0	0	0	0	0
	NPK	0	0	0	0	0	0	0	0
	Pesticide	10000	10000	15000	4000	4000	0	4000	4000
	Fungicide	0	0	0	0	0	0	0	0
	Total cost (shs)	**157000**	**214400**	**236900**	**125750**	**95700**	**95800**	**180500**	**84350**
	Unit cost (shs per kg)	285	357	237	105	160	120	451	337
	Profit margin (20%)	57	71	47	21	32	24	90	67
	Recommended producer price shs	342	428	284	126	192	144	542	405

Similarly, the computation of processing margins is illustrated in Table 3.7.

Table 3.7: Average unit processing cost

A Buying storage and handling	(Shs)	(%)
Personnel costs	5.31	7.51
Operational costs	3.14	4.44
Transport of Kiboko	16.82	23.78
Transport of Clean	14.49	20.49
Materials	1.51	2.14
Repair and maintenance	5.12	7.24
Depreciation	3.46	4.89
Interest (Crop Finance)	2.03	2.87
Sub-total	51.88	73.36
B Processing		
Personnel	0.34	0.48
Operational costs	0.11	0.16
Coffee penalties	0.76	1.07
Repair and maintenance	0.23	0.33
Depreciation	0.18	0.25
Sub-total	1.68	2.29
C Factory administration		
Personnel costs	1.61	2.28
Operating costs	1.15	1.63
Materials	0.0	0.00
Repair & maintenance	0.01	0.01
Depreciation	0.0	0.00
Interest and bank charges	2.01	2.84
Sub-total	0.78	6.76
D Head office expenses		
Personnel costs	4.46	6.31
Operating costs	5.74	8.12
Materials	0.02	0.03
Repair and maintenance	1.16	1.64
Depreciation	2.97	1.37
Interest and bank charges	0.09	0.13
Sub-total	12.44	17.59
Total costs	**70.72**	**100.00**

Although we have said that the basic objective of introducing a more scientific way of determining producer prices was the creation of positive incentives for production, in practice, what actually happened was as follows:

i)   Coffee prices were being fixed well below the export parity price to raise the badly needed government revenue.

ii) Prices of food crops were being fixed well below the domestic free market prices and above the export parity price.

iii) Cotton prices were being fixed at a weighted export parity price for export of cotton and import parity prices for local sales.

iv) Prices announced were not covering the full cost of production (including family labour) because there was always a delay in announcing proposed prices; the government always trimmed the proposed prices arbitrarily, and in calculating costs, official exchange rates were used for imported inputs while farmers were buying them at parallel exchange rates in the open market.

(v) Margins given to marketing agents in the case of coffee and cotton did not cover the full cost of marketing and the marketing agents had to depend on other activities, windfall gains and even underpaying the farmers.

(vi) One price was usually fixed for the whole country regardless of storage, processing and transport costs differentials.[7]

All these were a consequence of the fact that, in practice, the final decision on prices, especially of coffee and cotton, the major agricultural exports, was being made, not by the Agricultural Policy Committee but, by the Ministry of Finance in accordance with Government's revenue objective which was considered paramount.

We can illustrate these shortcomings by reviewing the producer prices and processing margins fixed by government in any year of the 1980s.

Review of the adequacy or inadequacy of producer prices and processing margins

Table 3.8 below presents a comparison between the farmers' cost of production and prices announced by government in January 1988:

Table 3:8: The cost of production and prices of export crops

	Robusta	Arabica	Cotton (AR)
Labour, man-day/ha	450	405	220
Labour cost	45,000	40,500	22,000
Inputs	19,600	13,800	2,200
Total cost of prod.	74,600*	54,300	24,000
Yield kg/ha	1,500	750	450
Costs UShs/kg	50*	72	54*
Announced price			
Ush/kg	29	50	32
Producer			
Loss USh/kg	21	22	22

> * Excluding the margin for, or the cost of, farmer's management or
> entrepreneurship.

It is clear that producer prices announced by government fell short of the cost of production. The figures show that Robusta coffee and cotton prices were just over half the cost of production. The announced minimum prices for food crops were also substantially below the cost of production as shown in Table 3.9.

Table 3.9: Cost of production and prices of food crops, Ushs/h

	Maize	Beans	G/nuts	Simsim	Soyabeans
Labour mandays	190	180	250	185	190
Labour cost	19,000	18,000	25,000	18,500	19,000
Inputs	2,700	5,000	11,700	1,800	1,000
Total cost of prod.	21,700*	27,000*	36,000*	20,300*	22,000*
Yeild kg/ha	1,500	700	800	400	1,000
Cost USh/kg	14*	39*	54*	51*	20*
Announced minimum					
Price USh/kg	6	20	30	35	15
Produce loss					
UShs/kg	8	19	16	16	7

> * Excluding the margin for, or cost of the, producer's management or
> entrepreneurship.

As indicated earlier, besides the cost of production, other important parameters in setting relevant producer prices are export parity and import parity. The review is based on the world market prices as they were in 1988:

FOB price (US$/kg)

Coffee Robusta	2.31
Coffee Arabica	2.85
Cotton AR	1.57
Maize	0.12
Beans	0.50
Groundnuts	0.35
Simsim	0.76
Soyabeans	0.22

On the basis of these assumptions, export realisation and export parity prices for coffee were as shown in Table 3.10.

Table 3.10: **Export realisation and producer prices at the 1988 official exchange rate of UShs.60 Per US$**

	Robusta UShs/Kg	Arabica UShs/Kg
Export realisation (2.31 resp 2.85 USh/kg)	139	171
Export marketing margin	17	17
Processing margin	10	17
Primary society commission	2	1
Export parity price, clean coffee	110	136
Export parity, *Kiboko**	59	109
Announced price*	29	50
Government tax*	30	59

* per kg of unprocessed (Kiboko) otherwise clean

Table 10 above shows that coffee export parity price at producer level was Shs. 59 and 109 for Robusta and Arabica coffee respectively but the announced producer prices for these two commodities were Sh.29 and Sh.50, and, therefore, substantially lower. The government retained the difference. Accordingly, producers paid a government tax of more than 50 percent of the export parity price. Another important consideration in agricultural commodity pricing is the exchange rate. Table 3.11 below shows how the producer price was being affected by the exchange rate.

Table 3.11:   Export parity price at different exchange rates

Export price	Official exchange rate shs 60/$	Open market rate 350shs/$
Export price US$/kg	2.3	2.3
Export price Ushs/kg	139	805
CMB costs, Ushs/kg	17	17
District union costs, Ushs/kg	10	10
Primary societies costs, Ushs/kg	2	2
Export parity price, clean Ushs/kg (producer level)	110	776
Export parity price, Kiboko Ushs./kg (producer level)	59	419
Announced producer price, Ushs/kg	29	29

The table below demonstrates how the foreign exchange rate was influencing the distribution of benefits.

Table 3.12: Export realisation and producer prices at the exchange rate of UShs.200 per U.S.$

Export realisation (2.31 resp. 2.85/kg	Robusta US$/kg	Arabica
Export marketing margin	462	570
Processing margin	17	17
Primary soc. commission	10	17
Export parity price, clean	2	1
Coffee (producer level)	433	535
Export parity price*	234	428
Announced producer price*	29	50
Government tax*	30	59
Subsidy to other sectors	174	319

* per kg of Kiboko, otherwise clean

In January 1988 the official exchange rate was Shs.60 per US dollar. The rate used in Table 12 is Shs. 200 per US dollar because by 1988 this figure was close to the average between the open market rate and the official exchange rate. Table 12 shows that coffee producers were heavily subsidising other sectors that were beneficiaries of foreign exchange allocations.

The analysis of the consequences or distortions of a given price policy does not eliminate the dilemma of governments in poor countries where, as Peter Timmer puts it, 'the need to tax' may be inevitable. The important point to note is that policy makers should understand the likely consequences of their actions. If it is not possible to achieve the optimum, they should, at least, endeavour to do what is 'satisficing'. Belshaw expressed the same point when, in 1963, in reference to the level of incentives as a constraint to agricultural production in Uganda, he said:

> Economic analysis does not have the last word in policy formulation. It is only preliminary to the decision making which is the art of political economy. If economic analysis tells us that policy A will generate new wealth at 8 percent per annum and policy B at 4 percent, it does not follow that policy A must be chosen. What economic analysis has told us, what we did not know before, is how much we are sacrificing by choosing policy B. Whether the price is too high is a question for the political conscience of the country to ponder.[8]

The analysis in this chapter has empirically demonstrated not only farmers' response to (or behaviour in the light of) changes in relative profitability as influenced by the cost-price relationship but also, what had already been pointed out in chapter two that by over - emphasising the government fiscal objectives at the expense of economic motivation and the need to provide or allow for incentives to the producers, the policies undermined the enhancement of capacity for production, thereby negatively impacting on the development effort.

Notes

1. P. Streeten, (1987). *What Price Food?: Agricultural Policies in Developing Countries*, London: Macmillan Press.
2. C.P. Timmer, (1986). *Getting Prices Right: The Scope and Limits of Agricultural Price Policy*, Codell University Press.
3. J.R. Bibangambah and B.E. Jansson, (1988). 'Foundations of Agricultural Price Policy with special Reference to Producer prices', *UCA Developing Paper No 3*, and International Federation of Agricultural Producers (IFAP), (1984). *National Agricultural Pricing Policies for Developing Countries: A Basic Strategy for farmers organisations*, IFAP.
4. Commonwealth Secretariat, (1979). *The Rehabilitation of the Economy of Uganda*, London.
5. Agricultural Secretariat, Bank of Uganda, (1985). Agricultural Price Policy - Methodologies and Issues in Price Determination, Kampala.

6.   Other alternative pricing methodologies include the terms of trade; the crop parity; the consumer price; and the border pricing approaches. The last approach is considered the ideal method by the advocates of a market oriented policy.
7.   Report of the Technical Committee on *Crop Marketing in Uganda*, March 1989.
8.   D.G.R. Belshaw, (1963). 'The level of Incentives: A Factor Limiting Agricultural Production in Uganda,' A paper presented at the Annual Conference of the Uganda Agricultural Association.

4

Government Intervention in Factor Markets

Uganda's agriculture is more dependent on nature and as such it is not yet science-based. Accordingly, the use of agricultural inputs and improved production practices in Uganda is among the lowest in Africa. Additionally, productivity-enhancing technologies fell into disuse during the years of misrule, leaving Uganda's yields much lower than those of other developing countries with similar climatic conditions.[1] As a consequence, the national fertilizer consumption has fallen from an average of 1.4 kg/ha in the 1960s to just 0.2 kg/ha in the 1990s. This is among the lowest levels in the world.[2] Total annual expenditure on agricultural inputs (fertilizers, implements and agricultural chemicals) averages only $10 - $15 per smallholder household. A survey of inputs' use, undertaken in 1992, found that only 16 percent of the 282 randomly selected farm households in six districts had bought any fertilizer in the previous five years. Only 8 percent used commercial seed every season. Most smallholders that use agricultural chemicals are producers of either cotton and vegetables or producers of milk from grade/exotic cattle.[3] Staple food production continues to be dependent upon traditional varieties of seed and complementary factors supplied by nature.

The underutilisation of improved or high-yielding agricultural inputs is responsible for the low productivity of Uganda's agriculture. The utilisation trends can be previewed in three periods.

Before 1971

Agro-chemicals
The decades preceding the military coup of 1971 were characterised by steady development in the agricultural input procurement, handling and distribution systems. Nevertheless, input usage among smallholders was generally low. A major exception was the popular use of cotton spraying chemicals which picked up remarkably immediately after World War II. This was further strengthened as a result of trials in Serere Research Station in the 1950s. Farmers were recommended to spray their cotton with DDT four times during the growing season. This spraying regiment resulted in considerable increases in cotton yields. However, mainly because of its adverse effects on human health, DDT has since been banned not only in Uganda but in many other countries as well. The second most popular agro-chemical to be used in the country was cuprous oxide. The use of this chemical for cotton seed dressing began in the early 1950s and has since then been used by ginneries and unions throughout the country with beneficial effects.

63

In general, apart from the cotton case described above, before 1971 the use of chemicals was skewed in favour of cash crops by progressive farmers particularly in the Central region. There was minimal use for food crops other than horticultural crops in peri-urban areas. Typical of most African countries, the quantities of chemicals involved were by and large small. For instance, in 1970, demand averaged 400 tons of insecticides, large proportion of which was DDT for cotton spraying.

Fertilizers

A somewhat similar scenario to the chemical situation also prevailed for Fertilizer usage was some what similar to that of agrochemicals. Most of the fertilizers were being used on large estate farms. For instance, total fertilizer consumption in 1969 was estimated at 26,700 tons and 80 per cent of this was used for sugar-cane, tea and tobacco. The rest of the crops accounted for only 20 per cent of which 72 per cent was used in Buganda alone.

Agricultural implements

Ox-ploughing was introduced in Uganda in the 1920s. By 1971 it was well established and integrated into the farming systems of north-eastern Uganda. Not only is the topography of this region suitable for ox-ploughing but the small farmers possessed large herds of cattle from which oxen were selected and trained for ploughing.

Though tractors were also introduced in the 1920s, the suitability of this technology in the Ugandan farming environment remains to be rationalised. Two large-scale experiments have so far been carried out in an attempt to help popularise the use of tractors. The first experiment called the Tractor Hire Service (THS) was initiated in 1948 with the hope that it would gradually be taken over by commercial enterprises. By 1962, it was only working on a modest scale, even in Lango and Acholi where most of its efforts were concentrated (see Table 4.2).

Following the call by the Minister of Agriculture in 1961 that the 'plough must replace the hoe', substantial purchases of tractors were made and the acreage covered by the service increased throughout the annual cropping areas of the country. However, the increased acreage was accompanied by accelerating costs in the operations of the service. Even though this exercise was a major drain on government resources, it was never accompanied by appreciable increase in output from those who benefited from the service. The main reason is that the THS intervened only in primary cultivation. But, since other operations such as weeding and harvesting absorb a substantial part of the total farm labour, the mechanised service made very little contribution to total farming pattern. The second experiment involving tractors was carried out in 1963 in the form of the Group Farm Project (GFP).

It sought to integrate tractors into the Uganda farming systems by bringing farmers together into groups so that their plots would be cultivated as single units [4]. Also large resources, in the form of manpower and bilateral aid finance, were involved in the project. The commitment of considerable national resources on group farms was not matched by substantial increases in output and, accordingly, in 1969 the scheme was abandoned.[5] Like the THS, the biggest weakness of GFP was that it took care of primary cultivation and planting only, without taking account the cost of weeding or harvesting. In consequence, group farms suffered from serious bottlenecks which hampered overall agricultural production.

Input networks and local production

By 1971, Uganda had a well-organised inputs supply and distribution system consisting of both the co-operatives and private companies. The Uganda Central Co-operative Union was handling inputs for co-operative unions and societies. Private farms such as Jaykay Agencies, Mackenzie Ltd., Windmill Ltd., Universal Farm Supplies, Uganda Farmers Trading Association and Twiga Chemicals handled and distributed inputs to farmers through private intermediaries. Some inputs, for example, hoes at Chillington in Jinja and UGMA in Lugazi; animal feeds at Uganda Feeds Ltd, Jinja; and fertilizer (single superphosphate) at Tororo, were manufactured locally. After 1971, many of the firms ceased operation and the whole input supply system became disorganised. This was a serious setback to the process of upgrading agricultural operations through more effective implements.

From 1971 to 1979

As a result of economic mismanagement, most of the achievements regarding agricultural inputs attained prior to 1971 were lost during the 1971-1979 period. Generally, the supply was haphazard and inputs were in very short supply.

Average annual demand of fertilizer was estimated at about 30,000 tons, but most of this demand was not met as annual supply was only about 22 per cent of annual demand (6,300 ton per year). The single superphosphate factory at Tororo which was established in 1962 with an installed production capacity of 25,000 metric tonnes per year was closed down in 1978 due to lack of spare parts and foreign exchange. Since then it has never been re-opened despite the fact that there is adequate market potential in neighbouring PTA countries.

The supply of basic tools such as hoes and pangas between 1971 and 1975 met only a small fraction of estimated demand. Annual average supply was 52,200 hoes and 300,000 pangas. The local production of hoes at Chillington (Jinja) and UGMA Ltd (Lugazi) stopped after the expulsion of the Asian owners and owing to lack of foreign exchange.

The supply of agricultural chemicals suffered and the demand was generally not met. Between 1971 and 1975 the annual demand for chemicals was estimated at 379 tons of fungicides, 60 tons of herbicides and 408 tons of insecticides. Most of this demand was not met. During the years following 1975, the supply became erratic and in most cases ceased altogether.

Ox-ploughs, which have historically been used in Teso, Lango and Acholi, were estimated at 90,000 in 1969. Due to lack of spare parts and failure to replace them on regular basis, the number had declined to between 20,000 and 30,000 by 1980.

The THS also declined drastically in performance due to lack of maintenance facilities and spare parts. At any one time, at least half of the tractors were not working and those that were in good condition averaged only 600 hours per year before 1975 which is only 50 per cent of the tractor operating capacity. The number of working hours declined to less than 90 hours per year (less than 10 percent tractor capacity) after 1978.

The supply of improved seeds from national research stations as well as imports were also drastically affected between 1970 and 1980. Many varieties of improved seeds e.g. beans, cowpeas, groundnuts, simsim, sorghum and maize were lost, neglected or just let to mix freely with local varieties. In 1970, the government, with assistance from the British government, established the Uganda Seed Project (USP).

The primary objective of the USP was to increase production of improved seeds (e.g. maize, beans, soyabeans, groundnuts, sorghum and simsim) and make them readily available to farmers. There was a steady increase in production mainly through the use of contract farmers. Production levels peaked in 1974 but, thereafter, the scheme's seed output declined steadily mainly in tandem. Seed production under the USP came to a complete halt during 1980.

Data on the inputs situation between 1975 and 1980 are not readily available. As Amin's rule intensified, no attempts were made to monitor and analyse the input situation in the country. However, it is generally known that as the economy deteriorated, supply of all inputs declined drastically. By 1979, most agricultural inputs were virtually non-existent in the country.

From 1980 to the present

Owing to the general economic decline during the 1970s, the country faced serious input shortages by 1980. However, from 1980 onwards, the government and several donor agencies and private traders resumed the importation of inputs. Table 4.1 gives estimated values of inputs imported into the country between 1981 and 1990. Importation picked up from 1984 mainly because of increased disbursements from donor projects such as the Agricultural Rehabilitation Project (ARP), and those funded by IFAD and EEC.

Table 4.1: Estimated value of inputs imported into Uganda, 1981-1990

Year	US$
1981	13,821,000
1982	11,166,290
1983	13,477,210
1984	22,571,503
1985	46,265,444
1986	31,068,452
1987	33,248,850
1988	46,153,222
1989	38,811,400
1990	32,446,430

Source: Agricultural Policy Secretariat, 1991

The agricultural inputs imported into the country included tractors and farm machinery, processing equipment for food and industrial crops (e.g. maize mills, shellers, coffee hullers) farm implements (e.g. hoes, pangas, axes, shovels, spray pumps), chemicals (e.g. fertilizers, pesticides, veterinary drugs), seeds, animal feeds, and improved livestock.

Prior to the introduction of the current liberalisation and privatisation policies, agricultural inputs imported into the country were distributed through six distinct agencies: (1) government ministries, (2) parastatal companies, (3) donor agencies/projects, (4) co-operative movement, (5) private traders/ companies, and (6) non-governmental organisations as shown in Figure 4.1.

Figure 4.1: Agricultural input flows in Uganda before liberalisation

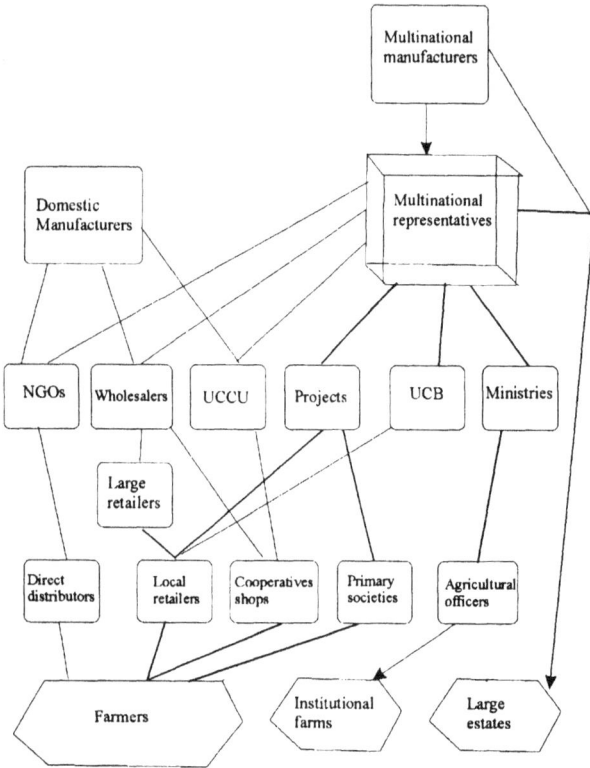

Source: Adapted from R. Laker-Ojok[6]

The image created by this elaborate network is very deceptive. The multiplicity of flow-channels suggests enhanced delivery effectiveness. However, dominance by official channels means disproportionate delivery in favour of officialdom.

The results of a survey by the National Inputs Co-ordination Unit (NICU) summarises the relative importance of the various agencies involved in importation of agricultural inputs between 1990 and the first quarter of 1992.

Table 4.2: Value of agricultural inputs imported by various agencies, 1990-92

Agency	1990 value (US$000)	1990 %	1991 value	1991 %	1992 (Jan-Mar) Value (US$000)	1992 %
Ministries	8,060	19.5	2,559	9.2	0	0.0
Projects	8,080	19.6	694	2.5	1,789	53.2
Parastals	11,340	27.4	15,539	56.2	1,362	40.5
Coope-ratives	330	0.8	148	0.5	8	0.2
Private	13,280	32.1	8,532	30.9	193	5.7
NGOs	260	0.6	181	0.7	12	0.4
Total	**41,350**	**100.**	**27,653**	**100.0**	**3,364**	**100.0**

Source: National Inputs Coordination Unit, the Agricultural Secretariat, Bank of Uganda.

The next section looks at each of these channels in more detail to find out their advantages and disadvantages in terms of relative performance and efficiency.

The established channel for the distribution of inputs by government ministries is presented in Figure 4.2.

On arrival, crop inputs would be stored in Ministry of Agriculture (MOA) central stores at Kawanda and Namalere. The Ministry Inputs Committee would then allocate the inputs to the various districts and institutions using such criteria as:

(a) crop acreage,
(b) human population, and
(c) district specific requirements.

The inputs were supposed to be delivered to the district headquarters using government vehicles. However, in practice, most district agricultural officers (DAOs) hired transport whose cost was subsequently met by the DAOs office. The transport cost was normally not reflected in the price of the inputs in any given location because of the pan-territorial pricing policy of MOA.

Figure 4.2: Established government channels for distribution of agricultural inputs

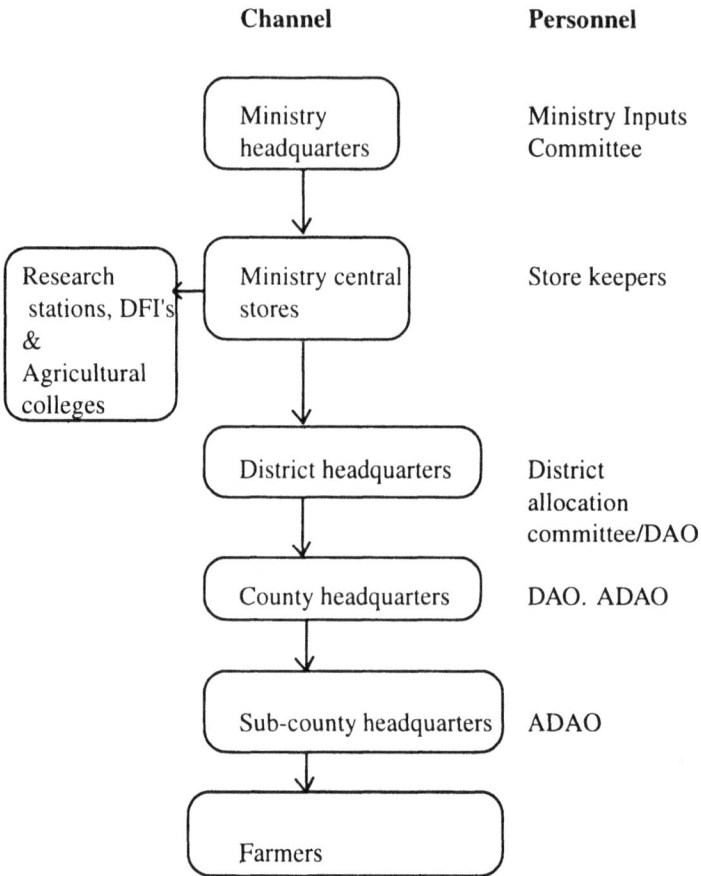

Channel   Personnel

```
                   ┌─────────────────┐
                   │ Ministry        │      Ministry Inputs
                   │ headquarters    │      Committee
                   └────────┬────────┘
                            │
                            ▼
┌──────────────┐   ┌─────────────────┐
│ Research     │◄──│ Ministry central│      Store keepers
│ stations, DFI's│ │ stores          │
│ &            │   └────────┬────────┘
│ Agricultural │            │
│ colleges     │            ▼
└──────────────┘   ┌─────────────────┐
                   │ District headquarters│ District
                   └────────┬────────┘      allocation
                            │               committee/DAO
                            ▼
                   ┌─────────────────┐
                   │ County headquarters│   DAO. ADAO
                   └────────┬────────┘
                            │
                            ▼
                   ┌─────────────────────┐
                   │ Sub-county headquarters│ ADAO
                   └────────┬────────┘
                            │
                            ▼
                   ┌─────────────────┐
                   │ Farmers         │
                   └─────────────────┘
```

The disadvantages of input handling by government ministries included:

• irregularity and inadequacy of supply;
• inputs are sold below the open market price and dissuade private dealers from entering the market; and
• government participation distracts government and civil servants from their established roles - i.e. agricultural research, extension, sector planning and monitoring.

Distribution and delivery by parastatals
UCB-Development Finance Group: From the mid-1980s, UCB became increasingly more involved with agricultural inputs importation, handling and distribution. In the recent past, input procurement by UCB-Development Finance Group has been through financial assistance from:

i)   World Bank/IFAD (SWRARP project)
ii) World Bank/IFCDF (ARP project)
iii) World Bank (small-scale industries & agro-processing)
iv) USAID Rehabilitation of Productive Enterprises.

In all cases, UCB-Development Finance Group through ICB and CTB acted as the main procurement agent for the named projects. The inputs were kept in warehouses in Kampala while awaiting distribution. Inputs distribution for specific projects such as SWRARP, RPE, RFS and the small-scale agro-processing industries projects financed by the EEC and the World Bank was always stipulated by the project sponsors.

UCB-Rural Farmers Scheme (RFS): Under this scheme, which no longer exists, inputs would be procured by UCB-Development Finance Group on the basis of needs assessment from participating UCB branches. On arrival, inputs would be stored by RFS department at the headquarters and distributed to branches for onward distribution to farmers.

Uganda Hardware Ltd: This firm used to deal mainly in building materials and agricultural implements such as shovels, wheel-barrows, axes, and pangas. The inputs were distributed through direct sales to end-users from its headquarters in Kampala or agents in various towns.

Inputs distribution by donor-funded projects
South Western Region Agriculture Rehabilitation Project (SWRARP): Inputs for SWRARP, which was funded by World Bank/IFAD at US$ 27m, were being procured by UCB. The inputs would be transported by UCB to the main SWRARP warehouse at Ndaija, Mbarara, from where they would be distributed in the SWRARP project area (Mbarara, Bushenyi, Kabale and Rukungiri districts).

SWRARP mainly used private traders to distribute inputs in the project area. Private traders would buy and stock inputs in their farm supply retail or general shops in the district towns. From these shops, traders, operating at the rural market level, would buy inputs for resale to farmers. In many instances, rural traders also would buy directly from the SWRARP warehouse. Farmers could also buy directly from district level stores, but were not allowed direct purchases from the SWRARP central store.

Figure 4.3 : Main channels for agricultural-inputs distribution under SWRARP

Channel	Market Level

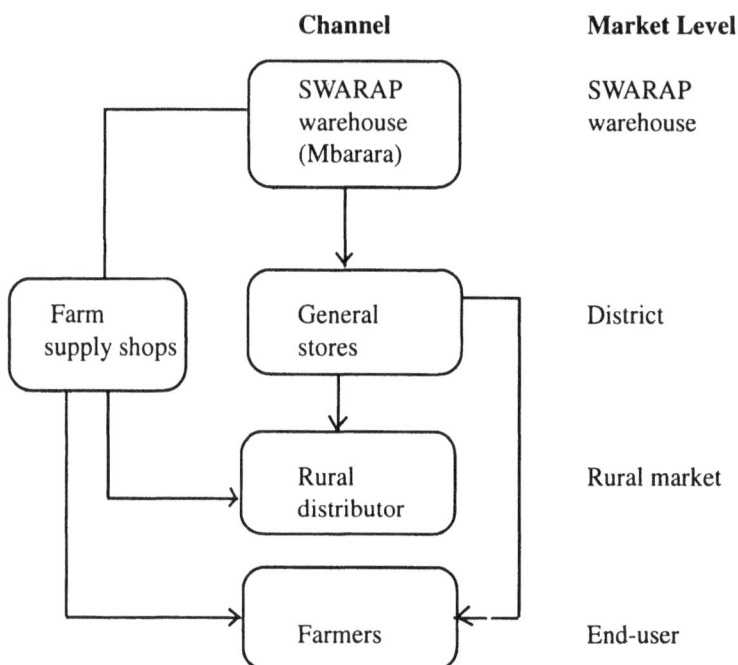

The Agricultural Development Project (ADP) was responsible for the distribution of inputs in the war-ravaged areas of northern and eastern Uganda. It was funded by the World Bank and IFAD. Inputs would be ordered CIF Tororo, Soroti, or Lira and, on arrival, they would be stored in big warehouses in the respective zonal headquarters. From zonal stores, inputs would reach the farmers through five principal channels, i.e. (a) primary co-operative societies, (b) women groups, (c) sub-county chiefs (d) direct sales to farmers from warehouses, (e) in rural markets.

Since one of the original intentions of the project was to help people in the war-ravaged areas of northern Uganda restore their agricultural productivity as quickly as possible, inputs were sold in project areas below the market price (about 5-20 per cent subsidised).

Rehabilitation of Productive Enterprises (RPE): The USAID-financed RPE project was jointly executed by UCB (60 per cent), UDB (35 per cent), and Bank of Baroda (5 per cent) under the supervision of the Development Finance Department (DFD) of the Bank of Uganda (BOU). It continued to supply a wide range of inputs to a number of farmers in various locations in the country.

Under the scheme, the loan to purchase inputs would be assessed by commercial banks and sent to DFD for approval. Once approved, and subject to the availability of funds, procurement and importation would be handled by DFD and, when the goods arrived, banks would be informed to request their clients to collect inputs from clearing /handling agents.

Input distribution and delivery by co-operatives (UCCU)

Under the Co-operative Agriculture and Agribusiness Support (CAAS) project, the co-operative movement in Uganda in 1988 received both financial and commodity assistance from USAID to a tune of US$ 20,766,600. The distribution of the inputs procured under this project was entrusted to the then Uganda Co-operative Central Union (UCCU). In addition to distribution through the co-operative network, UCCU would distribute some inputs to the general public and private traders mainly from its godown in Kawempe, Kampala.

Inputs distribution by private companies

A number of private traders and companies were involved in the distribution and delivery of agricultural inputs even before liberalisation of trade became official policy.

British American Tobacco Company

BAT distributes inputs only to tobacco growing areas comprising:

a)   West Nile (Arua and Nebbi districts).
b)   Middle North (Gulu and Apac districts).
c)   Bunyoro and Mubende districts.
d)   North Kigezi (Rukungiri district).

The BAT input distribution and delivery system is closely tied to its extension service. Input procurements are made according to estimates determined at the Annual Managers' Leaf Conference in June/July. The inputs are received and kept in the warehouses at Arua, Gulu and Rukungiri from where they are distributed to the societies through the tobacco co-operative unions.

Inputs are delivered to farmers under the close supervision of the company which often supplies the inputs on interest-free loan deductible from the delivered tobacco. This seasonal credit model adopted by the BAT has been very successful under Ugandan conditions. Unfortunately, and for a long time, BAT has used its monopsonistic power to keep tobacco farmers' price low. Whereas BAT is a big contributor to national treasury, it has not done the same to the tobacco farmers in their search for prosperity.

Other firms dealing in agro-chemicals consist largely of branches and/or representatives of multinational companies such as Twiga Chemicals Ltd, Shell Ltd, May and Baker, Ciba Geigy, Cooper Ltd, Industries & Agricultural Chemicals Ltd. Their main distribution channels have been supplies to government ministries and parastatals usually on contract; distribution to farmers through appointed private agents operating in strategic towns or locations; and direct sales to farmers.

Input distribution by NGOs
NGOs that have participated in inputs distribution and delivery include:
a)   Red Cross
b)   World Vision
c)   Church of Uganda
d)   Catholic Church
f)   Accord
g)   Lutheran World Federation

These NGOs have supplied and distributed inputs mainly in the war-ravaged areas of Luwero and north-eastern Uganda. They have provided basic inputs such as hoes, seeds, pangas and live animals to beneficiary farmers.

Input marketing constraints
In a well structured marketing system the input marketing chain would normally comprise: input importers/local producers; wholesalers; and retailers/distributors. There would also be adequate vertical and horizontal competition and co-ordination as well as market information flow with the following essential factors fully integrated into the marketing system:

a)   Marketing finance for prompt purchases and payments for crops and distribution of basic consumer goods.
b)   Credit for input dealers and farmers with appropriate repayment periods.
c)   An active and functioning advisory service to promote and advise on proper use of inputs.
d)   Adequate storage and processing facilities for inputs and produce.
e)   A well-developed transportation system to facilitate movement of inputs and outputs between traders and farmers.
f)   An enabling macro-economic environment which allows for planning in the short, medium, and long term with reasonable amount of certainty.

In general, the inputs marketing system in Uganda is still rudimentary, highly fragmented and, there is no clear definition of functions. Importers sometimes act as wholesalers, retailers and distributors. Inputs imported directly by the MOA have been funded mainly by a Japanese grant, while veterinary and livestock inputs have come mainly from EEC/EDF and Canada. Due to budgetary constraints, very little money has come from the Uganda government treasury for agricultural inputs importation.

Input importations by UCB on behalf of the MOA under ADP and SWRARP projects have come specifically for the north-eastern Uganda. From the experience of the last few years, direct involvement by the MOA and UCB has often led to poor sequencing of imports due to lengthy importation procedures and bureaucratic red tape resulting in shortages when critical inputs are needed. Direct distribution of agricultural inputs by MOA has also not been successful either because of two major reasons namely: a) the MOA inability to provide sufficient vehicles to distribute inputs to all areas of the country; and b) MOA's policy of pan-territorial pricing which leads to diversion of cheaper ministry inputs to the open market. The net result is that many inputs handled directly or indirectly by the MOA did not actually reach the small farmers in rural areas. Instead, they got lost in the marketing chain in the urban and peri-urban areas.

At the moment, most of the large private firms mainly import through tendering for government requirements as well as those for donor-funded projects. Very few of these firms import directly using their own funds. Neither do many firms use suppliers' credit. In general, private traders still regard input business as too risky and unreliable for investment. Besides, the high cost of loans discourages traders from borrowing for inputs importation.

Service delivery in Africa has always been skewed in favour of political bureaucratic and social elites, because they dominate non-market delivery channels. This bias limits the access of the majority of the population whose capacity enhancement would have created a critical mass for economic transformation.

This limited access and other constraints or inadequacies regarding the supply or marketing or availability of inputs need to be addressed because they are a hinderance to commercialisation and transformation of agriculture.

Government intervention in credit markets

Government intervention in credit markets through rural finance programmes and institutions in developing countries, including Uganda, has been aimed primarily at resolving perceived market failures. These failures are commonly attributed to two main factors; (i) shortage of short and long-term credit at interest rates low enough to encourage economic development, especially in the agricultural sector and (ii) absence of private rural finance due to an unfavaourable financial environment and a high level of transaction costs associated with the delivery of financial services in rural areas. Thus, the rationale for intervention in credit markets which initially started as an attempt to resolve a general shortage of investment finance subsequently shifted to channelling subsidised credit to what were believed to be *under-serviced priority sectors and targeted clientele.* The perception that some priority sectors, such as agriculture or the rural sector, are under-serviced or under-supplied with credit has empirical support. Using the ratio of sectoral credit to sectoral value-added as a measure of credit adequacy, it has been found that bank credit to sectoral value-added ratios in Uganda show that most sectors, with the exception of trade, but including marketing, operate with little bank credit as illustrated in Table 4:3.

Table 4.3: Relationship between sectoral GDP and commercial bank Credit

	Agriculture	Industry	Trade	Transport	Construction	Others	Total
Year	Credit/ GDP Ratio	Credit/ GDP Ratio	Credit/ GDP Ratio	Credit/ GDP Ratio	Credit/ GDP Ratio	Credit/ GDP Ratio	Credit/ GDP Ratio
1970	11.34	16.15	7.79	8.61	10.10	26.18	12.08
1974	14.84	32.63	10.36	11.45	10.00	20.90	16.45
1983	0.40	21.96	47.27	21.15	42.20	0.38	7.17
1984	0.46	28.04	22.28	23.63	7.53	1.18	6.14
1985	0.66	22.56	28.66	10.62	4.91	0.50	5.84
1986	0.52	17.15	36.95	7.80	8.25	0.16	7.15
1987	1.18	24.76	20.97	9.20	5.37	0.03	6.11
1988	1.03	9.40	14.74	9.37	3.89	0.00	3.95
1989	0.82	10.17	14.78	16.76	7.90	0.00	4.11
1990	1.11	10.11	18.22	9.17	7.59	0.01	4.54
1991	0.89	12.84	26.14	7.97	8.51	0.09	5.45
1992	0.44	11.89	25.85	7.00	7.29	0.04	5.06
1993	0.36	15.35	26.10	6.55	5.55	0.04	4.81
1994	0.24	14.05	26.27	4.32	5.80	0.04	4.71

Source: W. Odwongo, Problems of Developing Rural Financial Markets in Uganda[7]

However, Dale Adams has advised that by itself a small credit to output ratio is not proof of 'credit needed' as it is not a proxy for the rates of return that can be expected from investment in rural areas, and does not provide information on the credit-worthiness of potential borrowers. Instead, a small ratio may reflect low rates of return in farming, the lack of credit-worthiness among borrowers and the dorminance of subsistence agriculture[8]. It should be noted in passing that about 57 percent of Uganda's GDP is non-monetised.

Agricultural finance

The financing of agricultural development can be classified into: i) government financing of public services to agriculture; and ii) institutional financing (in the form of loans) to agriculturalists and agri-support activities such as processing and marketing as shown in Figure 4.4.

From 1950 to 1970 a variety of credit programmes/schemes were initiated in Uganda with the objectives of boosting agricultural output and also helping the rural poor. The discussion of the problems encountered and the evaluation of the programmes' performance will be presented in totality after outlining all the programmes.

a) *Uganda Commercial Bank*

The Uganda Commercial Bank (UCB) and its predecessor, the Uganda Credit and Savings Bank, have been in operation since 1950 to finance individuals and enterprises which could not, for various legal or institutional reasons, qualify for a loan from regular commercial banks - all of them expatriate banks. The expatriate banks were reluctant to provide loans to small farms for two reasons. First, they were accustomed to operate in a sophisticated environment where the range of collateral for loans and advanced loans was wide.

In Uganda, the only security available was land which could only be used to a limited extent, owing to legal complexities associated with the existence of various tenure systems. As a result, only very limited encouragement was given to potential local entrepreneurship, financing being accorded mainly to expatriate business. Secondly, the banks argued that the range of investment opportunities in the country was limited until the broadening of the economy following the high prices for Uganda's coffee and cotton exports in the late 1940s and early 1950s.

Figure 4.4: Flow of agricultural finance

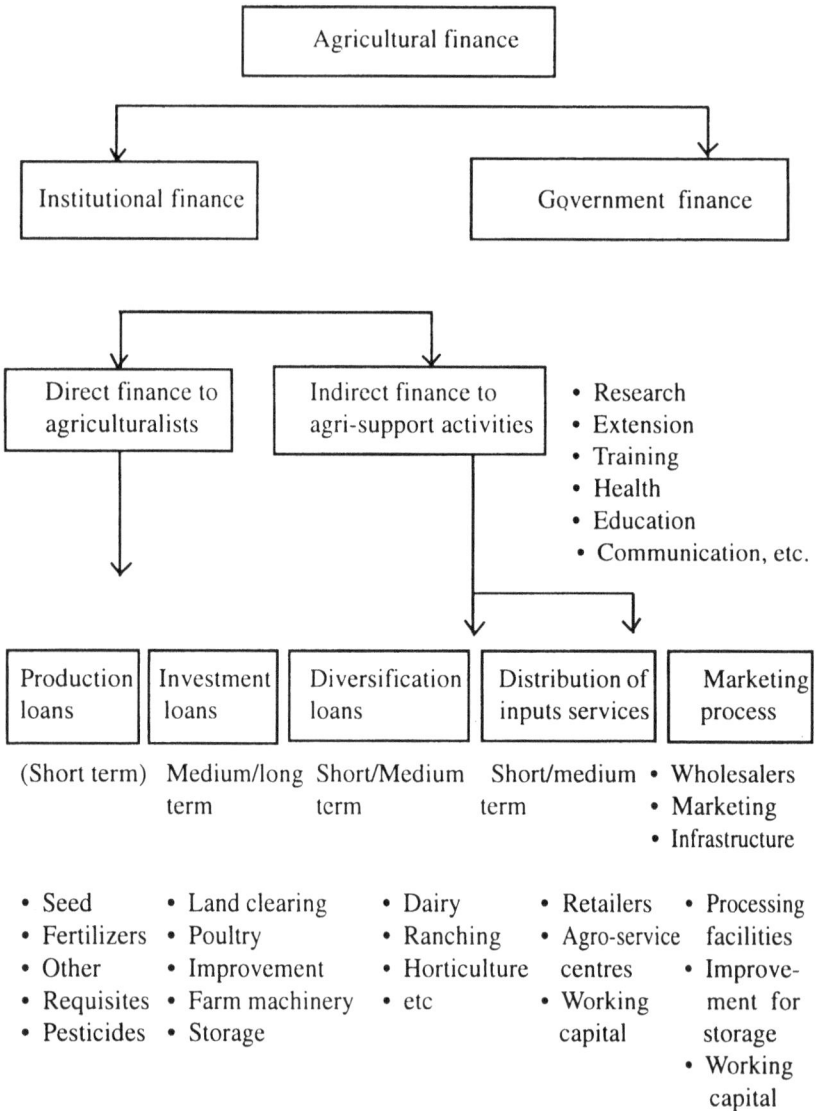

```
                    ┌─────────────────────────┐
                    │   Agricultural finance   │
                    └─────────────────────────┘
              ┌──────────────┴──────────────────────┐
              ▼                                      ▼
    ┌──────────────────┐              ┌──────────────────────┐
    │ Institutional    │              │  Government  finance  │
    │ finance          │              └──────────────────────┘
    └──────────────────┘
        ┌───────┴────────────┐
        ▼                    ▼
┌──────────────┐   ┌──────────────────┐     • Research
│ Direct finance│   │ Indirect finance │     • Extension
│ to            │   │ to agri-support  │     • Training
│ agriculturalists│ │ activities       │     • Health
└──────────────┘   └──────────────────┘     • Education
        │                                   • Communication, etc.
        ▼                    ┌──────┴──────┐
                             ▼             ▼
```

Production loans	Investment loans	Diversification loans	Distribution of inputs services	Marketing process
(Short term)	Medium/long term	Short/Medium term	Short/medium term	• Wholesalers • Marketing • Infrastructure
• Seed • Fertilizers • Other • Requisites • Pesticides	• Land clearing • Poultry • Improvement • Farm machinery • Storage	• Dairy • Ranching • Horticulture • etc	• Retailers • Agro-service centres • Working capital	• Processing facilities • Improvement for storage • Working capital

Adapted from L.E. Eturu, 'The Role of Central Banks in the Promotion of Investment and Financing'[9]

In 1972, government directed that all banking business and accounts of parastatals and co-operative unions should be transferred to the government-owned Uganda Commercial Bank. Consequently, expatriate banks were compelled to close their up-country branches and retrench to Kampala. The UCB took over some of the branches and in the process, expanded its network from 18 to 28 branches and 2 agencies by June 1973. By 1990, the UCB branches had increased to 188 (i.e. 81 percent of the country's 233 commercial banks' branches) by 1990. This expansion of financial services, especially in rural areas, was a positive response to the issue of under-serviced sectors and clientele raised above. It ameliorated the problem of both the availability and accessibility of investment finance.

In the 1980/90s, the UCB was the primary agricultural lender. In terms of number of loans made, UCB's Rural Farmers Lending Scheme was its most important rural credit programme. Most funds borrowed were provided by the African Development Bank. Originally, the RFS commenced with a revolving fund of Shs. 60 million contributed by the bank's own resources. The scheme subsequently received donor support to the tune of US$ 23 million. At its peak, in 1990/91, the scheme was operating out of about one-quarter of UCB's 190 branches, many of them in small towns and villages. Unfortunately, agricultural marketing constraints, including the unavailability of market outlets at remunerative prices, prevented the full realisation of the expected benefits from the scheme and, consequently, its impact on agricultural development was very limited.

Under the RFS, lending was based on the character of the borrower, his social standing in the community, his ability to undertake the proposed activity, his habits on handling funds, and viability of the project. Although character loans based on personal reputation and peer pressure have been claimed to be 'effective collateral substitutes' based on the so-called 'best practice principles' claimed to have been derived from experiences worldwide, Uganda's experience with character loans is totally different. More than 20,000 small-scale farmers have failed to pay off loans totalling over Shs. 6 billion. These are part of UCB's non-performing loans of Shs 67 billion (US$ 67 million) which constitute 80 percent of the bank's loans and advances that have made the bank insolvent. As a result of this massive defaulting, the RFS was suspended, and with the privatisation of the bank, the revival of a similar approach can be expected only in micro finance institutions.

(b) *The Bank of Uganda*

Established in 1966, the Bank of Uganda (BOU) is the country's central bank. It is responsible for issuing legal tender, maintaining external resources, promoting the stability of the currency and ensuring a sound financial structure.

It has been involved in agricultural financing (of farmers and agro-industries) mainly through the operations of its Development Finance Department (DFD) established in the early 1980s, with the major objective of putting in place a credit system in the country which would facilitate the flow of loanable funds to priority sectors of the economy, especially agriculture and agro-related industries. Thus, its involvement was a response to credit constraint. The DFD was also set up to mobilise resources from both external (donor funds) and internal sources by creating a Development Finance Fund.

From 1985 to mid – 1994, the DFD, under its rehabilitation of productive enterprises (RPE) programme, provided funds through the Bank of Baroda, the UCB and the UDB for financing the rehabilitation of existing and new agricultural enterprises in the private sector. The programme, funded by USAID grant of US$ 18.2 million, funded 223 enterprises in 20 districts by the time it was terminated in June 1994. Other schemes operated by the DFD include Development Finance Fund (DFF) and Refinance Scheme which by October 1994 had benefited 20 projects involving a refinance amount of Shs. 2.9 billion out of a total contribution of Shs. 3.9 billion, Export Refinance and Export Credit Guarantee Scheme which was established in 1992 to assist and encourage commercial banks to finance export development and diversification and the Investment Term Credit Refinance Fund (ITCRF), established in 1993 with financial assistance of US$ 25 million under the IDA Enterprises Development Programme, to provide refinance to the banks or credit institutions to lend for investment on viable enterprises.

Following severe problems in the crop financing system (especially because co-operative unions which were the major borrowers of marketing finance had become unbankable as they suffered chronic liquidity problems, low profitability and heavy indebtedness), the BOU, at the request of the government, went beyond assisting commercial banks through refinancing and bill discounting or providing loans to the marketing boards against Treasury guarantees, and took over the responsibility of coffee financing from commercial banks in 1989. This responsibility involved the BOU acting as banker to the CMB and providing funds to:

- clear CMB's outstanding liabilities to commercial banks, co-operative unions, primary societies and private processors.
- to cover CMB's financial position pending payment by the Treasury for the large volume of barter sales effected by the Board on behalf of the government and its agencies.
- finance working capital needed by the Board to pay for its inventories of coffee.

Secondly, the BOU became responsible for providing guarantees to commercial banks for lending to co-operative unions considered uncredit-worthy by banks. Thirdly, it was responsible for lending to some primary co-operative societies through commercial banks.

Arising from this involvement, BOU's outstanding loans for crop finance increased from Shs 2.3 billion in 1988 to Shs 18.7 billion in December 1989. Furthermore, the Bank got involved in direct payment to farmers through marketing boards. With structural adjustment, crop financing facilities were transferred back to the commercial banks in 1991 and central bank involvement in the provision of marketing finance ended.

Whereas it is true, as Table 16 shows, that the credit/GDP ratio failed to recover to the levels of the late 1960s and early 1970s - years of relatively impressive economic growth – the trend could have been worse if these schemes had not existed. In turn, the shortage of investment finance would have setback the much wanted economic progress. It can also be deduced from this multiplicity of credit schemes that, whereas credit availability and accessibility is very important, it is the failure to use the credit productively that is a more critical constraint to our development efforts.

(c) *The Uganda Development Bank*
The UDB was established in 1972 as a fully government-owned development finance institution with the main purpose of facilitating, promoting and financing the development of the various sectors of the economy. During the last 20 years, it has been a source of medium-term loans for medium and large-scale agricultural projects. A typical UDB agriculture loan is for five years with the principal repayment deferred for one year. It has no branch offices. Since 1987, it has relied on money from the DFD of the BOU to fund its agricultural lending. The main sources of these funds have been World Bank, Islamic Development Bank and the OPEC Fund. During the 1970s, with the financial assistance from IDA, the UDB financed establishments of large-scale government-owned ranches and dairy farms. In the early 1980s it implemented the ADB ranching rehabilitation projects involving a total outlay of US$ 13 million. The UDB also actively participated under the USAID-RPE project. In the 1990s the UDB has experienced serious loan recovery problems with recovery rates of less than 20 percent which has made it deeply indebted to external lenders and government. The UDB has accumulated US$81.5 million (Uganda Shs.82 billion) in non-performing loans. In September 1997, it was closed to the public for a week to enable a team of experts to reorganise its management and operations (i.e. restructure it) as a prelude to its privatisation.

(d) *The Co-operative Bank and the Co-operative Credit Scheme*

The Co-operative Bank was established as a co-operative society under the Co-operative Societies Act for the purpose of carrying on banking business for the benefit of its members. It was linked to the government by the control exercised by the Ministry of Co-operatives and Marketing and its participation in the administration of some of the funds on-lent by government through the central bank. Administered loans constituted 5 percent of total advance portfolio in both 1990 and 1994. The administered funds, sourced locally and which amounted to Shs 1.0 billion, came from the government as contribution to ADB ginnery rehabilitation loan, the BOU Crop Finance Support Fund and BOU/ DFF. The externally sourced funds mainly came from the African Development Bank, EEC and IDA/IFAD. Its total advance portfolio was Shs 20.75 billion in 1994. With 24 branches, the Co-operative Bank has been having second largest branch network (i.e. second to UCB) and it has also been the number two lender for agricultural purposes mainly through co-operatives. Unfortunately, it was closed in May 1999 for what the Central Bank called insolvency.

The Co-operative Credit Scheme (CCS) was started in 1961 with the aim of providing short-term production loans to farmers through primary co-operative societies. A revolving fund of Shs. 13 million was then established for the purpose. The scheme was originally implemented by the credit section of the Ministry of Co-operatives and Marketing on pilot basis involving about 100 primary societies. By 1973 the scheme was serving 506 primary societies and had served 39,881 members. During this period, the scheme was very successful (in fact it was regarded as the most successful in Africa) with average rate of default below 2 percent. But defaulting increased with Uganda's economic crisis of the 1970s and the scheme was almost abandoned. However, it was revived in 1988 with a USAID grant of Shs. 80 million under the PL-80 programme. Additional funds came subsequently from Swedish Co-operative Centre and the USAID PL-80 programme. By the end of 1993, CCS had disbursed credits to 29,717 farmer members of primary societies amounting to Shs 2.3 billion.

The magnitude of resources mobilised from external sources by government and associated development institutions for government use and credit lending since independence is shown in Table 4.4.

Table 4.4: Aid Commitments to Uganda (million US$)

	1962-71	1972-78	1979-85	1986-97
Creditor/donor				
European Union			100.6	693.5
EU Countries			100.8	1942.8
Japan				197.2
North America			23.3	458.5
Russia	19.8			0.3
Eastern Europe			9.0	34.9
China				174.6
Asia (excl. Japan)			8.0	93.5
Multilaterals				
o/w IMF		182.4	307.4	507.6
World Bank			206.3	1694.3
ADB	4.3	23.6	133.9	476.4
Others		27.1	216.9	7002
Arab countries		99.4	20.4	167.3
Other Bilaterals				49.1
Total	**24.1**	**332.5**	**1127.6**	**7190.4**

Source: L.A. Kasekende and M. Atingi-Ego, Bank of Uganda Memo (1998)

Why credit programmes failed

In both the pre-1970 and post-1980 periods, credit programmes were prominent development tools, but, in both cases, they failed to achieve the desired effectiveness owing to:

a) Limited population coverage.
Out of 2.5 to 3.0 million farm households in Uganda, it is estimated that only about 2 percent have been serviced with credit.

b) Funding instability or lending surges.
A substantial part of funds used in agricultural lending has been provided in fits and starts by the BOU or donors. Combined with inflation and loan recovery problems, this resulted in substantial variations in the real value of flows of rural lending. This has caused the formal financial system to create rural lending capacity that is difficult to reduce when flows of funds diminish. The resulting under-utilised capacity increases the average cost of lending. Combined with weak deposit mobilisation efforts, this means that scale and scope economies are difficult to realise. Irregular flows of funds also lessen the expected value of borrowers maintaining excellent credit ratings with formal lenders and this contributes to default problems.

c) High costs of delivering financial services
It has been estimated that even in efficient programmes the costs of providing loans to low-income farmers can range from 10 to 20 percent of the value of money lent. If the loan is accompanied by technical assistance the cost may increase to 20 - 30 percent of the loan value. Rural transportation deficiencies, inflation, defective collateral, and loan default add further to the real costs of these programmes. If these costs are not covered by interest earnings, the lending agency suffers decapitilisation or becomes addicted to continual infusions of outside funds.

d) Persistent loan non-performance and loan defaults
Virtually all formal credit programmes in Uganda had chronic problems of loan-non-performance and loan default.[10]   Non-performance[11] is the loan's lack of capacity to generate enough income to repay the principal and interest to the lender. It represents failure of a loan to service debt obligations as they fall due regardless of what security a lender may hold on the facility. In other words, it represents project failure or wilful avoidance of repayment. An advance is termed non-performing or sticky when it shows no signs of disengaging from the hands of the borrower and sticks to the bank's books.

In Uganda, two criteria have been used to detect non-performing credit facilities. First, a credit facility with a pre-determined repayment schedule is considered non-performing when:
– The principal and interest remain outstanding for 180 days or more.
– The principal and interest payments outstanding for 180 days or more have been capitalised, refinanced, re-negotiated, restructured or rolled over contrary to original terms.

Secondly, a credit facility such as an overdraft or any other open-ended credit without a pre-determined repayment schedule is non-performing when:
– The credit facility exceeds the customer's established borrowing limit of 180 consecutive days or more.
– The customer's borrowing line has expired for 180 days or more.
– Interest is due and remains unpaid for 180 days or more.
– The account or overdraft remains inactive with no deposits or the deposits made are too little to cover interest capitalised over 180 days.

To a bank, the identification of non-performance per se is not enough. It is necessary to determine the severity of non-performance in order to take appropriate corrective action. This is to say that standards are necessary for proper recognition and classification of non-performing loans. When no such standards are set for non-performing assets, banks may well fail to recognise problem advances or may even delay corrective action.

The Bank of Uganda and Financial Institutions Statute of 1993 introduced a code system to classify loans under three adverse categories: substandard doubtful, and loss.

Substandard

The objective criteria of recognition rest with the period of arrears of principal and interest for 180 days or more but less than one year. Subjective indicators include weaknesses such as inadequate cash flow to service debt; undercapitalisation and insufficient working capital; absence of financial information or security documentation; irregular payment of principal and interest; and inactive overdraft.

Doubtful

This category represents loans with arrears for one year or more but less than two years. Subjective indicators include those under substandard but, more importantly, there is deterioration to the extent that full repayment is unlikely or releasable security values will be insufficient to cover the bank's exposure.

Loss

This is the most adverse category, and it represents loans whereby repayment of the principal and interest remains outstanding for two or more years. The recognition of non-performing assets stimulates collection efforts and reduces the possibility of loss on such assets.

The growth and magnitude of non-performing loans in Uganda has been rising steadily since 1981 and reached alarming proportions by December 1993. It is estimated that the UCB which held 40 percent of total deposits of the banking sector had almost 80 percent of its loans and advances in the non-performing category. When the UCB is excluded the rest of the commercial banking sector had 28 percent of its loans non-performing. It is reported that even the best performing foreign bank - Standard Chartered - had 13.2 percent of its portfolio in non-performing loans.

When the Non-Performing Assets Trust Bill was tabled in the NRC the discussion indicated that a staggering sum of over Shs. 100 billion was being locked up in non-performing loans, with about 80 percent of the bad loans in two of the twenty commercial banks operating in the country.

Common causes of non-performance in Uganda can be categorised as political, institutional, technical and economic. They can also be categorised, for purposes of analysis, as lender or borrower-based and, therefore, cultural. On analysing these causes, it is important to note that non-performance does not necessarily mean project failure because there are many cases of successful projects on which repayment is not made. Thus, non-performance must include both default due to project failure and wilful avoidance of repayment.

A politically inspired credit scheme tends to beget non-performance especially if its timing coincides with or follows a major political event such as war, elections, or civil strife. Experience in Uganda shows that recipients tend to perceive such loans as reparations for damages or inducements or rewards for political support[12]. The following selected cases illustrate the point:

- The Group Farming Loans Scheme (1964-68)
- The Beef Ranching Scheme (1970s)
- Tobacco Development Loans Fund (1966-1970)
- Agricultural Development Project (1980s)
- USAID Luwero Triangle Economic Recovery (1986-88)
- Crop Finance Scheme (1988-90)
- UCB Rural Farmers Scheme (1987-1993)
- *Entadikwa* Credit Scheme 1996

The recovery of loans given under these schemes was below 50 percent. Political pressure on loan allocation tended to impinge on appraisal, targeting, collection and restricted the lender from exercising prudent judgement.[13]

Coups and wars in Uganda since 1971 have seriously disrupted the environment for making good use of loan funds to generate repayment. Productive assets created by the loans were wantonly looted or destroyed. To escape death or persecution, borrowers fled the country leaving sticky loans on the bank's books. These loans progressively weakened their capital base.

Other political causes of non-performance include government excessive taxation policy; sudden changes in exercise duty structure forcing prices to go upwards thereby dampening product sales; sudden ban of manufacture of a product as was the case of polythene, and government failure to exercise financial discipline resulting in inflation and upward shifts in factor prices. There is also the problem of government creating excessive competition through its licensing policies. Liberal projects licensing as has been the case for coffee exporters, tends to lead to over-supply or excessive competition in the market which may seriously dampen sales income.

Lender-based causes of non-performance are perhaps the most serious and reflect to a large extent the infancy of the banking business in Uganda. Institutional capacity, for example, relating to banking laws and their enforcement, organisation, manpower and equipment which would ensure prudent management of bank funds, has been generally lacking. In Uganda, there is no legal framework to enable loan defaulters to be effectively and quickly dealt with. The present legal system is slow and costly and favours defaulters.

The World Bank diagnostic studies of the banking sector indicate that this problem is largely a result of management deficiencies and inherent weaknesses in lending operations. In particular, risk assessment in loan appraisal, credit analysis and sanctioning techniques are lacking. Effective loan supervision is very weak especially in the case of administered loans resulting in low loan recovery rates. Credit control and portfolio monitoring systems are inadequate or inappropriate. There is also the problem of lending pressures in relation, but not limited, to administered lending operations.

One of the most critical problems in Uganda is that banks are established with inadequate capital. The position has been more acute with domestic banks most of which have had negative capital base especially after the devaluation exercise in 1987. Faced with a serious lack of internal resources, banks are inadequately equipped in terms of personnel, equipment and related logistics. This is where the problem of non-performance begins.

The absence of an adequate pool of trained bank staff and the relatively slow growth in training programmes aggravate the situation especially if such inadequately capitalised banks rapidly expand their branch networks in an environment characterised by poor transportation and slow development in computerised banking operations. In one sense, therefore, non-performance is a consequence of the teething problems of new financial institutions and the generally low development of banking in Uganda.

Loan appraisal, sanction and disbursement procedures and loan appraisal capacity in banks is generally lacking especially in the case of long-term loans. Commercial banks for the most part lack capacity and experience to appraise term loans, having been trained to extend and manage overdrafts and short-term working capital facilities and other retail banking procedures. The inspection of loan files in banks indicates serious shortcomings in risk assessment and compliance with prudential norms.[14]

The absence of information, to banks, of key values used in project preparation creates a serious problem in appraisal as borrowers in Uganda have been demonstrating in their projects a much higher financial return than is actually possible. The projection of high financial returns about what a typical borrower will be able to achieve is usually based on unrealistic assumptions. This is especially true of projects in industry and agriculture.

Project design often excludes detailed consideration of results which occur in the field. Bank appraisal of projects tends to be confounded when the expected mean or average sector cash flow is used as a basis for project formulation. Here, the problem stems from a range of results actually achieved by ultimate borrowers. It takes an experienced loan officer to scrutinise cash flows from the very successful to the worst failures.

In Uganda, getting a bank loan is a an expensive and time consuming process. Loan applicants have to wait long hours to initiate a transaction. They may have to pay 'facilitation fees' to process the paper work and they have to follow up the approval ladder. Delays in loan approval and tedious disbursement procedures tend to slow down or even to stall project implementation which means that the borrowers find it hard because they are unable to realise investment within the agreed time frame and to keep with the loan repayment schedule.

The tendency of banks to tailor loan maturities to book-keeping convenience rather than the borrower's cash flow patterns begets debt collection problems. Due dates at close of accounting quarters may be harmonious with book-keeping rhythms of banks but may not coincide with peaks in the borrower's liquidity circles. Periodic instalments of equal size are easier to handle by the lender but the cash flow available from loan-supported enterprises may not conform to this ready pattern.

The coordination and timing of disbursement is crucial to loan performance. Inordinate delays in disbursement, poorly coordinated distribution or acquisition of production inputs have been a common cause of non-performance of administered term loans. Such problems tend to depress borrower cash flows and reduce their repayment capacity.

Inspection reports of banks indicate that loans are generally poorly documented and this delays accurate and prompt action to enforce repayment. With inadequate documentation, banks cannot administer loans or follow up defaulters effectively.

Documentation and accounting standards are the basis for monitoring and supervision. A commonly reported problem in Uganda is the serious lack of accounting standards. When no standards have been set for non-performing assets, banks fail to recognise problem advances which in turn causes delays in taking corrective action. Poor accounting standards coupled with insufficient supervision by lenders, and, to some extent, by the BOU have accentuated non-performance in Uganda.

A serious cause of non-performance is generally the poor payment system in the country. Delays in effecting payments to suppliers by government, parastatals and related institutions are or constitute a destabilising factor in loan collection by banks. Interest burdens created by such delays explain the distress and indebtedness of the coffee and cotton sub-sectors to banks in the 1990s. This is, therefore, an area which economic reforms in the country must tackle in order to redress the problem of non-performance in banks. The situation was equally bad in Japan until the Prompt Payment Act was enacted. Similarly, legislation was adopted in India to assist banks and borrowers on debt collection.

Non-performance of advances to industry and agriculture is largely a consequence of low returns and lack of production-increasing and cost-reducing innovations. Disruption of research capacity resulting from two decades of war and political chaos imposed serious restrictions on the productivity of agriculture and industry. Consequently, yield and key values in project proposals presented to banks cannot be reproduced in the actual project situation, and often lead to overestimation and project failure. Other technical causes of non-performance include down time due to delays in receiving inputs; non-availability of important facilities such as power, water, and transport; and lack of proper maintenance leading to frequent break-down of plant and machinery; improper selection of plant and machinery or improper plant layout; and lack of proper systems of quality control and testing.

A convenient remainder of the factors considered by lenders in deciding whether or not to approve a loan is that of four 'C's. These are the conditions within which the borrower will be operating for the duration of the loan; the character of borrower, income-generating capacity of the project, capital (borrowers' investment or equity, his liquidity and solvency), and collateral (i.e. borrower's assets which could provide tangible security for a loan and which could be sold to repay the loan if necessary). The main economic conditions that have affected loan-performance and repayment in Uganda are exchange rate variations, inflation and interest rates. For foreign denominated loans, on which the borrower bears the exchange risk, repeated and sharp devaluations throughout the 1980s dramatically increased the debt burden. Difficulties of non-performance which banks have faced on foreign lines of credit are essentially a consequence of exchange risk exposure. Similarly, the repayment capacity of commodity exporters have been eroded whenever the Ugandan shilling has depreciated.

For over two decades (1970s and 1980s) inflation had its toll on loan performance. Interest rates charged on loans were negative in real terms. Nominal interest rates exceeded by the rate of inflation, encouraged borrowers to wilfully delay repayment because they could obtain a profit by employing cheap funds at higher rates of return.

The second critical economic factor is the income-generating capacity of investments. Dale Adams[15] has suggested that chronic loan recovery problems may reflect a paucity of high return investment opportunities. He holds that low average and highly variable rates of return may make it difficult for borrowers to repay loans and may also lessen the value of borrowers maintaining their credit-worthiness with formal lenders by fulfilling debt obligations.

The third economic factor is insufficient equity. There is a serious problem of borrowers' dependence on bank funds. In financing terms, credit far in excess of the borrowers' contribution imposes debt servicing obligations which are large relative to their cash flows and increases the probability of failure to repay as scheduled. Overloading a borrower with debt is one way to expose the lender to the risk of ownership in the borrower's undertaking or of ensuring poor loan collection performance.

The fourth factor is dissension among partnerships. Partnership firms are particularly vulnerable to failure because conflicts among partners and heavy withdrawals by outgoing partners preempt project objectives and lead to non-performance. If partnerships do not split, they take up expansions by setting up similar units in different names. Such expansion creates difficulties in controlling the account, and may lead to diversion of funds, divided attention and other problems which may adversely affect the operations of the first enterprise.

The discussion on causes of non-performance or loan recovery problems has, so far, been largely within the economic and management contexts. But credit availability, its use and repayment also have cultural contexts. These are the behaviour and practices of lenders i.e. creditors' culture and those of borrowers (i.e. borrowers' culture).

Our concern with the borrowers' credit culture relates to how credit is used and social attitudes to indebtedness.

The productive use of credit depends not only on what we have called 'conditions' -the supply/demand situation and the environment - but also the capacity, values and attitudes of the borrower. The conditions for the farmer, for instance, include size of land holding, security of land tenure, soil fertility, sources of water, control of pests and diseases, freedom from debilitating illness, price stability, variations in demand for farm products, access to markets information and access to suitable productive technologies. The type of farm enterprise being undertaken places important constraints upon farming operations. The seasonal cycle of labour requirements vary according to the crop grown. Peak labour demand, the need for specific inputs such as seeds, fertilizers, pesticides and the time of harvesting depend largely on the seasonal cycle. If the farmer is not able to maintain his minimal requirements until he has harvested his new crop, he will be most concerned about obtaining credit for 'consumption' purposes to tide him over. Thus production credit offered at the wrong time of the year is quite likely to be used for other purposes.

In Uganda, credit 'diversion' to 'consumption purposes' is not peculiar to farmers. Stories about acquisition of luxury cars and expensive 'good time' by the elite in commerce, industry and the service sector are common. Attitudes towards work and division of labour, time and thrift; credit and indebtedness, as well as towards governments in general, are all critical factors influencing borrowers' use of credit and willingness to repay.

Values relating to work and leisure condition both the kind and amount of activity that requires credit. To some people, hard work signifies low economic status; leisure is seen as a luxury of the more well-to-do. It seems to be true that in many areas of Uganda, men have only a minimal interest in hard work in farming, and may well resist changes which would require additional time, labour and managerial inputs.

The time concept also affects borrowers' approaches to innovations and credit use. The new investment based on credit may well exceed what are culturally defined limits on how long certain work or tasks should take. In Uganda, this is true of dairy farming based on exotic or grade cattle and modern poultry farming. Some people feel that the related farming operations constitute real 'detention'.

Attitudes towards thrift vary significantly from one individual to another, but in some cases such attitudes become cultural norms. We have already noted that culturally-determined values which do not favour thrift and saving are responsible for the 'cancer of low saving' in Uganda. An extremely important issue of attitude relates to the meaning given to credit. To those who provide credit, it is usually viewed as an input to assist the producer in raising his production and income. Unless a borrower perceives credit as an input, he/she cannot see the need for productive use and the obligation to repay.

In an effort to gain political support, governments make promises of benefit to people. Loans from banks and credit schemes may, therefore, tend to be viewed, erroneously, as government grants or gifts in fulfilment of promises by politicians, This may easily be part of the problem of loan delinquency in the UCB and the UDB. Development finance, whether it is for agriculture or any other sector, is necessary but it cannot succeed in an environment characterised by a culture of non-repayment of loans by wilful defaulters. Non-repayment of loans cripples and eventually wipes out financial intermediaries. The bad loan explosion into a crisis began with a closure of a local bank, followed by a take over of others by the BOU climaxing with the institution of the Non-Performing Assets Recovery Trust (NPART) for UCB and closure of the UDB, the International Credit Bank, Greenland Bank, and the Co-operative Bank.

Government intervention in foreign exchange markets

As in the commodity markets, during the pre-reform period, government intervention in foreign exchange markets was in the form of statutory monopoly, controls and administered prices. Prior to the economic reforms that were launched in the 1980s, only the BOU could sell foreign currency, and it monopolised the control of all foreign exchange received into the country. The exchange rate was fixed and over-valued as evidenced by the gap between the official and parallel (or black) foreign exchange rates.

In 1982 government introduced a dual exchange rate system consisting of a lower rate (termed window 1) to be used to import aid-financed priority inputs and petroleum products and a higher rate (termed window 11) determined by supply and demand through an auction market. Under window II, the exchange rate was determined by market forces. By 1986 when the NRM government came to power, inflation was in three digits (161 percent) and there was a balance of payments funding gap of US$ 200m. Clearly, there was need for breaking the inflationary spiral and for achieving external balance. To tackle the two problems, a choice had to be made between the control model and structural adjustment. The control model involved the revaluation of the exchange rate and the imposition of a regulated price regime. Advocates of this strategy were concerned that adjustments through devaluation would fuel inflation and hinder the recovery of the productive sector by raising the cost of imported industrial and agricultural inputs.

The alternative strategy of structural adjustment contained the devaluation of the exchange rate to restore the competitiveness of exports and import substitutes and thus to restore external balance; adjustment of monetary and fiscal policy to reduce the inflationary pressure arising out of excessive monetary expansion, particularly as a result of central bank financing of the national budget deficit; the restoration of positive real interest rates to stimulate financial saving and the process of financial intermediation, and the tackling of key structural bottlenecks, such as poor infrastructure and inputs and material shortages, in recognition that the restoration of appropriate price incentives was not a sufficient condition for economic recovery.

Initially, the government adopted the control model. The previous dual exchange rate system (introduced in 1982), which had an official rate at USh 1,480/US$ and a second rate at USh 5,000/US$, was abolished and the Uganda shilling was revalued to USh 1,400 per US$. As a consequence, inflation accelerated from 120 percent in May 1986 to 240 percent in May 1987 and the economy was brought to the verge of collapse. The May 1987 currency reform removed two zeros from the face value of the shilling; thus the exchange rate of USh 1,400 per US$ became equivalent to new UShs 14 per US$.

By this time the government had realised that the control model was failing to address the economy and, therefore, it turned to the alternative strategy. In June 1987, the government devalued the exchange rate from USh 14 per US$ to USh 60 per US $ as part of a sweeping package of the introduction of a new currency with one new shilling equivalent to 100 old shillings. The effects and impact of the exchange rate liberalisation will be discussed in Chapter Six.

Government control over land

The imposition of British colonial rule at the end of the nineteenth century marked the beginning of an evolution which entailed among other things the shift of land ownership from group rights (e.g. tribal, clan, village, family and official rights)[16] towards the individualisation of tenure. But more fundamentally, the British, through the Uganda Agreement of 1900, introduced a land tenure system[17] under which 50 percent of the land in Buganda became crown land. Under the terms of the 1900 Agreement, the division of land (in square miles) in Buganda between the British Crown, the Buganda chiefs and the missionary societies is summarised in Table 4.5.

Table 4.5: Allocation of land in Buganda under the 1900 Agreement (in sq. miles)

Forests under control of the Uganda Administration	1,500
Uncultivated land vested in Her Majesty's Government and controlled by Uganda Administration	9,000
Plantations and other private property of His Highness the Kabaka	350
Plantations and other private property of the Namasole	16
Plantations and the private property of the Namasole, mother of Mwanga	10
To the Princes: Joseph, Augustine, Ramathan and Yusuf-Suna, 8 square miles each	32
To the princesses, sisters, and relations of the Kabaka	90
To the Abamasaza (chiefs of counties), 20 in all, 8 square miles each (private property)	160
Official estates attached to the posts of Abamasaza, 8 square miles each	160
To the three Reagents, official property attached to their office, 16 square miles each	48
Mbogo (the Muhammedan chief) and his adherents	48
Kamuswaga, chief of Koki	24
One thousand chiefs and private landowners, estates computed at an average of 8 square miles per individual	8,000
To the three missionary societies, and in trust for the native churches	92
Government Stations (at Kampala, Entebbe, Masaka etc.)	50
Total	**19,600**

Sources: S.W. West[18] J. M. Opio-Odongo[19]

This land settlement in Buganda introduced a fundamental change in the traditional system. Instead of group ownership, land rights were conferred on individuals. Instead of Buganda's share of the land being held by the people as a whole or by the government on their behalf, it was held by the local ruling class which had to apportion it between its 3,700 individual members. People cultivating the land so allocated automatically became tenants to the grantees and hence were subject to pay rent. This conversion of customary owners into tenants has become a source of permanent conflict. The insecurity of tenure arising from the conflict has been a serious disincentive to investment and productive as well as sustainable use of the land by the user-occupiers.

To legalise and regularise these individual rights to the land, and to differentiate this freehold tenure from that of the freeholders in English law, a name was found for the system of land tenure in Uganda and a law defining it was enacted in 1908. The name is the word 'mailo'[20] and the law is Land Law of 1908. The main provisions of this law were that:

- an individual can own up to 30 square miles without special sanction of the Governor;
- a mailo land owner can transfer land by sale, gift or will to another person of the Protectorate but cannot transfer land or lease it to anyone who is not of the Protectorate without the special permission of the Lukiiko (Buganda Legislative Council) and the Governor;
- where a person leaves no will, succession will be ascertained by the customary rules of succession; and
- customary rights of the people to the use of roads, running water and springs are preserved.

The effects of both the Agreement and the Land Law were, on one hand, to confer property rights in perpetuity and, on the other hand, to take away land from the peasants and give it to the rulers and the churches. The position regarding government control over land in areas other than Buganda can be gleaned from part of General Notice No. 551 of 1950 and from subsequent developments. The Part of the General Notice read as follows:

His Excellency THE GOVERNOR wishes all the people of Uganda to understand the policy of His Majesty's Government and the Protectorate Government which has been followed in the past and will be followed in the future, in respect of Crownland outside townships and trading centres in the provinces other than Buganda. FIRSTLY, these rural lands are being held in trust for the use of the African population.

SECONDLY, although the right under Laws of the Protectorate is reserved to the Governor as representing the King (of England) to appropriate areas which he considers are required for forests, roads, townships or any other public purposes, yet it has been agreed with the Secretary of State that the Governor shall in every case consult the African Local Government concerned and give full consideration to its wishes.

Moreover, the Governor will not alienate land to non-Africans except:

a) for agricultural or industrial or other undertakings which will in the judgement of the Governor in Council promote the economic or social welfare of the inhabitants of the territory; and

b) for residential purposes when only a small area is involved.

THIRDLY, it is not the intension of His Majesty's Government and the Protectorate Government that the Protectorate of Uganda shall be developed as a country of non-African Settlement.

Although, in theory, land under the control of a Board of Trustees was for the native population and land under the control of the Crown was for free disposal, in practice, there was no distinction between trusteeship land and Crown land.

The 1908 land law defined the rights of landowners but it was the Registration of Titles Ordinance of 1922 which determined actual possession or ownership of a specialised landed property.[21] Registration removed or at least reduced ownership uncertainty although this was only for the local elites or political notables and not for the mailo tenants or peasants.

There is a wide-spread belief among development specialists that tenure security is an important condition for agricultural development. Secure rights are believed to:

i)   increase credit use through greater incentives for investment, improved credit-worthiness of projects and enhanced collateral value of land.
ii) increase land transactions, facilitating transfers of land from less significant to more efficient uses by increasing the certainty of contracts and lowering enforcements costs.
iii) reduce the incidence of land disputes through clearer definition and enforcements of rights.
iv) raise productivity through increased agricultural investment.[22]

The casual relationships summarised above are illustrated in Figure 4.8.

Figure 4.5: Conceptual model linking title and tenure security with agricultural performance

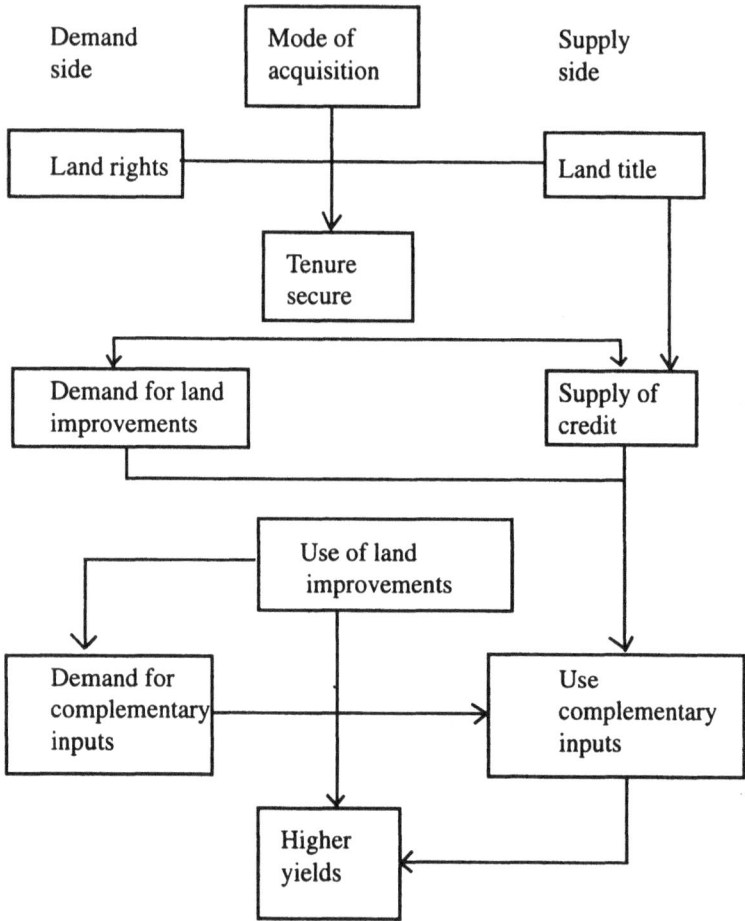

Adapted from: J.W. Bruce and S.E. Migot-Adholla: *Searching For Land Tenure Security in Africa,* 1994.

In January 1953, a Royal Commission was appointed to the East African countries to make recommendations for the 'better economic development' of the land and to address all the problems relating thereto, including modification of the traditional tribal system of land tenure.[23] The resulting comprehensive report, published in June 1955, made a number of recommendations the principal of which were:

i)   Policy concerning the tenure and disposition of land should aim at the individualisation of landownership and mobility in the transfer of land which, without ignoring existing property rights, will enable access to land for economic use.

ii) Land tenure law cannot simply be left to evolve under the impact of modern influences. A lead must be given by governments to meet the requirements of the progressive elements of society by applying a more satisfactory land tenure law.

iii) Existing property rights must not be arbitrarily disturbed. Exclusive individual ownership of land must be registered, and government must not dispose of land without an established legal process of adjudication and registration of all interests in the land.

iv) There should be a prohibition on the registration of sub-divisions below a certain size.

v)   Land tenure rules to meet local circumstances must command a measure of local support, but no rules should be made which are out of line with the territory-wide policy and which would obstruct the eventual individualisation of landownership and access to land in the interests of the territory as a whole.

vi) Local land boards should be established to assist in interpreting and guiding local views and actions concerning land tenure.

vii) In so far as barriers to free land exchange are not removed, to that extent will the prosperity of the peoples of East Africa be retarded.[24]

In December 1955, the Uganda government published its 'Land Tenure Proposals' accepting the main recommendations by the Royal Commission. The objectives of these proposals were to:

•   redefine the status of land in Uganda and to afford greater local control over land administration subject to general directions of the then central government;

•   define the processes of law by which land may be disposed of by central and local governments; and

•   encourage individual landownership in such a manner as not to annihilate the goodwill of traditional authorities; nor to prejudice good husbandry; nor to abandon such safeguards as are essential for future progress of the people.

District councils discussed these proposals but, as this was the time of the Mau Mau unrest in Kenya, some councils were apprehensive that the proposals were a disguised attempt to introduce a 'White Highlands' into Uganda.

Nevertheless, the proposals were eventually accepted by the Kigezi District Council in 1958, and subsequently in some parts of Ankole and Bugisu mainly because of the population pressure and a multiplicity of boundary litigations and disputes. This paved the way for adjudication and registration pilot schemes of rights to land in Uganda. The machinery for adjudication of rights was established by the Crown Lands (Adjudication) Rules enacted in May 1958. The provision of these rules have been summarised by Morris[25] as follows:

> These Rules provided for the formation of adjudication committees chosen by a meeting of the adult males of the parish concerned and consisting of between ten and twenty tax payers, with the parish or village chief as chairman. Where, in any district to which the rules were applied, any person in occupation of any land by virtue of rules of any customary right wished to be registered as the proprietor of a freehold estate in respect thereof, he might apply to be adjudged the owner of such land by native custom. Such application would, after due notice, be considered by the adjudication committee of the area where the land was situated. The committee was to hold its hearing in public and anyone who wished could make representations to it. At the conclusion of the hearing the committee would determine whether or not the applicant was the person recognised as the owner of the land by native custom and would forward a certificate embodying their findings to the District Commissioner. The decision would then be published, and any person aggrieved by the decision could, within thirty days, appeal to the District African Court which would confirm the names of the persons adjudged to be the owners by native custom, after decision by the court where appropriate, would then be forwarded by the District Commissioner to the Director of Lands and Surveys. Any person whose name had appeared in such a notice could then apply to the Director of Lands and Surveys to be registered as proprietor of an estate of freehold in respect of the land of which he had been adjudged the owner by native custom and, on payment of the prescribed fees, would be entitled to the issue of a certificate of title to the land under the Registration of Titles Act.

The areas covered by the pilot phase of adjudication and registration were Rujumbura county in North Kigezi (now Rukungiri district), 6,400 titles; Shema county in West Ankole (now Bushenyi district) 1,500 plots adjudicated and surveyed; Bubirabi area, south-east of Mbale town at the foot of Elgon mountains (120 plots adjudicated, demarcated and surveyed) without prior payment of fees (Shs25 to 35/= per acre, inclusive of air photography, plotting and provision of survey control). [26]

By the time of independence, in 1962, the following main land tenure systems existed in Uganda. [27]

a)   Land alienated in freehold to both Africans and, prior to 1916, when the Secretary of State in Britain decreed against further alienation in freehold, to non-Africans.

b) Land alienated in leasehold which, under the Crown Lands Ordinance, were not to exceed the duration of 99 years. Such leases sometimes bore buildings maintenance, and other development conditions to be carried out by the lessees. Rent was chargeable with respect thereto, and unless express provision to the contrary were borne by the will, no assignment, except by will, would be valid without the consent of the Governor. Moreover, the lessee was under an obligation 'to use and develop the natural resources of the land with all reasonable speed'[28]

c) Land held under registered freehold title and formerly held under customary tenure. These were titles granted in 'pilot scheme' districts of Kigezi, Ankole and Bugisu.

d) Land held under tenures peculiar to Ankole and Toro (native freehold which were mainly creatures of tenure of the Toro and Ankole Agreements of 1900 and 1901 in favour of those who signed these agreements.)

e) Land in urban areas which were occupied by persons of any race provided that such persons had, from the protectorate government, valid leases or temporary occupation licences, the latter were renewable every year but always subject to termination if land was needed for some development purposes.

f) Crown land in rural Buganda were vested in the British government by virtue of the Buganda Agreement of 1900. This land was only occupiable, according to the Crown Lands Ordinance, by persons of any race provided they held valid leases or licences and temporary occupation licences were issued to African occupiers of this land, at an annual rental. The eviction of these persons was subject to the payment of appropriate compensation if the land was required by the government, could be imposed at any time.

g) Crown land in rural areas outside Buganda, which represented the bulk of the land in Uganda, was mainly occupied by Africans under customary tenure and without Protectorate government licences. Non-Africans could occupy this category of crown land only under a valid lease or licence.

h) And finally, the mailo land tenure of Buganda.

In 1969, the Public Lands Act was enacted vesting all 'public' lands and the former crown lands in the Land Commission and local land boards.

In 1975, fundamental legal changes were made in Uganda's land tenure system. Under the Land Reform Decree of 1975, all land in Uganda was declared public land (i.e. state-owned) to be administered by the Uganda Lands Commission in accordance with the provisions of the Public Lands Act of 1969. All freeholds, including mailo ownership that existed before the commencement of the decree, were converted to long-term leaseholds of 199 years for public bodies and religious organisations and 99 years for individuals. Written consent of the Commission was necessary before the lessee could transfer the whole of the lease for value. Any transfer of public land except under these conditions was an offence in law. No person would occupy public land by customary tenure except with written permission of the prescribed authority.

The fundamental legal change introduced by the Land Reform Decree was that no person other than the Uganda Land Commission (and therefore the state) could hold an interest in land greater than a leasehold and all leaseholds (both converted and first registrations) were deemed to have been granted by the Land Commission. There was also provision for anyone owning land under customary tenure to apply for a lease over his customary land-hold. The implication of this public ownership of land is that in case of compensation, the claimant could be compensated not for the land as such, but only for the developments on the land.

The process of obtaining a leasehold or registered title involved application to a district land committee (or land office in the case of urban areas) who were supposed to inspect the piece of land being applied for to ensure that it was not under any dispute. After the district land committee had satisfied itself that there were no encumbrances, it would recommend the application to the Land Commission for an offer of lease. After the Land Commission had approved the application, the land would be surveyed and mapped. This would be followed by the preparation of lease papers detailing the terms and conditions under which the lease would be granted. When these papers have been signed by the applicant and endorsed by the Land Office in the Department of Lands and Surveys, a title deed would be issued with the endorsement and seal of the Land Commission. The lease could be for 2 years, 5 years, 49 years and 99 years as the maximum.

Although the process of obtaining a leasehold appears to be clear, it has suffered from serious abuses and misuses. Firstly, the leasehold system unfairly and unjustly favoured the big, rich, powerful and political notables. They had the contacts, knowledge, power and money to expedite the processing of the lease title documents. Corrupt practices made the process of land registration long, expensive and cumbersome. By the time one got the title, the expense incurred – on transport between home and district headquarters, between one's district and the Lands Department in the capital city, tips, bribes, official and unofficial fees to surveyors and the Lands Department — amounted to about UShs 2.0 million which was a significant percentage of the value of the land itself.

While the process was too difficult and too expensive for the rural poor, many of the big, rich and powerful people succeeded in bribing their way through to acquiring thousands of hectares of land, in many cases, displacing peasants or turning them into squatters on land that by customary tenure belonged to those peasants. In this way, abuses of the rules and procedures governing land registration tended to concentrate land into the hands of a few financial, propertied and political magnets resulting in a landless class of rural dwellers. Since the cost of securing a title deed in effect prevented people from obtaining a freehold or leasehold, the 1975 Land Reform Decree was a constraint to development. Consequently, a study[29] that was sponsored in 1987, under the Economic Policy Reform Programme, to assess the effects of land registration on tenure security, credit use, and agricultural investment, recommended four policy options.

a) Decreasing the cost of land registration by reducing direct application fees and the transactions costs of time and travel involved in the application process.
b) Increasing the efficiency of the land registry to reduce costs.
c) Easing procedures and conducting information campaigns to improve farmers' awareness of registration.
d) Reforming the 1975 land law to again allow freehold registration on demand.

Beyond abuses and transaction costs, there were objections to the 1975 Land Reform Decree that were more fundamental.

Firstly, the Land Reform Decree violated the principle that a land tenure system should protect people's rights in land i.e. protect people from eviction, especially those who have no other way to earn a reasonable living. This means that the land tenure system should protect people from eviction if there are no other income-earning alternatives available in the non-farm sector of the economy. But as we have noted above, it led to land concentration, increased marginalisation and landlessness as people in possession of economic and political power took advantage of the less powerful and bought them out.

Secondly, the Land Reform Decree, which included a provision for possible leasing of land held under customary tenure, increased fear and insecurity for the peasants as there was an overhang of the danger that they would wake up one morning only to find that some rich person had, through corruption, obtained leasehold over their land without their knowledge. In a number of cases this fear became a reality and peasants were turned into squatters. The decree also vested land in the state. This was tantamount to state take-over of property without compensation.

Furthermore, the decree not only increased the cost of land administration by requiring periodic renewal of leases but, more importantly, it constrained agricultural development as it interfered with the land market which should ideally allow a progressive farmer easy access to land through purchase. The decree required written consent of the Land Commission before ownership of land under leasehold could be transferred. The decree also did not provide for the mailo owners to sell to sitting tenants or for tenants to buy their parcels from the mailo owners. Lastly, the decree never tackled the problem of 'mailo' tenants. The 1900 Agreement, which converted land previously held under customary tenure, into privately owned mailo land in Buganda remains a serious source of contention or land crisis.

The most critical case is that of Kibale district which from 1900 to 1964 was part of Buganda. Although the people of this area were predominantly Banyoro, they were reduced to tenants when Baganda who had collaborated with the British to defeat Kabalega and his forces, were rewarded with mailo land in what is now Kibale district. The transfer of Kibale back to Bunyoro in 1964 did not alter the land tenure situation. The people of Kibale continued to resent and have therefore been agitating for the return of the land to its legitimate owners.

The framers of the 1995 constitution dodged the issue of mailo tenants by stating that the problem would be resolved by the first parliament under the 1995 constitution within two years after the election of that parliament. Thus, although the 1995 constitution asserts that 'land in Uganda belongs to the people of Uganda',[30] thus reversing the position established by 1975 land reform law which decreed that land belongs to the state, this is in accordance with the land tenure systems of mailo land, leasehold, customary and freehold. The assertion in the constitution does not help mailo tenants, especially in Kibale district, since it retains the validity of mailo land. As one commentator put it, the 1995 constitution brought hope to many but also brought anxiety to some. The 1998 Land Act was expected to eliminate this anxiety and translate hope into reality. But it remains to be seen whether the land grievances of the people of Kibale will be resolved without antagonising the absentee landlords.

In order to assess the efficacy of the 1998 Land Act, it is necessary to recapitulate the causes of disenchantment with the previous position. From the perspective of promotion of economic developments, the call for rationalisation of the laws governing peoples rights to the land was needed to:

- liberate peasants from being 'mailo tenants' to being ordinary freeholders;
- provide remedy for the land alienated from peasant customary owners through leaseholds acquired corruptly or fraudulently;
- resolve the issue of vast amounts of land in some parts of the country where the land title holders have neither been using the land nor leasing it out, thereby depriving the country of development opportunities;
- convert customary communal ownership into individual freeholdings without upsetting the traditionalists;

- remove gender iniquities in landownership; and
- reduce the cost of land registration or titling to make it affordable by the poor, and ease procedures to facilitate freehold registration on demand.

Both the 1995 constitution and the 1998 Land Act restored the control over land to the citizens of Uganda. They both state that 'all land in Uganda shall vest in the citizens of Uganda'. They have changed the overall power to regulate rights to the land. However, both the constitution and the Land Act have not changed or restructured the tenure systems or legal rights themselves.

The two legal landmarks hold that land shall be owned in accordance with the land tenure systems of customary, freehold, mailo and leasehold - the very tenure systems that were in existence by the time of independence in 1962. Hence the two legal landmarks do not constitute a land reform or a final tenure settlement. In particular, by retaining the mailo land tenure system and its heirachial ownership structure, the change did not go far enough to emancipate peasants on mailo land from the non-landed class into which they were converted by the 1900 Uganda Agreement [31]. The only hope for eventual liberation now lies in the Land Fund created by the Act and intended to:

i) give loans to sitting tenants to enable them to acquire registrable interests;
ii) enable tenants to acquire certificates of title; [32]
iii) resettle persons who have been rendered landless by government action, natural disaster or any other cause; and
iv) assist other persons to have their land surveyed for the purpose of acquiring certificates of title.

But the Land Fund, whose objective is to attain freehold status (or powers of full ownership) for all, has been too overloaded to function effectively. Given the magnitude of the assignment, the pace is bound to be so slow that the goal will not be accomplished in the foreseeable future. Besides the impediments of corruption and the usual bureaucratic inefficiencies, the attainment of freehold tenure for all is encumbered by the condition that tenants must secure the consent of their landlords. In practice this will frustrate the objective of the Fund. Already, government is finding it hard to raise US$22 million (approximately USh 33 billion at the time of writing) to compensate absentee landlords who may lose land[33], educate the public about the Act and create land boards as well as land tribunals. This is the budget for the next five years 1999/2003. It was part of the US$ 1 billion that was sought from the consultative donor conference held in Kampala from 7 to 11 December 1998.

The issue of land alienated from peasant customary owners through leaseholds acquired corruptly and fraudulently (i.e. the issue of cleaning the registry) did not receive the attention it deserved, although it is stated, under the special powers of the registrar, Section 92 of the Act, that 'The Registrar shall, where a certificate or instrument (e) is illegally or wrongfully obtained or (f) is illegally or wrongfully retained, call for the duplicate certificate of title or instrument for cancellation or correction or delivery to the proper party'. Surely this is not an express order for the land registry to be cleaned.

Furthermore, in the interests of political stability the legislators remained completely silent on the issue of land title holders who have kept vast amounts of land idle, thereby depriving the country of development opportunities. On a positive note, the Act provided for the issue of customary communal ownership certificates of customary ownership and has granted freedom to a customary owner to apply for freehold tenure.

The call to remove gender iniquities in landownership was partially answered through Section 40 of the Act which provides that no person shall:

a)   sell, exchange, transfer, pledge, mortgage or lease any land or

b)   enter into any contract for the sale, exchange, transfer, pledging, mortgage or lease any land;

c)   give away any land inter vivos, or enter into any other transaction in respect of land-
     in case of land which the person ordinarily resides with his or her spouse, and from which they derive their sustenance, except with prior consent of the spouse.

But this does not constitute co-ownership between spouses (i.e. by husband and wife) which the women of Uganda wanted.

The call to reduce the cost of land registration is assumed to have been answered through a provision under the Land Fund which stipulates that loans be given to enable people to have their land surveyed for the purpose of acquiring certificates of title. But this is part of the overload hardly expected to be delivered.

To ease freehold registration procedures, the functions and the process of land management were decentralised down to the parish level closer to the people. But the range of procedures and the bureaucratic red-tape that is involved makes the process as cumbersome as under the previous leasehold law.

To conclude this section, we wish to emphasise; first, that although the 1998 Land Act has not restructured the land tenure systems which existed prior to the Act and that, therefore, it has not brought about significant land reform, still, it is a step forward towards freehold tenure. Second, in as far as its provisions enhance the degree of tenure security through the formalisation and strengthening the legal status of the relationship between registered owners and user-occupants, it reduces the uncertainty and anxiety of the end-users and increases their stake in the management of the land resource. This will promote productive use of the land. To the extent that the provisions of the land can facilitate land transfers and market transactions (though these are still heavily encumbered), it will encourage investment in the land which is a desirable process for development. Its promotion of change from customary communal ownership towards individual ownership is a promotion of a modernisation that the promoters of development have been seeking to foster since the advent of agricultural policies in the country.

The effects of a state dominated development strategy

For a hundred years, since 1890, the development strategy in both Uganda and the whole of Africa was dominated by the state through its control not only of the macro-economic environment, but also the economic commanding heights of production, marketing and distribution. This approach made both positive and negative contributions which are partly responsible for the way African development has proceeded; the setbacks it has suffered; and the progress or lack of it, it has made so far. We say 'partly' because Africa's development pace has been dictated by both endogenous and exogenous determinants. The endogenous determinants include structural, historical and geographical circumstances[34] (according to Harvad's Prof. Jeffrey Sachs); poor policymaking and defective policy implementation; incompetent political leadership, interest group conflicts, inappropriate attitudes and values (lacking a work ethic, without thrift or frugality unlike the north east Asians and without entrepreneurial skills); and managerial and technological incapacities and incapabilities in terms of limitations of knowledge, skills and experience. Of the inappropriate or inadequate policies, the most critical have been a consistent bias against agriculture in pricing, taxation and exchange rate (as shown in our review and analysis of government intervention in product and factor markets); and neglect, especially by colonial governments, to get Africa effectively inducted into the industrial culture.

An additional but critical endogenous factor is population growth. It affects the balance of supply and demand, both for goods and labour (at macro-level) and leads to increased dependency ratios, land fragmentation and diminishing returns to labour (at micro-levels). Also population pressure forces people to marginal lands and patterns of land use that create serious environmental problems.

The exogenous determinants include colonialism and imperialism; external shocks and crises; and the external debt. Colonialism led to an international division of labour that suited the requirements of the coloniser - an industrial producer - by converting 'one part of the globe into a chiefly agricultural field of production for supplying the other part which remains a chiefly industrial field'[34.] Even as the twentieth century comes to an end, agriculture still dominates the occupational structure of Africa except in countries with substantial mining such as Zambia, South Africa, Zaire and Libya. In African countries, less than 10 percent of the population is urban and over 75 percent is primarily agricultural. We do not mean to imply, of course, that agriculture itself generates poverty or promotes under-development. What we mean to stress is that there are certain circumstances and growth processes associated with agriculture which generate or sustain poverty, e.g.. vulnerability to seasonality, vulnerability to parasitic extraction, adverse terms of trade, limited wage employment etc.

As a consequence of colonialism, African countries were not industrialised because Africa's 'role in the world system was to provide cheap raw materials to the metropolitan industries and to yield high profits for the metropolitan - based merchant capital'. In the words of M.D. Kingue:

> The trading economy, which marked economic relations between colonisers and colonised until the second world war, and which survived until the colonies became independent, placed the colonised country in a state of total dependence on the colonising country. The organisation of the colony's economy reflected the needs of the metropolis, the local trade buying only for export and selling mainly imported produce. Agriculture was oriented not toward meeting the food needs of the native population but toward meeting the requirements of the metropolis. A large number of countries have thus become specialised in one or two cultivations, which characterise the structure of their exportations even today: groundnuts in Senegal and Niger; coffee in Burundi, Ethiopia, Uganda and Rwanda; cotton in Upper Volta, Chad, Niger and the Sudan; palm oil in Dahomey; bananas and sugarcane in Somalia.[36]

The non industrialisation policy is responsible for one of the most outstanding contradictions in Africa's path of development. That contradiction is urbanisation before industrialisation leaving the continent without capacity to provide employment and the required urban services.

Non-industrialisation, encouraged by colonial authorities, is the best representative of externally induced policies. However, despite the process of decolonisation, in the 1980s external influence over domestic policies became a critical factor again in connection with structural adjustment programmes (SAPs). A team of eminent economic analysts, who did a study for UNICEF, found that though the initial principal aim of adjustment policies was through short-term demand management measures, it soon 'became clear that such policies caused considerable losses of output without, however, removing the underlying causes of balance of payments dis-equilibria .... By the mid-1980s these therefore gave way to a second generation of more comprehensive policy packages aimed at structural adjustment' and subsequently 'a third 'generation' of adjustment policies which squarely acknowledged the importance of social factors as well as the need for structural change and long-term sustainable growth'. According to the same UNICEF study, only one country - Mauritius - appeared 'to have simultaneously achieved the four objectives of stabilization, growth, the protection of vulnerable groups and structural adjustment'.[37]

The UNICEF study on Africa's recovery[38] in the 1990s, found that the continent had suffered four major external shocks in the 1980s. These were:

- African exports had stagnated and lost market share;
- the increase in the prices of manufactured products and the fall of African traditional exports, namely cocoa and coffee, had made terms of trade deteriorate further;
- nominal interest rates on debt had mushroomed to record levels; and
- gross and net inward capital flows had dropped drastically.

These external shocks reinforced or were reinforced by the severe effects of the drought of 1984/85; the development of the aids pandemic and civil strife in several countries.

One of the causes of Africa's perpetual failure to graduate from poverty is the external debt burden which is a result of two causes: the inability to export enough to cover the cost of our imports and the chronic deficits in national domestic budgets resulting from the tendency to consume more than we produce. The servicing of this external debt consumes resources that would have been used to improve and expand physical and social infrastructure and productive capacity.

The UNICEF study also found that by the end of 1992 sub-Saharan Africa was bleeding by a yearly outflow of about US $ 9 billion in financial resources to pay debts. Since then the outflow has worsened. According to the World Bank in its Global Development Finance 1998, the outflow has sharply risen to US$ 14.5 billion. The burden (US$ 235 billion) and the haemorrhage are so great that they have compelled James Grant, the Executive Director of UNICEF to bravely state that to accept a situation where the poorest continent in the world pays such an amount to countries that are 50 or 100 times richer – sub-Sahara Africa has a GDP equivalent to that of Belgium - 'must rank on the scale of moral disgrace, if not with slave trade, at least with the worst of the nineteenth century excesses when, in the early days of capitalism, exploitation new few limits. For this to be part of the required processes of the financial system as we know it, it simply shows how far we have yet to travel in developing international codes of behaviour which accord with national codes'.

In summing up, we conclude that government policies - price controls, inefficient crop marketing boards, over taxation of agricultural exports, and urban bias (the consequence of which is poor rural infrastructure and lack of basic facilities in rural areas) - that dominated both the colonial era and the first two decades of the post-independence period (1960 - 1980) distorted or reduced farmers' production incentives by intervening in the operations of commodity and factor markets. This, in turn, undermined efforts to commercialise agriculture, promote agricultural investment, adopt new technologies to increase productivity and output and change farming practices to sustain soil fertility. The net result of internal structural factors, inappropriate interventions that did not provide for economic motivation or the creation of a critical mass for sustainable economic growth, internal and external shocks, colonial neglect of capacity enhancement and finally the external debt burden, is the African economic crisis whose symptoms are:

- having the largest number of the poorest countries in the World – 32 of the 47 least developing countries according to the UN classification.
- being the only continent where economic production per person declined throughout the 1980s.
- having an agriculture that depends on basic or rudimentary technology with the lowest per hectare production in the world.
- whose industry, small and light, is overlay dependent on imports of capital, skilled labour, technology and spare parts.

Given the intensity of this African crisis, it is no wonder that the continent's quest for prosperity is still a distant dream. This is both a consequence and an indicator of failures of the control model which had guided Africa's development strategies and management approaches from the colonial period to the 1980s.

Notes

1. Rita Laker-Ojok, (1996) *'Managing Input supplies for small farmers in Uganda: A problem of institutional charge'* in P.L Langseth et al (eds), Uganda: *Landmarks in Rebuilding a nation,* Kampala: Fountain publishers
2. Rita Laker-Ojok, *Ibid.*
3. Rita Laker-Ojok, *Ibid.*
4. Steven Carr, (1982). Impact of government Intervention and Small holder Development in North and North East Uganda, ADO Occasional Paper No 5, Wye College, London.
5. S. Carr, *Ibid.*
6. Rita Laker-Ojok *'Managing Input Supplies for small farmers in Uganda' op.cit.*
7. W. Odwongo, (1996). 'Problems of Developing Rural Financial Markets in Uganda', *The Ugandan Banker,* Vol 4 No 1.
8. Dale W. Adams, (1991). 'Rural Finance in Uganda: Question and New Options,' Mimeo.

9. L. Eturu, (1986). 'Role of Central banks in the promotion of Investment & Financing of Agriculture, Industry and Exports', Agricultural Secretariat, Bank of Uganda.
10. W. Dale Adams has remarked that what is particularly puzzling about the chronic loan recoveries problem in Uganda is that it occurs in formal credit programmes whereas large amounts of loans and deposits are handled with few irregularities by the informal financial markets, in many cases by individuals with little education.
11. The presentation on loan non-performance greatly benefited from Joseph Nsereko's article, (1995). 'Problems of non performance Advances' in the *Ugandan Banker*, Vol 3, No 1.
12. A debtor to Uganda Commercial Bank is quoted to have said recently in 1997 that he could not be made to repay when he had guaranteed his regions electoral support for the President.
13. The World Bank's review of Uganda's financial sector (1990) noted that in Uganda, there is such a thing as "Lending to meet social objectives" involving abandoning strict commercial criteria, allegedly under pressure from officials in high places.
14. While poor loan appraisal is definitely a key factor in loan defaults some analysts have pointed out that the problem may have little to do with lack of skills training; that it has more to do with the values and attitudes and therefore behaviour of staff. In a number of cases the information received is not verified; in some cases it is 'doctored' or falsified in collusion with borrowers, and yet in others it is already 'cooked' Thus the 'Moral Hazard' is itself a key factor. J.R. Bibangambah, (1995). 'Towards optimum utilisation of credit in Uganda 'In the *Ugandan Banker*, vol 3, No 1.
15. Dale Adams *op.cit.*
16. James Obol Ochola, (1969). 'Ownership of land in African Customary Tenure' in J. Obol Ochola (ed). *Land Law reform in East Africa*, Kampala MOF; A.B. Mukwaya, (1953). *Land Tenure in Buganda*, Eagle Press.
17. Land Tenure refers to the legal rights and institutions that determine how land is owned and operated; whereas land reform is a basic restructuring of the land tenure systems; thereby meaning redistribution of land or property rights.
18. H.W. West, (1972). *Land Policy in Buganda*, Cambridge University Press.
19. J.M. Opio-Odóngo, (1992). *Designs on the Land*, Acts Press, 1992
20. 'Mailo' is derived from the English word mile used first to mean one square mile and finally to describe and differentiate this particular form of land ownership.
21. It is claimed that it was in Buganda that one of the very first British attempts was made to record the rights in land held by an African People. See H.W West, *Op.cit.*
22. Results of empirical tests of these casual relationships have been impressive in Asia (1994) but have not been conclusive in Africa. (See J.W. Bruce and S.E Migot - Adholla, (1994) *Searching for Land Security in Africa*, Iowa Kendall Publishing Company.
23. As noted above, Uganda was already having substantial land under individual and registered tenure - the mailo land of Buganda. The 1955 Report of the East African Royal Commission was therefore urging broader individualisation programmes.
24. East African Royal Commission, (1955) report Gud. No 9475 London: HMSO.
25. H.F. Morris and S. James Read, (1966). Uganda: *The Development of its Laws and Constitution*, London: Stevens and Sons.
26. Other efforts made to transform tenure arrangements in Uganda were in the context of land consolidation as the Bufumbira Pilot Land Consolidation scheme in 1959 which flopped and resettlement programmes which led to the resettlement of people from highly densely populated districts of Kigezi to Toro and Bunyoro.
27. The summaries are reproduced from J.L. Kangwanyi, 'The Harmonisation of Land systems in East Africa' in J. Obol Ochola, *Land Law Reform* in East Africa, *op.cit.*
28. Morris and Read, *op.cit*
29. Michael Roth *et al*, 'Tenure Security, credit use and farm Investment in the Rujumura Pilot land registration scheme, Uganda'; in J.W. Bruce and S.E. Migot - Adholla (eds), *op cit.*

30.   The constitutional position is a notable improvement over the 1975 position as it insists on immediate compensation to property owners in case of any takeover by the state. However, the state contends that this position is disadvantageous to development arguing that it denies the state the opportunity to acquire land immediately for promotion of investment, especially industrial investment.

31.   In a sense, the restoration of control over land to the citizens is a partial one as the reversal was politically feasible only for the 1975 land law and not for the 1900 Land settlement. The truth is that no real land reform can ever occur without reforming the structures created by the 1900 settlement.

32.   Paragraphs (i) and (ii) apply to all tenants by occupancy in all regions of Uganda including those of Kibaale district which we identified as the most critical case. However, the Ministry of Water; Lands and Environment has proposed UShs. 15 billion ($ 11 million) as a special fund for the 'lost land' in Kibale district.

33.   Kibaale district alone requires US$ 11.0 million or half the budget for the next five years to compensate absentee landlords.

34.   J.L. Gallup and Jeffrey D. Sachs with A.D. Mellinger, (1998) 'Geography and Economic Development', Annual World Bank Conference on Development Economics.

35.   Karl Marx, *Capital* vol 1, as cited by W. Kaberuka, (1990). *The Political Economy of Uganda 1890-1979: a case study of colonialism and underdevelopment*, New York: Vintage Press.

36.   M.D. Kingue, 'The three types of poverty', Ceres May-June 1975.

37.   Quoted in C. Lopes, (1994) 'Enough is enough; an alternative diagnosis of the African crisis', Discussion paper No 5, The Scandinavian Institute of African Studies.

38.   G.A. Cornia, R. Hoeven, T. Mkandawire, (1992). *Africa's·Recovery in the 1990s,* New York: UNICEF.

5

The Economic Crisis in Uganda 1971-1990

In a predominantly agricultural economy, an agricultural crisis is both a cause and consequence of a general economic crisis.[1] Thus, the agricultural production crisis (that is, decline or deterioration in agricultural production or output) discussed in Chapters Five and Six concerning traditional export crops like coffee, cotton, tea, and tobacco is an integral part of a wider economic crisis that Uganda experienced over two decades from 1970 to 1990.

Uganda's agrarian crisis (i.e. agricultural production crisis conditioned by structural and technological stagnation) has its roots in the colonial economy which kept Uganda's agriculture under a peasant mode based on production of primary agricultural commodities by means of resource factors provided by nature, and characterised by a low degree of commercialisation and technological backwardness. The control of processing and marketing these commodities, both for local consumption and export, were monopolised by the Asian merchant class and a few European import and export companies.

African entrepreneurs were barred from processing, and directly trading in agricultural export commodities. This discouraged the emergence of an African commercial capitalist class capable of mediating between small peasant producers and the market. The bulk of capital accumulation from agricultural trade by the Asian merchant class was not re-invested in agricultural production and processing but in import substitution industries which were not foreign exchange earners. To further marginalise the Africans who had been agitating to enter import/export trade, in the mid-1940s, the colonial regime through legal and administrative measures, brought under state control African co-operative societies and unions and restricted their operations to collection and delivery of agricultural produce to state marketing boards.

At the level of production, Ugandan agriculture has, over the years, experienced competition for labour between production for consumption and production for the market. Because of heavy reliance on rudimentary technology, a dependency on cheap family labour, which also provides its own subsistence, means that at best production can only be sustained if it is first and foremost contributing to family's sustenance and, secondly, if it is not putting a lot of demands on the peasant's labour. At worst, however, production in the areas of export crops was mainly maintained through coercion and intimidation.

Although both the colonial and post-colonial regimes later attempted to use incentives in the form of administered prices and subsidised inputs to maintain high production levels, as shown in Chapter Three, the prices never adequately covered the producer's labour input. Nor were the agricultural inputs generally available to all producers as Chapter Four has clearly shown. Agricultural inputs were selectively and discriminatively given to the so-called progressive farmers i.e. the large producers as an added incentive to maintain good quality.

The pricing policy that left the bulk of the agricultural export proceeds in the hands of the marketing boards and the state did not encourage peasants to continue producing for the market. The poor local terms of trade, which included late payments for deliveries in the case of peasant producers and poor returns to labour in the case of labourers on agricultural plantations, the lack of infrastructural support in form of extension services and agricultural inputs, the lack of effective marketing strategies, the poor international terms of trade resulting from the decline in prices of primary commodities in the 1970s and the political turmoil that the country faced from 1971, severely affected agricultural production.

The problems in processing and marketing compounded the agricultural crisis. They increased collection, delivery, and marketing costs which, in the process, affected the profitability of the enterprises, both public and private. In turn, this affected the income levels of peasant producers who moved away from commodity production whose marketing and processing were directly controlled by the state. Peasants shifted to those crops which permitted some degree of independence in marketing. They also completely neglected crops like cotton which were labour intensive. Agricultural wage labourers withdrew their labour and turned to working their small plots or simply moved to the urban centres for petty employment and trade in the informal sector. These factors, coupled with other natural disasters like drought, completed the decline of agriculture - the principal source of Uganda's foreign exchange earnings, thus intensifying the country's balance of payments crisis.

Uganda's economic crisis[2] has been marked by structural deterioration and the consequent intensification of absolute poverty. Banugire[3] has distinguished three stages of economic decline in an agrarian economy. The first is the recessionary stage which consists of a general decline in the rate of growth of incomes, usually associated with one or a combination of the following: a fall in export prices, a fall in demand for agricultural and mineral products, severe supply bottlenecks, crop failures due to drought, and abnormal dislocations such as political disturbances and wars. The second is the structural decline stage where persistent recessionary decline and structural dislocations generate substantial changes in the roles of the various production, consumption and trade components of the economy. In particular, the leading dynamic sectors and sub-sectors decline in relation to the traditional and informal sectors in both rural and urban areas. Persistent structural deterioration eventually leads to the third stage, that of the regressive or *magendo* economy.

In Uganda, the crisis in the 1970s and 1980s was set off by economic repression in the form of:

- partial nationalisation (in 1970) by government buying 49 shares in all major industrial enterprises, companies and banks;
- restrictive economic policies using the instruments of price controls and a fixed exchange rate;
- Amin's war of economic independence against the Asian community; and
- economic mismanagement especially in the form of inappropriate price policies, excessively low producer prices, excessively high export taxes, and an overvalued currency.

The consequent collapse of the Asian-controlled commercial and industrial sectors (or modern sector) and the collapse of the production of agricultural export crops,[4] spread through the infrastructure and the export sector and produced macro-economic vicious circles and hyper-inflation bringing ruin to the entire economy. The chain of events and the macro-economic vicious circles constituting Uganda's economic crisis are presented in Figure 5.1.

Uganda's crisis illustrated by the chart can be summarised as follows:

i)   Decline in GNP per capita estimated at a rate of 1.1. per cent per annum during the 1970s and early 1980s.

ii) Decline of per capita agricultural and food production by 2.1 and 1.0 per cent per annum respectively between 1970 and 1982.

iii) Deterioration in export performance in volume terms because of dislocations in the production process and shifts away from non-food cash crops especially coffee, cotton, tea and tobacco to food crops.

iv) Poor export performance in value terms plus a drastic fall in net capital inflow, generating a steady decline in import values and rising import prices.

v)   Extreme difficulties in getting imported inputs, spares and materials.

vi) Abnormally high rates of inflation (3 digits) and declines in income aggravated by an absolute decline in industrial output due to lack of investments and low levels of capacity utilisation.[5]

vii) Intensified problems of low income and absolute poverty.

Figure 5.1: Uganda economic crisis 1970 - 1985

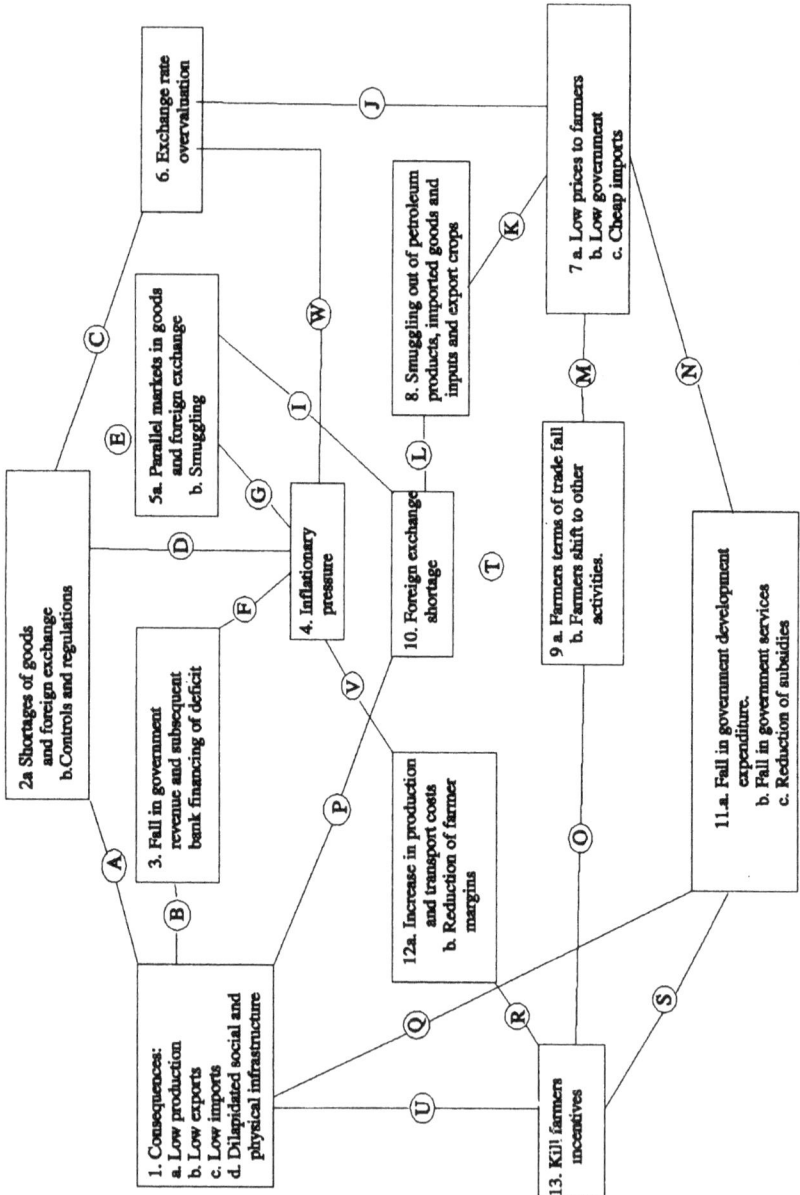

In short, institutional capabilities, infrastructures and social values and standards in Uganda decayed. Services deteriorated or vanished, unemployment escalated and poverty intensified. As Professor Mazrui puts it, 'it certainly looks as if the whole post colonial euphoria about modernisation has been a mere illusion of modernity, a mirage of progress, a facade of advancement'.

In rural areas, people's response to the crisis was manifested in the outflow of resources from the agricultural export sector into subsistence and the informal sector, eventually leading to the collapse of the export sector. In urban areas, the response by urban workers and poorly paid civil servants, caught up in hyperinflation, took the form of informal activities, including subsistence agriculture in an urban setting.[6] One of Uganda's important peculiarities is the tendency for a single household, or in many cases a single individual, to join the informal sector without giving up formal employment. The informal sector, especially subsistence agriculture in urban areas, subsidises the unbearably low wage formal sector.

The structural decline, resulting from political anarchy, inappropriate economic policies, technological and managerial inadequacies, confirms the view that while internal and external imbalances are an important dimension of Uganda's as well as African economic crisis, a much more fundamental aspect of the crisis is the fact that no fundamental transformation of the inherited political economy has been brought about. Fundamentally, therefore, the crisis should be attributed to the neglect by colonial and post-colonial regimes to create indigenous capacities and capabilities for development management. It is documented that although the colonial government in Uganda, laid the basic foundation for possible future development by promoting cash crop production, 'the administrators made little effort to revolutionise the economic structure beyond primary production'. Agricultural technology remained rudimentary and no manufacturing industry, not directly related to the extension of the primary exporting economy, was developed. In a speech to the House of Commons in 1925 the British colonial secretary made the following remark:

> I am perfectly certain that it is most important to-day that those in this country who have money to invest should invest that money not only where it may be that orders will be bringing in trade which in the future will mean complementary and not a conflicting trade .... Last year, for example, or quite recently, the people of Uganda took from us between 6000 and 7000 bicycles in six months when Uganda is producing that cotton which in the long run Uganda will be able to produce, we shall not only be selling bicycles to them but Morris cars, therefore in the administration and development of these colonies the duty of Colonial Administration and the interests of British industry should march hand in hand.

This is clear testimony that the main reason for Uganda's failure to industrialise was a deliberate colonial policy – the British sought to develop their colonial economies in a manner that did not make them future competitors in the same market.

In the case of Uganda, macro-economic constraints have been reinforced by several regressive tendencies; namely,[8] the systematic 'privatisation' of the public sector by those who manage it (i.e. prebendalism)[9], the personalisation of the private business sector (i.e. bias against the corporate approach) and the exploitation of the peasants by the state bureaucracy and business interests. The prebendalism syndrome weakened the social services and public sector enterprises, reducing them to private estates of politicians, bureaucrats and managers. The tendency towards personalising the private enterprises militates against the establishment and consolidation of the corporate mode of management necessary for a dynamic, vibrant and responsible private enterprise sector. Both the public and private sectors must be held responsible for the misuse of foreign exchange earned by the peasants through the production of coffee. The two must also be blamed for lack of proper maintenance of the basic infrastructures.

The important lesson to be learnt from Uganda's crisis, both agricultural and economic, is that it was a result of policy failure in terms of inappropriate development strategies and inadequate incentives, abuse of state power, chronic political instability and lack of economic management capacity, conflict between development and political objectives, the prevalence of non-developmental values and attitudes, and Uganda's position in the international economic system as already discussed with respect to the African continent as a whole.

As will be explained in Chapters Six and Seven of this book, the years of destruction and national decay were followed by reconstruction and recovery efforts and todate Uganda is passing through a period of renewed development.

Although the economic downturn in the 1970s and 1980s was most severe in Uganda, it was by no means limited to that country. It affected the whole of sub-Saharan Africa (excluding South Africa) where annual growth rates in GDP of the region dropped from 3.9 percent in 1960-70 to 1.6 percent in 1970-1979 and -0.7 percent in 1980-1985.

Although Africanist analysts maintain that this economic crisis was basically from the structural deficiencies of the African economies, other analysts (mostly of the neo-classical economics school) especially those from international financial and development institutions, perceived the crisis in terms of internal and external imbalances: budget deficits, inflation and balance of payments deficits.

The remedy proposed by IMF and World Bank was a free market approach through structural adjustment programmes.

An alternative approach put forward by African governments under the auspices of the Organisation of African Unity (OAU) was the 1980 Lagos Plan of Action. Its basic thrust was long term restructuring of African economies – the achievement of more self reliance, more economically integrated Africa by the year 2000.

Notes

1. V. Jamal, (1987). 'Ugandan Economic Crisis, Dimensions and Cure', in P.D. Wiebe and C.P. Dodge, *Beyond Crisis: Development Issues in Uganda*, Kampala: Makerere Institute of Social Research; V. Jamal," (1991). 'The African Context of the Ugandan Crisis', in H.B Hansen and M. Twaddle (eds), *Changing Uganda*, Kampala: Fountain Publishers.

2. An economic crisis has been defined as a situation of an economy where:
   a) Sufficient exports cannot be generated in the medium term to pay for basic imports (raw materials, spares and replacement equipment and basic needs and to service existing debt (net of capital flight);
   b) Supplies of basic needs (food, health, transportation, education, housing and so on and their distribution at levels accepted as adequate for that society cannot be maintained and raised with population growth).
   c) The state cannot rectify this condition rapidly because of the social conflict over how adjustment should be made, or because it lacks resources (through fiscal crisis) to do so; leading to a lack of "relative autonomy" necessary for the required degree of intervention (Fitzgerald 1991).

3. F.R. Banugire, (1987) 'The impact of the Economic crisis on Fixed Income Earners', in *Beyond crisis,* op.cit; F.R Banugire, (1989) 'Uneven and Unbalanced Development: Development Strategies and conflict', in K. Rupesinghe, *Conflict Resolution in Uganda*, Kampala: Fountain Publishers.

4. J.R. Bibangambah, (1992) 'Macro-economic constraints and the Growth of the informal Sector' in J. Baker and P. Pedersen (eds), *The Rural Urban Interface in Africa*, Uppsala: Scandinavian Institute of African studies,

5. D. Mwesigwa, (1987). 'The structural and Spatial Significance of the small scale Economic Sector in Kampala City, Uganda', Unpublished M.A. Thesis. Dept. of Geography University of Dar-es-Salaam.

6. J.R. Bibangambah, 'Macro-economic constraints' op.cit.

7. W. Kaberuka, (1990) *The Political Economy of Uganda 1890-1979: A case study of colonialism and underdevelopment,* New York: Vintage Press.

8. F.R. Banugire, 'Uneven and Unbalanced Development....' op.cit.

9. R.H. Bates, (1991). 'Agricultural Policy and the Study of Politics in Post -Independence Africa,' in D. Rimmer, *Africa 30 years on* , London: the Royal African Society.

10. M.D. Kingue, (1975). 'The three types of Poverty,' CERES May-June.

6

Responses to Poor Economic Performance

It has been said that a negative feeling, especially a feeling of defeat, is not an appropriate anchor for a forward looking vision. However, we would be dishonest if we did not admit that feelings of defeat and perceptions of a failing cure or an incurable patient have occurred both on the continent and outside it.[1] Africa's socio-economic challenges have remained resilient for an intolerably long time. Africa has continued to trail all the other continents in most respects despite its supposed 'immense potential'.

The analysis in the foregoing chapters of this book has recognised that the failure for the development mission to be accomplished, so far, is multi-faceted; there are endogenous as well as exogenous factors; there have been inappropriate values and policies; there have existed incapabilities and incapacities leading to ineffectiveness or failure to advance and there have been externally induced problems.

We need to point out, however, that no consensus has emerged regarding the failure to reach the destination. There are analysts who attribute the failed 'prescriptions' to the wrong diagnosis of the African crisis. They particularly blame any analysis of development that is not done in the light of history. In 1975, for instance, M.D. Kingue, the then Assistant Administrator of the UNDP and Regional Director for Africa, said:

> The reasons behind the African countries' poverty cannot be readily understood unless some thought is given to their people's past, the stirring history of the contacts between these people and others in the course of the last five centuries and also the way they attained statehood.

However, half a century of diagnosis (including a closer look into history) has not as yet produced a mirror for, or a torch into, the future of Africa. Even Carlos Lopes' article 'Enough is Enough' has turned out to be just another diagnosis, and not a beginning of a descent to the 'hidden treasure'. In the meantime, and in the last quarter of the twentieth century, most African countries, (or at least more than 30 since the publication of the World Bank study, *Adjustment in Africa: Reforms, Results and the Road Ahead*, covering 29 countries[2], have accepted to be guided by a development paradigm that represents a consensus that people (i.e. ideas and actions), institutions, technologies and policies are the key determinants of economic performance and hence the prime movers of development. In the words of one commentator, the current consensus on development has shifted away from planning to policy orientation, from discretionary government intervention to a greater acceptance of market forces, from controls and administered prices to transparent fiscal incentives and disincentives, from public to private ownership of the means of production and from increasing public investment toward private sector development.[3]

The early 1980s (1981 - 1984)

As a result of external pressure and change in government, Uganda began to respond to the economic crisis in 1981. By restoring formal sector economic activity, and raising the level of production through the creation of incentives for Ugandan producers and foreign investors. Additionally, the reform of the management and policy-making machinery of the country was also seen as an important priority. Other priorities were the restoration of confidence in the Uganda shilling, elimination of price distortions and the improvement of fiscal and monetary discipline.[4] With a view to halting and reversing the economic crisis in the first half of the 1980s, the Uganda government implemented the first phase of a stabilisation and adjustment policy package with the advice, guidance and assistance of the IMF and the World Bank.

The UPC government, which took over power in December 1980, adopted the following measures:

- the realignment of external value of the shilling resulting in a depreciation of the external value of the shilling by 41 times in only three years;
- the dismantling of price controls;
- the rationalisation of the internal distribution system and the machinery for importation/procurement;
- the provision of incentives through upward adjustment and realignment of producer prices;
- the improvement of the governmental budgetary performance and the curtailment of subsidies to inefficient public enterprises;
- the introduction of policies to encourage foreign investment and the return of companies, which were nationalised during the military regime, to their original owners; and
- progressive increases of interest rates with a view to mobilising savings and achieving greater efficiency in resource allocation.[5]

The above measures achieved some short-term success in reviving the economy i.e. in moderating inflation, in reducing the parallel market activities and smuggling and in improving the balance of payments position. The country, therefore, seemed to be steady on the path to stabilisation.

Despite these measures, the economy collapsed again in June 1984 for the following reasons:

- the programme depended for its success on continued inflow of foreign finance and yet not enough of it was forthcoming on a continuous basis;
- the programme was altogether misplaced as it overloaded a single policy instrument - the exchange rate – to correct a wide range of distortions, some of which had little to do with the foreign sector;
- the guerilla war pushed government expenditure beyond planned limits and consequently the earlier deceptive show in meeting IMP performance criteria was now clearly lacking; and
- the reform or stabilisation programme was never fully implemented and was actually abandoned after June 1984.

The transitional period (1985 - 1986)

The fall of the Obote government in July 1985 was followed by yet another period of chaos. Mainly due to shortages caused by increased insecurity and the looting that followed the change of government, inflation rose to unprecedented levels. There was also disruption in export trade as part of the coffee was smuggled out of the country. The flow of imports was also disrupted.

The first year (1986) year of the NRM government was characterised by debate and indecision. At first it was unwilling or reluctant to accept the IMF/ World Bank conditionalities for African countries wishing to borrow money from the these institutions. The conditionalities included:

i) promoting trade deliberisation by abolishing price and, foreign exchange controls, import restrictions, and abandoning trade protectionism; devaluing the local currency to raise the price of imports and lowering the price of exports in terms of foreign currencies;
iii) instituting anti-inflationary programmes such as control or elimination of government budget deficits, and withdrawing of subsidies on education, health, agriculture etc;
iv) effecting anti-inflationary control of wage increases by dismantling price controls and minimum wages, leaving all prices to market forces;
v) allowing foreign investors including multi-national corporations to operate in the country and repatriate profits to their own countries;
vi) reducing spending on public services especially defence; and
vii) privatising the economy including sale of public enterprises to local and foreign investors, thus reducing and even eliminating direct government involvement in the economy.

The 1986 budget abolished the dual exchange rate system introduced in the early 1980s and fixed the exchange rate at Uganda shillings 1,400.00 to the US dollar. It increased salaries by 50 percent, introduced price controls, and extended state monopoly over internal and external trading. For instance, it gave the PMB monopoly for the internal and external marketing of maize, beans, soyabean, groundnut and simsim. Similarly, Uganda Hardware was given monopoly for timber, hides and skins.[6]

Unfortunately, the fixed nominal exchange rate severely penalised the producers. Coffee producers were unable to gain from the coffee boom and the suspension of the ICO quota. Non-traditional exports came to a standstill. The restoration of price controls merely boosted the flourishing black market. In short, the economy was back in the vicious circles of the 1970s and early 1980s.

While the economy was continuing to deteriorate, a serious economic debate was also taking place. From the point of view of the NRM government, the factors generating the crisis such as the distortions in the pattern of economic activity created by the colonialists, economic mismanagement during the previous regimes, the wars of liberation, lack of economic integration and transformation and the deterioration in terms of trade were mainly historical. The IMF view was, as usual, that the crisis was being perpetuated by lack of incentives to producers, monetary indiscipline and excessive government interference with the market system through the use of administrative controls.[7]

The recovery programmes 1987 (onwards)

As part of its Economic Recovery programme (ERP), the NRM government finally accepted the IMF diagnosis and approach. It had no choice. The demand for foreign exchange to rehabilitate and reconstruct the country's infrastructure and to revive, basic manufacturing facilities, was overwhelming. The government launched its ERP in May 1987 and an IDA economic recovery Credit of SDR 50.9 million and an African Facility credit of SDR 18.8 million were approved in September 1987. A second economic recovery credit (ERCII) of SDR 98.1 million was approved in January 1990. The ERP was subsequently supported by structural adjustment financing facility arrangements from IMF/ World Bank, and assistance from other multilateral and bilateral donors.

This phase of the implementation of policy reforms, which was an intensification or renewal rather than a beginning of macro-economic reforms under the NRM administration, was based on two main policy packages. One of these was macro-economic stabilisation policies aimed at demand management in order to restore financial equilibrium. These policies included the devaluation of the Uganda shilling; liberalisation of the foreign exchange rate (i.e. moving to market-determined foreign exchange rates); reduction of fiscal deficit by implementing revenue enhancing and expenditure controlling measures; and curbing inflationary crop financing.

The second was structural adjustment whose aim was to promote accelerated and sustained economic growth. This included liberalisation of trade by abolishing export and import licensing; the abolition of price controls; the repealing of Industrial Licensing Act; the promulgation of a new investment code; the return of the expropriated Asian properties; the privatisation of industrial public enterprises; abolition of export and distribution monopolies; the overhaul of the civic service; the restructuring of the tax system and the improvement of tax administration.

Given the causes of the agricultural crisis discussed in Chapter Three, reform and its significance as an integral component of the general economic crisis discussed in Chapter Five had to be directed or focused at the improvement of producer incentives, increased efficiencies in the processing of agricultural products and improvements in marketing arrangements for agricultural products. Accordingly, the areas of sectoral policy or institutional reform were identified as agricultural pricing; trade liberalisation and promotion; restructuring of marketing boards; rationalising crop processing capacity; financial rehabilitation of co-operative unions; and strengthening agricultural research and extension institutions. Action steps to formulate, review, adopt and implement specific policy measures covering the above areas constituted Uganda's agricultural sector policy agenda[8] for the period 1989/90 - 1991/92.

The state in Uganda, as elsewhere in Africa has, both in colonial and post-independence periods, regulated commodity flows and prices via monopolies granted to parastatal marketing boards, via export taxes, via control of prices to processors and consumers, via licensing and via the exchange rate. Thus, the system of administering coffee prices to be paid to farmers, processors, and marketing agents had stemmed from the centralised system of procurement and export which was introduced in the 1940s and early 1950s. The purpose of reform, therefore, was to bring about more competitive and open market arrangements with prices at various market levels being determined by the competitive market forces, reflecting not only domestic but also movements in the international prices for agricultural products.

Following the work of nine working groups established by the Agricultural Policy Committee (APC) under the Action Plan for the implementation of the agricultural sector policy agenda, a project called the Agricultural Sector Adjustment Credit (ASAC) was formulated and under this project, IDA made available approximately US$100 million to the government of Uganda. Of this amount US$85 million was for support of the adjustment component of the project and US$15 million was for the investment component.

One of the main objectives of ASAC was to support the coffee sub-sector reforms in the area of liberalisation of coffee marketing, the provision of adequate incentives to sub-sector participants, and streamlining the marketing finance arrangements. In 1991 coffee marketing was liberalised. This meant that whereas prior to 1991 coffee pricing, transportation, storage and final export were centrally organised and controlled by CMB, thereafter state monopoly was abolished and marketing (both internal and export) became open to any interested operator. In otherwards, coffee farmers became free to sell to any buyer - primary co-operative societies, private buyers, and agents of a restructured CMB[9] as shown in Figure 6.1. Similarly, primary buyers became free to sell to any processors or exporters.

Subsequently, and in response to liberalisation, the coffee sub-sector was flooded by operators, both for internal marketing and for export which, in turn, created a competitive environment, especially price competition and prompt payments. The number of registered coffee sector participants is shown in Table 6.1.

Table 6.1: Coffee sector participants

Category	1990/91	1991/92	1992/93	1993/94	1994/95	1995/96
Exporters	1	21	34	86	117	167
Export grading facilities	2	7	7	9	17	17
Hulling factories	n/a	136	142	163	204	400
Buying stores	n/a	185	200	214	159	*
Roasters	4	5	5	5	3	9

Up to 1995, the export market share of private exporters was progressively rising while that of CMBL, and co-operative unions fell from 84 percent and 12 percent in 1991/92 to 3.9 percent and 4.3 percent in 1995/96 respectively, an indication that the more efficient exporters, in this case the private sector, were increasing their export market share while the less efficient were losing it. This is a clear case of gainers and losers from the adjustment policy reforms. The growth in the share of private exporters in the coffee sub-sector is shown in Table 6.2.

Figure 6.1: The post-liberalisation coffee marketing structure

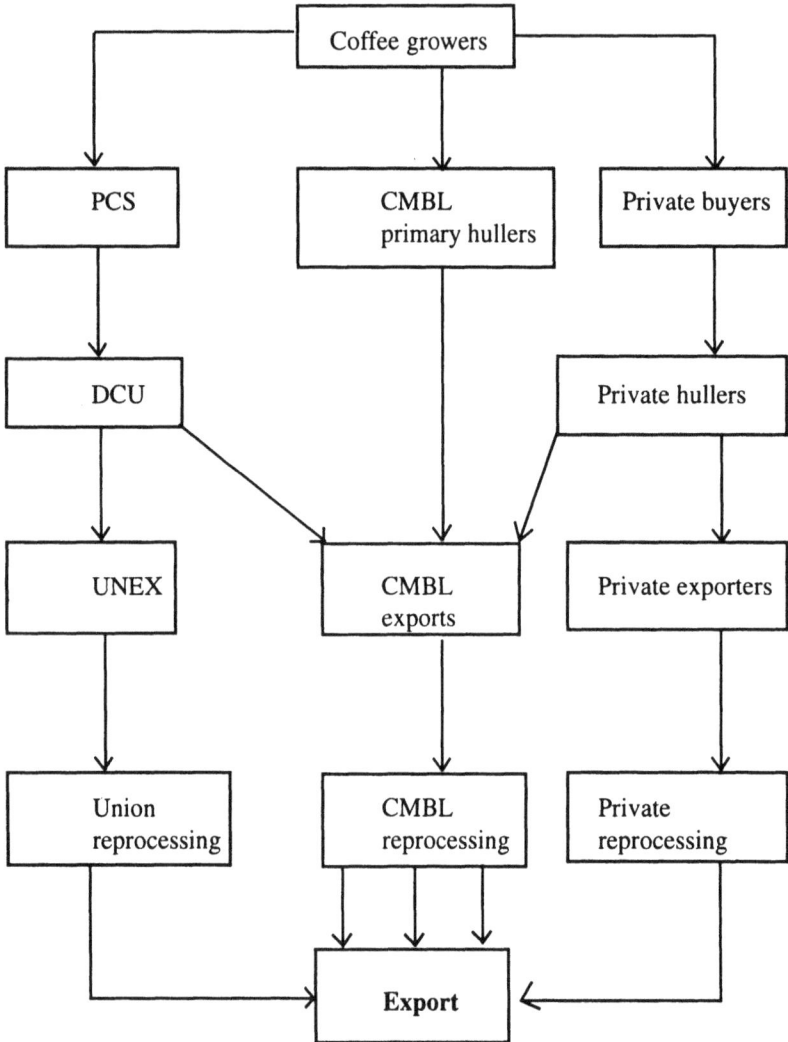

The figure shows that the marketing structure has changed from that of a single buyer (monopsony) or a few buyers (oligopsony) to that of many buyers (competition) with prospects for increased marketing efficiency and better or higher prices for the producers. The figure also shows that exporting coffee has become a multi-channelled process.

Table 6.2: Export market share (%)

Exporter	1990/92	1991/92	1992/93	1993/94	1994/95	1995/96
CMBL	92	83.7	39.3	16.1	9.7	3.9
UNEX	8	11.9	16.0	11.3	11.2	4.3
Private	0	4.4	44.7	72.6	79.1	91.8
Total	100.0	100.0	100.0	100.0	100.0	100.0

Source: UCDA Reports, 1995/96.

By 1996 the number of registered exporters had increased from 21 in 1992 to 167 indicating that the number of people whose livelihood depends on working in coffee export business and the expected returns on the capital management skills devoted to that business was increasing. The major exporters are shown in Table 6.3.

Table 6.3: Major exporters of coffee in Uganda in the wake of liberalisation

Buyer	Share (%)
Volcafe	18.8
Coffee Commodities	10.7
Sacadec	9.7
Bernard Rothfos	8.1
Drucafe	7.1
Phibo	6.3
Forward Exploration	4.9
Bouvery	4.3
E.A. Commodity	2.7
Sucafina	2.5
Unicof	2.2
Tamari & Sons	2.1
Eurocafe	2.1
Others	18.5
Total	**100.0**

Source: UCDA Quarterly Reports.

The majority of these exporters are nationals from other countries who have either gone into joint venture with local Ugandans or have registered in the country as coffee exporters. At present there are nine roasters actively buying coffee in Uganda.

Before liberalisation, the government retrieved, as coffee export tax, any surplus of sales revenues over the sum of producer prices and processing and marketing margins. This is to say that the government fixed a 'threshold price' supposedly covering the cost of producing, processing and marketing coffee. If the coffee was sold at or below the threshold price, then no tax was paid. If the coffee was sold above the threshold price, then 70 percent of the difference would go to government in export duty. The consequences of this system were:

a) Tax burden fell heavily on those producing fine qualities.

b) Tax burden fell very heavily on producers when market prices rose.

c) Arbitrary tax rates changes created uncertainty in the market.

d) The residual nature of the tax failed to reward efforts to upgrade product quality or maximise the unit value of sales.

e) Coffee exporters were precluded from realising trading profits and this discouraged entry into the export trade.

Government subsequently accepted, in principle, that the residual export taxation system should be replaced with an *advalorem* system (percentage tax) regardless of the sale price, the advantages being low taxation rate, equitable sharing of the tax burden by everyone in the industry, simple tax calculation and collection; and certainty and stability. The advalorem system meant that the fixed marketing margins for exporters would be abolished, and the export price, less the aggregate of tax payable to the government, producer price, and margins payable to processors, would accrue to export agents as trading profits. With liberalisation, export tax and the system of administered margins for processors and fixed prices for farmers have been discontinued. As producer prices are no longer fixed by government, sellers and buyers are free to agree or bargain over prices. This means that producers are in a position to directly benefit from opportunities or favourable changes in the world market for coffee.

In general, the prices that buyers offer take account of world price less marketing costs; prices paid by competitors; average prices realised over a given period and costs of production of the commodity.

Like coffee, cotton marketing, has been liberalised. Cotton farmers can now dispose of their cotton seed to private buying agents and are no longer restricted to sell through the co-operative union ginneries. All ginneries, previously owned by co-operative unions, are now free to sell lint directly to local textile mills or to export, rather than through the LMB which has been restructured, in a manner similar to that of CMB, into two separate organisations namely the Cotton Development Organisation (CDO) to carry out regulatory functions, and the Cotton Marketing Company Limited (CMCL) to handle trading and export functions. The CMCL will eventually be privatised. As in the case of coffee the expected benefits from the liberalisation of the cotton industry are the elimination of monopoly inefficiencies in marketing and better prices for the producers. The government's price/margin system has been abolished. The cotton price to the farmer will henceforth be determined by market forces operating through the parameters similar to those of coffee.

The internal marketing of food crops was never a subject of government monopsony because the state marketing organisation – the PMB – operated alongside private traders as shown in the diagram below:

Figure 6.2: Food crops marketing channels

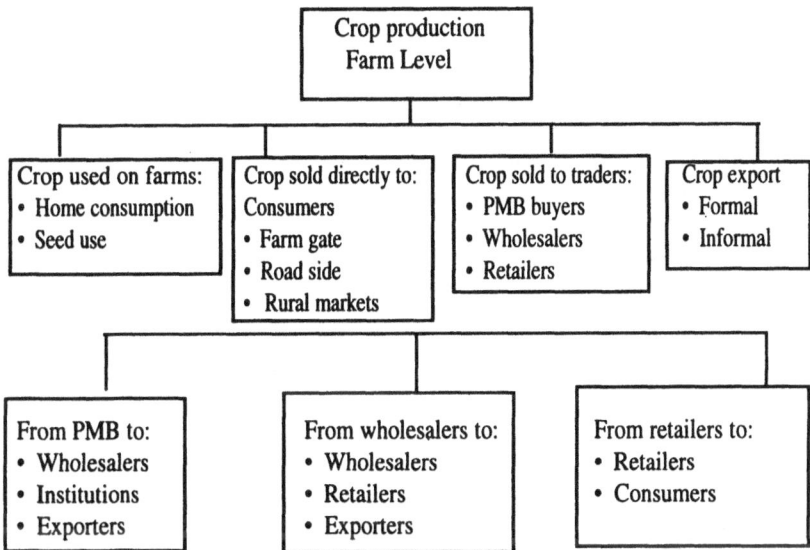

```
                        ┌─────────────────────┐
                        │  Crop production    │
                        │  Farm Level         │
                        └─────────────────────┘

┌──────────────────┬──────────────────┬──────────────────┬──────────────┐
│ Crop used on     │ Crop sold        │ Crop sold to     │ Crop export  │
│ farms:           │ directly to:     │ traders:         │ • Formal     │
│ • Home           │ Consumers        │ • PMB buyers     │ • Informal   │
│   consumption    │ • Farm gate      │ • Wholesalers    │              │
│ • Seed use       │ • Road side      │ • Retailers      │              │
│                  │ • Rural markets  │                  │              │
└──────────────────┴──────────────────┴──────────────────┴──────────────┘

┌──────────────────┬──────────────────┬──────────────────┐
│ From PMB to:     │ From wholesalers │ From retailers   │
│ • Wholesalers    │ to:              │ to:              │
│ • Institutions   │ • Wholesalers    │ • Retailers      │
│ • Exporters      │ • Retailers      │ • Consumers      │
│                  │ • Exporters      │                  │
└──────────────────┴──────────────────┴──────────────────┘
```

The diagram above shows that, for food crops, even before the reform process there was a multiplicity of market outlets and a diversified market structure favouring competition. It also shows that the PMB and hence the government was not a dominant player. The PMB export monopoly has been abolished in favour of opening up the export trade to private sector initiatives. Incentives for such participation have been established under the Agricultural Non-Traditional Export Promotion Programme in the form of 100 per cent foreign exchange retention privileges and associated import entitlements. The PMB, like the CMB and the LMB, is undergoing divestiture to phase it out of the export trade and allow its former roles to be played by the private sector.

In tea processing, the export monopoly of the Uganda Tea Authority has been abolished. Measures have also been taken to revive the Uganda Tea Growers Association as a service organisation financed through cost recovery from outgrowers and to return the ownership and management of its tea factories to the private sector.

Finally, in dairy marketing, the Dairy Corporation no longer enjoys monopoly in milk collection, handling and processing. The government objective is encouraged by private sector participation in the dairy industry. Private investors have already assumed ownership and management of a substantial number of milk collection centres in competition with the Dairy Corporation. To formalise this, there is a draft Dairy Industry Bill (1997) seeking to repeal the Dairy Industry Act of 1967 which gave the Dairy Corporation a monopoly to control the production and marketing of dairy products. By April 1999 the expected enactment has not taken place.

Overall, Uganda's economic reforms have included the following:

i)   Currency reform and liberalisation of foreign exchange;
ii) Trade liberalisation ;
iii) Privatisation and divestiture of public enterprises;
iv) Re-organisation of tax revenue collection through setting up of the Uganda Revenue Authority;
v)   Streamlining investment policy through the setting up of the Uganda Investment Authority and introduction of an investment code;
vi) Reform and reorganisation of civil service;
vii) Reduction in the size of the army; and
viii) Rehabilitation of the socio-economic infrastructure.

The impact of the reform process

Almost everyone agrees that globally Uganda's economic performance has markedly improved, and that this improvement is due to the economic reform policies implemented by the government since 1987. However, there is no unanimous agreement on the real impact of this successful reform process for two reasons. First, there is no agreement on the choice of the most appropriate impact indicators. The World Bank, IMF and all 'economic growth fundamentalists' regard macro-economic growth rates as the key test. But developmentalists or structuralists point to structural transformation, reduced poverty and reduced vulnerability as the real indicators of positive impact. As one commentator has pointed out, 'the degree of satisfaction with a given performance depends on the perceived nature of the task and the evaluative criteria which are employed'. [10]

Secondly, there is no unanimous agreement because of the following paradox: on the one hand there is impressive economic performance and on the other there is deepening object poverty, human deprivation, vulnerability and inadequate social services.[11] One commentator has depicted these two faces of Uganda as follows:

> There is a Uganda with high prospects for the future, which despite a difficult starting point has staged a remarkable economic recovery and is moving toward self-sustainable development... In this Uganda which has benefited from trickle-down policy of structural adjustment, the economy has been liberalized, private sector developed, investment boomed, import business flourished and even casinos mushroomed. These are good reasons for structural adjustment advocates to be satisfied.
>
> There is another Uganda which is still one of the poorest countries in the whole world. The present is uncertain but the future is even less reassuring. Economic growth has been substantial but it was basically due to support from foreign aid, and anyway has not significantly reached the majority of people living in rural areas or depending on agriculture. [12]

In short, the 'Ugandan paradox' is the dichotomy between macro-level performance and micro-level realities. In spite of an impressive growth rate of 6.5 percent since 1987, there is widespread poverty with over 55 percent of the population classified as poor, of which 15 percent belong to the category of the 'core poor'. This reality inevitably leads to the conclusion that the reform process has produced mixed results.

Two of the main objectives of structural adjustment policies - i.e. economic stabilisation and reversal of decline have been achieved. From a negative growth rate of -12.6 percent in 1979, the economy has averaged an annual growth GDP growth of 6.5 percent since 1987. From a three-digit inflation, the annual inflation rate has averaged 6-10 percent in the period after 1993. Interest rates for commercial banks lending dropped from 40 to 23 percent and foreign exchange rate has stabilised between Uganda shillings 1000 and 1500 per US dollar.

Macroeconomic stability has led to increased investment rates and faster economic growth as shown in Table 6.4.

Table 6.4: Key indicators of economic trends in Uganda between 1987 and 1996

	Average 1986/87-1991/92	Average 1992/93 - 1995/96
Recurrent revenue (as % GDP)	6.2	10.2
Total expenditure (as% GDP)	14.61	9.8
Domestic financing (as % GDP) % per year	1.2	-1.5
Growth average level 2 Money supply (M2)	105.5	31.8
Average end-period inflation	107.6	5.6
Private investment as % of constant price GDP	6.6	10.0
Growth in GDP (%GDP per year)	5.2	8.1
Growth in industrial production	11.81	6.2
Private Transfers to Uganda (US$m)	104.8	356.8
Non-coffee exports (US$m)	31.9	105.2

Source: Adapted from Uganda Human Development Report, 1997.

The reform process has positively affected the agricultural export sector in a number of ways. Through liberalisation of trade and foreign exchange, an improvement has been made in the incentive structure. Prices paid to farmers in Uganda today are in line with international prices. Coffee farmers earn between 60 and 70 percent of the world price up from a mere 20 percent before liberisation. Farmers have positively responded to higher prices by increasing coffee output enabling the country to export 4.15 million bags of coffee in 1997 which is the highest figure since the introduction of the crop in the country. Uganda has now surpassed the Ivory Coast to become Africa's leading coffee producer. With the abolition of export taxes on agricultural products, agricultural producers are no longer overloaded with the bulk of the country's taxation. Farmers and farmers' organisations are now in a position to directly benefit from improvements in their work performance or market changes. Farmers and their organisations are now strategically exposed to determinants of profitability and business performance. This means they are no longer mere participants but contestants in the market.

However, whereas the reform process has restored stability, reversed decline of capacity to generate exports and has propelled growth, benefits from the trickle-down policies of structural adjustment have failed to match peoples perceived and actual needs. Besides, initially (i.e. prior 1992) the reform process produced shocks that intensified food insecurity for more people in the country and entrenched poverty. These shocks were the immediate adverse effects of some of the conditionalities associated with adjustment lending by the World Bank and IMF. Those which have turned out to be particularly adverse included the removal of subsidies and price controls on agricultural inputs; the divestiture of input supply, credit and seed production to the private sector; the supplying of farm credit on commercial terms; and the introduction of user charges for government services previously supplied free of charge or at highly subsidised rates.

An assessment of the effects of these conditionalities can be gauged from results of a survey of farm households in five districts selected from three regions of Uganda for the period 1990-1992. For the districts of Mubende, Mbale, Lira/Apac and Tororo, the study revealed that the use of fertilizers (a purchased input) was very low (7, 8 and 10 percent of the respondents in 1990, 1991, and 1992 respectively. Nobody reported using fertilizers in Tororo, one of the main cotton/maize growing areas. The use of spray chemicals was also not widespread - a rather disturbing factor for a crop like cotton where spray chemicals are essential. The high costs of spray chemicals (in the absence of subsidies or price controls) were blamed for its low use. The purchase of oxen was also very low (8, 3 and 3 percent) during 1990, 1991 and 1992). All the three variables considered indicate an agriculture dependent on nature rather than a science and technology-based agriculture.

That the cost is a barrier in the transition to a more productive and technologically developed agriculture is further confirmed by the way the farmers themselves perceive their production constraints.

Table 6.5: Problems of production and percentage of respondents

Problem	Mubende	Mbale	Tororo	Lira/Apac
Expensive input	95.0	85.3	69.2	80.5
Lack of capital	35.0	29.4	51.3	26.8
Lack of transport	45.0	14.7	38.5	12.2
Low prices	15.0	8.8	25.6	4.9
Lack of land	0	14.7	7.7	2.4
Poor storage	0	0	0	0

Source: J.R. Bibangambah, 'The Impact of Structural Adjustment', 1993

The majority of respondents (80 percent) said expensive inputs was the main problem hindering their production. The problem was also common in all the four districts surveyed with percentages ranging from 95 percent in Mubende to 69.2 percent in Tororo. Most respondents' complaint about lack of capital came from Tororo district (51); and Mubende had the highest percentage of respondents complaining about lack of transport. The percentage of respondents who mentioned low prices was relatively small: 26 percent in Tororo, 15 percent in Mubende, 9 percent in Mbale and 5 percent in Lira/Apac. The lack of land was mentioned by 15, 8 and 2 percent of the respondents in Mbale, Tororo and Lira/ Apac respectively but nobody in Mubende mentioned it.

When asked to suggest possible solutions to the production problems/ constraints, 76 percent of the respondents suggested re-introduction of subsidies. This response was common in all the four districts 80 percent: in Mubende, 76 percent in Mbale, 74 percent in Tororo and 76 percent in Lira/ Apac. Dr Uma Lele met a similar response in Malawi.

The development of indigenous capacities was undermined by colonial policies and neglect. As a consequence, the local private sector is not an effective contestant in the investment and trade markets. The excessive dependence on foreign aid not only by government but also by all 'associations' (including our manufacturers/industrialists), non-governmental organisations, churches and individuals is clear evidence of incapacity to sustain the delivery of essential services. In short, during the transitional period when central public institutions are being dismantled and the private sector is not yet in a position to replace such bodies, productivity will be adversely affected to the extent that it depends on high-yielding purchased inputs.

Uganda's low productivity agriculture is associated with utilisation of backward and less productive technologies and excessive dependence on nature. The spread of modern technologies into Uganda's agricultural sector has been limited so far by the peasants' low level of education and low purchasing capacity. This means that since the majority of the people lack the purchasing power to buy the necessary inputs, they use low yielding technologies resulting in low productivity, low incomes, low savings and low farm investments, hence lack of assets and, therefore, poverty.

New technologies in the form of new or better seeds, feeds, fertilizers and pesticides inputs cost money. Thus, innovations must necessarily be associated with investments of funds and effort. Hence, it is important to facilitate the acquisition of the necessary inputs and technologies and, therefore, break the vicious circle.

Commercial terms make credit as expensive as the other inputs we have already discussed and produces the same effect. The reduction in credit and increases in interest rates may limit seasonal and long-term borrowing for agricultural purposes. Fifty six percent of respondents in the already mentioned four district case studies suggested government guarantee for production loans as a means of ameliorating the production credit constraint.

The development of new sources of revenue raising (for the government) such as cost- sharing, will tend to reduce disposable income for input purchase, as well as probably reducing labour productivity via foregone health care. In the four districts we have studied, we found that the income level of respondents was still low with 83 percent earning less than US$500 per annum. Only 9 percent of the respondents earned above US$1,000 per annum, 1 percent earned less than US$ 100. It was also found that a simple subtraction of income declared by respondents and expenditure incurred revealed that 55 percent of the respondents were spending more 'than their income' (i.e. were in deficit). This could be genuine deficit or could be due to income under-declaration. Our probing also revealed that only 6 percent of the respondents found income from crops sufficient, while 89 percent found it insufficient to meet their requirements.

Other adverse effects of structural adjustment included the introduction of service user charges which curtailed the wellbeing of large sections of society by denying those people access to health services and education (before the introduction of Universal Primary Education – UPE) because they were already living in financial deficit and retrenchment of the civil service by over 50 percent which not only greatly increased unemployment but also created income and food insecurity for ex-civil servants.

Although the capacity of the economy has recovered and improved to some extent, the actual structure has remained disproportionately agricultural. The lack of capabilities to operate and maintain the necessary transformation processes, especially in manufacturing, is a fundamental missing link. It is not enough to simply talk or sing of having provided an 'enabling environment'. As Nobel Prize winner Theodore Schulze has counselled, there is need to allocate effort and capital to do three things: increase the quantity of reproducible goods; improve the quality of the people as productive agents and raise the level of the productive arts. While it may be argued that government efforts to attract foreign investors, and support and promote education (e.g. through UPE and training) indicate its full appreciation of the task, developments in this direction are not yet substantial.

Rural poverty persisted or worsened as costs of inputs and imports increased much faster than the returns from the country's tradables (both food and non-food), even though government insists that overall the population below the poverty line has declined from 56 to·44 percent.

Liberalisation by itself does not guarantee competition and efficiency. Imperfect markets have prevented the assumed positive effects on farmgate prices to be fully passed over to the farmers. The necessary conditions of a suitable environment – that markets be contestable[13], that mobility of both resources and goods be perfect or convenient, that required public utilities (e.g. electric power, gas, water, telecommunications utilities) be available and functioning effectively, that the environment be stable and secure (i.e. outcomes be predictable with certainty) – are yet to be attained. Under these conditions, there is fear that the free market will tend to marginalise further the already marginalised and to enhance economic injustice.

Notes

1. In his article, 'Enough is Enough', (1994) Carlos Lopes gives a list of recipes-intensive agriculture, grassroots initiatives, infrastructures, high-tech solutions, industrialisation, structural adjustment and democracy-which participants, at a round table conference on *Democratisation of Africa*, said had failed to awaken the continent from its lethargy.
2. C. Jones and M.A. Kinguel, (1994). 'Africa's Quest for prosperity: Has adjustment Helped?', *Finance and Development*, Vol 31, No 2.
3. I G Patel (1993). 'Limits of the Current Consensus on Development', Proceedings of the World Bank Conference on Development Economics.
4. D.G.R. Belshaw, (1988). 'Agriculture - led Recovery in Post Amin Uganda: The causes of failure and the basis for success' in H.B. Hansen and M. Twaddle (eds) *Uganda Now: Between Decay and Development*, Kampala: Fountain Publishers.
5. J. Hinderick and Sterkenburg, (1987). *Agricultural Commercialisation and Government Policy in Africa*. London: KPI Limited.
6. E.O. Ochieng (1985). 'The Uganda government measures to Rehabilitate and Revive the Uganda economy' in P. Ndegwa *et al* (eds), *Development Options for Africa in the 1980's* OUP.
7. E.O. Ochieng, (1991). 'Economic Adjustment Programmes in Uganda 1985-1988' in H.B. Hansen and M. Twaddle (eds), *Changing Uganda*, Kampala: Fountain Publishers.
8. The task of formulating detailed policy programmes was assigned to nine agricultural policy working groups (established for the purpose as follows)
    i)   Rationalisation of coffee processing capacity (WG 1)
    ii)   Coffee Marketing Strategy and Organisation (WG 2)
    iii)   Financial restructuring of co-operative unions (WG 3)
    iv)   Agro-economic study of cotton production (WG 4)
    v)   Rationalisation of cotton processing capacity (WG 5)
    vi)   Restructuring of Lint Marketing Board (WG6)
    vii)   Restructuring of Uganda Tea Growers Association (WG 7)
    viii)   Restructuring of Produce Marketing Boards (WG 8)
    ix)   Agricultural research and Extension Planning (WG 9)
9. The liberalisation process led to the restructuring of the former CMB into CMBL which is a commercial entity and Uganda Coffee Development Authority (UCDA) a promotional and regulatory body to monitor, regulate and promote the development of the coffee subsector.
10. D.G.R Belshaw, (1996). 'Sectoral and Institutional Pitfalls for the unwary macro- economist', *Structural Adjustment Forum Newsletter* No. 6.
11. UNDP, (1997) *Uganda Human Development Report*.
12. T.A. Nguyeni (1996). 'Food Security and Exports: contribution to a National Food Strategy to meet the challenges of poverty reduction and growth' *EPAU Policy Paper, No. 4*.
13. Jones. S, (1991). The road to 'Privatisation', in *Finance and Development*, vol 28, No 1.

7

Response to Medium and Long-term Challenges

Responses to food insecurity

National food security is an overriding concern for all countries and all governments. In Uganda, this concern is even expressed in the national constitution[1] as one of the national objectives and principles of state policy. Uganda, the Pearl of Africa, is a country endowed with some of the finest natural resources in sub-Saharan Africa. Under diverse ecological and cultural determinants, it evolved, over time, four main food production systems[2], characterised by varying degrees of vulnerability. The four food systems are:

- Banana-based food system hinging on a perennial banana grove that yields on a year-round basis resulting in a reliable supply of food. Bananas are produced by more than 75 percent of the farmers in the high rainfall areas of central, southern and south-western Uganda. The country is the world's largest producer of the crop and accounts for 6.5 million tons annually. The banana-based food system is supplemented by sweet potatoes.
- Cereal or grain-based food system based on millet (finger and pearl), maize and simsim produced in the drier and less fertile areas of eastern and northern Uganda. The cereal-based food system is supplemented by cassava and potatoes.
- Milk-dominated food system of the pastoralists in the areas of livestock dependency (>50 percent gross household revenue or >20 percent food energy[3]) in the north east (Karamoja) and parts of Mbarara, Masaka and Rakai districts in the south. It is supplemented by cassava and sorghum.
- A new food system that has emerged in Uganda is a rice-dominated system, a product of 'adjustment' not by World Bank/IMF or Government of Uganda but by peasants themselves. As shown by studies by M. White[4] and Zie Gariyo[5] in eastern Uganda, with the breakdown of cotton marketing during the years of misrule (1971/1985) peasants in eastern Uganda switched to production of food crops especially maize and rice, increased their own consumption and improved their levels of nutrition.[6]

Food security - the assurance of a minimally adequate level of food consumption - concerns not only supply security through expansion of production and support measures, but it also involves marketing and distribution issues, such as storage and infrastructure development as well as people's purchasing capacity.

Food security is achieved 'when all people at all times have both physical and economic access to sufficient food to meet their dietary needs for a productive and healthy life'.[7] This is to say that food security is access to quality food in sufficient quantities at all times for people to lead an active and healthy life. Thus the two essential determinants of food security are adequate and stable availability determined by own food production and market supply while access depends on food prices and household income.[8] The food insecure are, by implication, those people who have lost or at risk of loosing availability of and access to food. This is to say that food insecurity affects households that lack the ability either to produce their own food or to buy enough. It results in an inadequate diet.

Two kinds of food insecurity are distinguished: chronic and transitory. Chronic food insecurity describes a continuous inadequate diet, whereas transitory food insecurity focuses on a temporary decline in a household's access to food[9]. A complementary view of food insecurity is in terms of the risk that certain social groups will confront starvation.[10] Food risk is measured as the probability that a given population, defined, for example, by geographical location, may experience inadequate access to food. This probability is, in turn, the product of environmental risk (i.e. the probability of crop failure) on the one hand, and income risk (i.e. the probability of failing to earn enough), on the other. Thus the task of a food security policy or strategy is to reduce the level of these probabilities[11]; and hence stabilizing supply and reducing the incidence of poverty are both necessary components of a food security strategy.

Food security can be analysed at several levels: national, regional, village, household and individual. To some extent, national/regional food security can be monitored by aggregated demand and supply indicators, e.g. per capita daily calorie supply as an indicator of food availability (derived e.g. from food balance sheets). However, food may be available at the national/regional level but not on the household level, due to low income. Thus, income is a complementary indicator to describe access to food. From national per capita income, averaged energy content of the daily diet and the relative prices of food, national food consumption (calorie consumption by income group) can be derived. But just as national per capita income is a poor indicator of the prevalence of poverty, so is per capita income a poor indicator of the number of people consuming inadequate amounts of food[12]. However, national/regional food availability remains one of the necessary preconditions for household food security.

This is surveyed usually by dietary intake in comparison with appropriate adequacy norms (e.g. for energy: percentage of calories consumed versus requirement), capturing both the households' food availability and the households' access to food. It is important to bear in mind that the first does not ensure the second since food may be available in markets, but the household may not have access to it owing to insufficient income. However, dietary intake implies more than availability of and access to food. It is necessary that the household desires to obtain the available food, and has the knowledge to use it in terms of adequate preparation, composition, and intra-household distribution.

Earlier interpretations of the concept of food security did not include food utilisation. This is what is conveyed in analyses which hold that food security is a necessary but not sufficient condition to obtain nutrition security.[13] It is thus held that the concept of nutrition security is more comprehensive than food security. In line with this view, Luther Tweeten has observed that 'some individuals with access to food do not utilize food properly because of illness, ignorance or culture'. This points to the importance of nutrition education and health programmes as means of improving food utilization[14.] It is held, therefore, that it is only by combining the determinants of food security with complementary aspects of caring capacity, health and environmental factors that we arrive at nutrition security as shown in the figure 7.1.

A national food strategy aspiring to work towards the maintenance of national food security was defined by the Netherlands' Royal Tropical Institute[16] as: 'a permanent instrument for policy planning and food sector management which ideally ensures the coherence of diverse technical actions, investments, social and economic policies related to a country's food and agricultural sector'. It was also pointed out in WCARRD Mission report[17] that the basic areas to be covered by a food security strategy include[18] the development of incentive-oriented food production policy; the prevention of food losses; improving marketing practices; and combating the immediate and long-term impacts of drought.

According to the Netherlands Royal Tropical Institute report a food strategy aspires to work towards the maintenance of national food security in three ways; namely, by establishing a framework for food production and consumption objectives, thus, helping to identify consistent policy priorities for achieving these objectives over time, specifying within this framework, short and medium-term programme and project action to accelerate the realisation of food policy goals; and providing a mechanism for the more effective implementation of specific programme and project proposals, both strengthening national institutional and management capabilities; and exploiting external development assistance to food and agriculture more productively.

Figure 7.1:   **Principal determinants of the Nutritional Status at the Household Level**

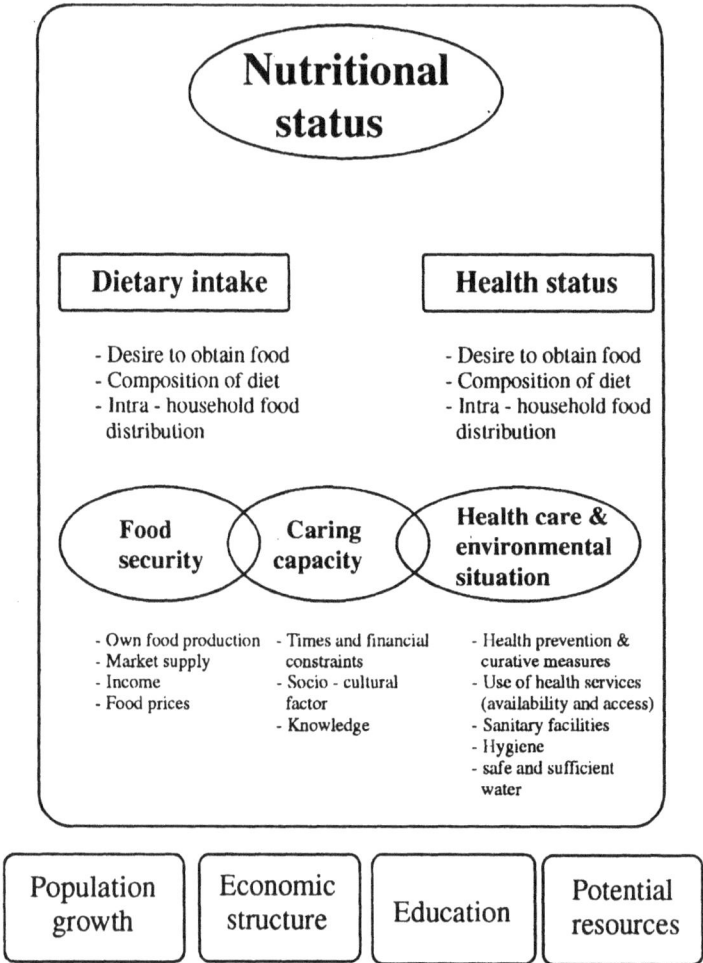

```
┌─────────────────────────────────────────────────────────────┐
│                   ╭───────────────────╮                      │
│                   │    Nutritional    │                      │
│                   │      status       │                      │
│                   ╰───────────────────╯                      │
│                                                              │
│   ┌─────────────────────┐         ┌─────────────────────┐   │
│   │   Dietary intake    │         │    Health status    │   │
│   └─────────────────────┘         └─────────────────────┘   │
│                                                              │
│   - Desire to obtain food           - Desire to obtain food │
│   - Composition of diet             - Composition of diet   │
│   - Intra - household food          - Intra - household food│
│     distribution                      distribution          │
│                                                              │
│   ╭─────────╮   ╭─────────╮   ╭─────────────────╮           │
│   │  Food   │   │ Caring  │   │  Health care &  │           │
│   │ security│   │capacity │   │  environmental  │           │
│   ╰─────────╯   ╰─────────╯   │   situation     │           │
│                               ╰─────────────────╯           │
│                                                              │
│  - Own food production  - Times and financial  - Health prevention & │
│  - Market supply          constraints            curative measures   │
│  - Income               - Socio - cultural     - Use of health services │
│  - Food prices            factor                 (availability and access) │
│                         - Knowledge            - Sanitary facilities │
│                                                - Hygiene              │
│                                                - safe and sufficient  │
│                                                  water                │
└─────────────────────────────────────────────────────────────┘

┌────────────┐ ┌────────────┐ ┌───────────┐ ┌────────────┐
│ Population │ │  Economic  │ │ Education │ │ Potential  │
│   growth   │ │ structure  │ │           │ │ resources  │
└────────────┘ └────────────┘ └───────────┘ └────────────┘
```

Source: Adapted from UNICEF[15]

Although some commentators (e.g. Lofchie[19], Nsibambi[20],) have asserted that post-independence African governments tended to pursue what Lofchie has described as 'almost anarchic *Laissez-faire*' food policy and actually abandoned the colonial food policy of 'famine reserves' and 'famine crops such as cassava', Uganda seems to have received inspiration from the World Conference on Agrarian Reform and Rural Development (WCARRD, 1979) and the food strategy approach initiated by the UN World Food Council for a positive intervention first adopted in Uganda's first recovery programmes of 1982-1984.

The food and agricultural considerations in the recovery programmes were subsequently followed by a food strategy study report titled 'Toward a National Food Strategy Vol. I & II' by the Royal Tropical Institute (Amsterdam) under an agreement between the government of Uganda (GOU) and the European Economic Community (EEC). In this 1984 report, the government's national food strategy objectives were to:

- achieve a satisfactory level of self-sufficiency in basic foodstuffs and ensure a supply of food in adequate quantities and quality to meet national nutrition requirements at all times;
- improve nutritional level of the population and nutritional values of the food consumption basket;
- improve food marketing and distribution in order to stabilize food availability and prices;
- develop the food processing industry along more commercial lines; and
- explore possibilities of food exports;

The report's main recommendations were that principal food strategy objectives should include increasing agriculture's contribution to overall economic development and rural incomes; boosting national food security and improving nutrition; the diversification of food and agricultural exports; and ensuring a more equitable distribution of income between different regions and reducing food supply imbalances.

It also recommended that priorities for policy implementation should be: the integration of the food production sector into a market exchange economy with a view to creating marketable surplus for food deficit areas, urban consumption and exports; putting emphasis on increasing yields through improved husbandry practices and input levels; preventing the decline of livestock population held by the small holders through the integration of livestock crop production activities at farm level; disease control, improvement of livestock marketing, improved fisheries management in the densely populated areas; providing an incentive policy package covering three interrelated aspects - pricing, market organisation including marketing efficiency and storage, including the operation of security and market intervention stocks;[21] providing a productivity policy package covering research aimed at development of improved low-cost technical packages for small farmer production; extension to provide the essential link between researchers and farmers in the generation, dissemination and utilisation of agricultural knowledge; input supply systems with emphasis on improving their effectiveness so as to promote a more regular flow of inputs to the rural sector.

Furthermore, the report recommended that, means be provided for reaching nutritionally vulnerable groups by establishing an autonomous National Food and Nutrition Council, with a mandate to take binding decisions concerning the planning, implementation and co-ordination of food and nutrition related issues, and an Institute for Nutrition and Food Science, at Makerere University, to carry out applied research, train staff at different levels and advise on implementation of food and nutrition activities, as well as expanding the primary health care system and linking its monitoring activity to a nation-wide nutritional surveillance system.

Although the Royal Tropical Institute study effectively carried out the work of analysing food and agricultural constraints, and made recommendations for policy and programme action to meet food and nutrition objectives, the civil strife and political instability in the country prior to 1986 was such that no specific action programme could be undertaken to implement the recommendations.

Despite the fact that the 1984 National Food Strategy study report had put more emphasis on productivity or yield increases, the 1990 USAID/GOU Uganda Accelerated Foodcrop Production Strategy Mission observes, (i.e. six years after the Royal Tropical Institute's report) that 'the recent recovery in foodcrop output is more the result of expanded conventional inputs (land and labour) rather than from rising yields' - an indication that not much had changed in terms of productivity.[22]

In 1990, it was still the case (as it is today) that the increase in productivity was the most critical requirement, not just for food availability but for ameliorating the general poverty, especially rural poverty. Accordingly, the report stated emphatically that 'raising per capita income and living standards requires an increase in productivity of the major portion of the nation's resource base – that devoted to foodcrop production.'

The objectives of the 1990 foodcrop production strategy were to:

•   provide food at affordable prices in sufficient quantities and with adequate nutritional values;

- increase farm income, national income and employment by improving food production technology, optimum allocation of resources and upgrading marketing technology;
- supply adequate raw materials for industries and save foreign exchange by producing crops more effectively; and
- diversify commodity exports with foodcrops produced more efficiently, thus freeing farm resources to produce additional export commodities.

The study found that foodcrop production in Uganda had been constrained by inappropriate macroeconomic policies, lack of improved technology including superior varieties, inadequate supplies of operating inputs ranging from hoes and pangas to fertilizers, pesticides and herbicides, deteriorating public services, infrastructure and market information, and lack of effective demand, leading to a stagnant foodcrop market compared to other countries.

The recommended foodcrop strategy covered four main areas. The first of these was foodcrop research, which would entail screening of high-yielding, disease and pest-resistant foodcrop seed varieties; adapting varieties from elsewhere to local conditions; breeding new varieties drawing on germplasm from domestic and international sources; developing strategies regarding cultural practices and appropriate technology; adapting equipment, soil conservation, crop rotations, use of manure, and economic use of fertilisers; developing indigenous agricultural industries to produce basic agricultural inputs such as lime for acid soils, Rhizobium bacteria for legume crops and nitrogen urea; raising research output by attracting, motivating, and holding in service the most able and qualified research scientists; and providing adequate, timely and consistent funding for research activities. The second was food crop extension, which would concentrate on proper funding through appropriate salaries and travel expenses paid on time; giving greater emphasis to extension programmes for women because of their major role in producing and marketing of food crops; reorganising and training underutilised staff; encouraging provisions of extension services by the private sector, improved co-ordination by unifying the extension service; linking foodcrop producers, researchers and administrators to set priorities and organise an outreach programme; rehabilitating the Information and Visual Aids Centre and farm demonstration buildings as some of the required facilities; and improving foodcrop seeds and planting material input delivery system. The third area was improving foodcrop marketing through the provision of information on current prices, crop conditions, regional crop deficits, transportation costs, etc; improving foodcrop quality, post-harvest handling, storage through research and extension working with producers, marketeers and consumers, giving due care to the need for marketing research and extension to give greater attention to the participation of women as deliverers and recipients of services;

and opening marketing to free competition. The fourth area was expanding availability of credit to foodcrop producers by providing secure title to farm real estate.

It needs to be noted, at this juncture, that both the 1984 and 1990 Food Strategy reports did not make any recommendations in respect of combating the immediate and long-term impacts of drought or any other unfavourable climatic conditions. This means the two reports did not examine or consider the criticality of environment or environmental risk in the availability of food and the vulnerability of the food systems stated earlier. This matter received more attention in the 1993 and 1996 Government of Uganda Food Security Strategy documents.

The 1993 document was basically a policy statement of what Uganda was formulating as a National Food and Nutrition Security strategy. It covered the food and nutrition policy objectives and an outline of main actions or strategies but left action programmes and their management to be formulated later.

Government stated, unambiguously, that the overall strategy was to:

- treat food as a national strategic resource;
- direct resources in the national development plan in order to facilitate attainment of food and nutrition goals;
- include food and nutrition issues in the national, district and sectoral development plans;
- ensure that nutrition issues are incorporated in formal, informal and non-formal training in order to improve the knowledge and attitudes of communities in nutrition related matters;
- ensure food security at household, district and national levels for purposes of improving nutrition status of the population;
- establish and maintain food and nutrition monitoring mechanisms;
- enforce the food and nutrition policy; and
- provide the political will and commitment to facilitate the translation of the policy into action programmes.

The specific policy objectives and proposed actions (not in any way different from those stated in the 1984 and 1990 documents except for food surveillance) covered areas of food supply,[23] food processing and preservation, food storage, marketing and distribution,[24] external food trade, food aid, food standards and food quality control, information, education and communication, women, food and nutrition, food and nutrition surveillance and research. Finally, the document gave a lay-out of the intended Food and Nutrition Management Structure which incorporated a National Food and Nutrition Council (NFNC) proposed in the 1984 Food Strategy report.

Another food and nutrition policy statement covering goals, specific objectives and strategies was produced in October 1996 under the auspices of National Food and Nutrition Council. It was the Uganda National Plan of Action for Nutrition (UNPAN) produced also in 1996 that went beyond a statement of objectives and strategies and specified what activities were to be carried out, where, by whom, and within what time frame. The activities were for:

- Improving household food security;
- Preventing specific micronutrient deficiencies;
- Protecting consumers through improved food quality and safety;
- Preventing and managing infectious diseases;
- Promoting child nutrition and development;
- Caring for the socio-economically deprived and nutritionally vulnerable;
- Promoting appropriate diets and health life styles;

A contentious issue among the considerations for ensuring food security is that of national food security reserves. In the 1990 study report, Professor Luther Tweeten and his team submitted that 'the cheapest national food reserve policy is a sound foodcrop production strategy, and good roads and communication along with currency reserves to enter the international market for imports when production fails'. The same view is expressed, on behalf of DANIDA, by consultants from the Carl Bro Group in their Uganda Master Plan and Investment Programme for the Grain Marketing Sector (Vol.I, II, and III) in which they state that 'Uganda can achieve the objective of food security without having to establish a national food security reserve which would be a costly exercise'.[25] In their view, 'The Government should follow a supportive approach - increasing food security by motivating and supporting development of production and on-farm and village storage'.

While the Carl Bro consultants acknowledged that local food shortage problems are potentially possible, they held that these could be solved by redirecting export stocks. They added that such occasional food problems by certain groups such as refugees and displaced persons should be addressed by a ministry responsible for social welfare and not a public enterprise/government parastatal such as the PMB. They also endorsed the view that the local food problems in Uganda are often not the result of a supply shortfall but, rather, are due to limited purchasing power e.g. among the urban poor. Thus, they contended that the food security problem is essentially a poverty/social problem and should be addressed as such. This was the approach subsequently adopted by government in the 1996 national food strategy.

In spite of the advice based on affordability, the urge for a national food reserve was not completely eliminated. The 1993 food policy document still included an action for 'studying overall storage requirements for strategic food reserves and establishing national food security and food reserve programmes' although the objective was scaled down to 'establishing and maintaining minimum strategic food reserves in stores located at appropriate levels'.

The contention that the food security problem is essentially a poverty problem and should be addressed as such is based on what has been termed a 'post-modern perspective'.[26] Under this perspective, the analysis of food security issues has shifted from a concern for aggregate food supplies at the global and national levels to what Prof. A.K.Sen has called entitlements i.e. the ability of households or individuals to command access to food.[27] From this viewpoint, food insecurity in LDCs is attributed to two major causes. The first is widespread poverty: people do not earn sufficient income to satisfy their minimum nutritional requirements. Moreover, because incomes are so low, people are unable to accumulate savings and are, therefore, much more vulnerable to shocks which adversely affect their ability to grow or purchase food. Consequently, poverty leads to both chronic food deficiency and transitional food insecurity, including vulnerability to famine.

The second cause involves major shocks which severely disrupt people's livelihoods and entitlements to food. Such shocks include drought and, in particular, internal conflicts. Improving food security necessitates alleviating poverty in LDCs, reducing the incidence of adverse shocks which disrupt people's livelihoods and putting in place mechanisms to mitigate the impact of shocks on entitlements to food.[28] The formulators of the 1996 document appear to have based their views on the neo-liberal paradigm or 'standard model' - which emphasises free market system and private enterprise as the best approaches to economic growth and poverty reduction.

In what he has called a food security synthesis, Luther Tweeten, one of the greatest advocates of the standard model, has summed up the food security issue as follows:

a) The principal cause of transitory and chronic food insecurity is poverty. People with adequate buying power overcome the frictions of time (e.g. unpredictable, unstable harvest from year to year) and space (e.g. local food shortages) to be food secure.
b) Poverty can be overcome through broad-based, sustainable, economic development.
c) The most effective and efficient means to economic development is to follow the standard model which assures an economic 'pie' to divide among people and among functions such as human resource development, family planning, a food safety net, or environmental protection. The standard model is applicable to any culture and provides 'a workable prescription

for economic progress ensuring buying power for self reliance and food security in any nation.'

Tweeten also holds that 'global trade liberalisation, which developed countries have led but for which developing countries also need to take initiative, has much to offer food security in all countries.'[29]

Tweeten's submissions, which are contained in the paper he prepared for USAID, seem to have influenced the thinking of those who formulated the 1996 national food strategy document under the sponsorship and guidance of USAID. In this document the strategy spelt out consists of three main components; namely agriculture-led development as a basis for industrialisation, export development and diversification, food production development, and food exports with a particular focus on non traditional agricultural exports especially maize and beans as a response to the challenge of growth and poverty and hence the need to improve household incomes.

Whereas the previous food security strategies were largely food-crop production strategies, the 1996 food security strategy is multi-dimensional. The formulation of the strategy was based on an integrated approach - meaning that both analysis and policy strategy formulation integrated stabilisation (an IMF priority) with growth (a World Bank focus), and with human development (a UNDP concern) to produce an integrated or balanced-policy approach.[30] This falls within a development paradigm which emphasises people, institutions, technologies and policies.

A new perspective of enhancing or promoting food security through poverty alleviation or poverty reduction policies is that of micro-level finance for stabilising consumption and reinforcing the households' wealth and income base. This entails a broadened role of rural finance to address not only credit and savings needs for agricultural production and off-farm enterprises but also other demands for financial services such as financing food consumption and health care as well as providing households with most effective savings, credit and insurance services for smoothing consumption, holding precautionary savings and diversifying the asset portfolio.

Since the incomes of most rural households in developing countries depend directly or indirectly on agriculture, they vary from year to year and from season to season. Such fluctuations in income translate into fluctuations in consumption if households have no savings or credit to fall back on. These periods of transitory food insecurity are experienced by many rural households in developing countries and can lead to chronic food insecurity and deprivation, forcing households to sell off whatever they possess.

Extensive and intensive household-level studies (especially by researchers from the International Food Policy Research Institute and the Department of

Agricultural Economics and Rural Sociology of Ohio State University)[31] in developing countries led some policy analysts and strategists to postulate that there is potential for improving household food security through rural finance. The underlying conceptualisation is that financial services could help prevent both transitory and chronic food insecurity in the following ways.

First, by providing access to credit, savings and insurance services, households could acquire inputs, labour and equipment to generate additional income. Second, access to credit, liquid savings and insurance services could increase their capacity to bear risk, enabling them to invest in new agricultural technology and off-farm enterprises. Third, improved access to financial services could help stabilise consumption of food and other essential goods more efficiently than existing informal services do.

This broader concept of rural finance and household food security provides a rationale for policies that aim at sustainably expanding credit, savings and insurance for the rural poor. A more comprehensive treatment of innovative approaches to financial services is given in a separate section on micro-finance.

From the early 1980s normative thinking led to positive interventions that marked the beginning of a real shift from a somewhat *laissez-faire* food policy to a food strategy approach. However, the implementation and effectiveness of this strategy have been more at the level of macro-economic management and less at the level of actual farming. Increases in agricultural output have continued to depend on extensive use of land and labour rather than from increased yields - an indication that not much has changed in terms of productivity except in the case of milk production where acquisition of higher yielding breeds of cattle and improved management have led to notable milk increases.

The unimpressive record of the food strategy approach is attributable to the failure by development promoters to get improved technologies transferred from reports in research stations to the Ugandan farmers. This is the greatest challenge that the National Agricultural Research Organisation (NARO) must address. With respect to food crop production, on-farm technical advice has been largely non-existent (inspite of the existence of administrative structures called agricultural extension), except recent efforts by non-governmental organisations such as CARE and other efforts by donor agencies like USAID, which is working on non- traditional (food) exports especially beans and maize, and DANIDA which is working through the Uganda National Farmers Association. Fortunately, the problem of limited on-farm technical advice has already been recognised and NARO is reported to have already worked out strategic plans to deal with it.

The post 1996 orientation from food crop production strategies to food security strategy intended to address both food supplies and purchasing power is now part of the Poverty Eradication Action Plan and relevant action programmes whose impact is yet to be realised. What is still unresolved is the problem of episodic events especially drought and, therefore, the problem of food shortages in drought -prone areas during periods of unfavourable weather. In July 1991 the National Early Warning and Food Information System (NEWFI) was established. This is under the FAO-executed regional project based in the Inter-governmental Authority on Drought and Development (IGADD) headquarters in Djibouti, funded by the Italian government.

The National Early Warning and Food Information Unit is charged with the responsibility of collecting agro-meteorological, nutritional, socio-economic and remotely sensed data assessment of the food situation in the country. The agro-meteorological data is derived from the National Meteorological Centre which receives weather data from up-country stations using radio calls. The remote data sensing is currently done by the FAO/IGADD regional project in Djibouti. The nutritional data is obtained from nutritional surveillance which is periodically carried out to assess the nutritional status of the people in a given locality. The socio-economic data is obtained from monthly reports as well as the market news service reports derived from the Ministry of Trade and Industry. More specifically, the National Early Warning and Food Information Unit carries out food assessment surveys, yield estimations, monitors seasonal crop areas, inputs, weather conditions and provides socio-economic data and nutritional data.

In theory, early warning should help the creation of preparedness, but by emphasising disaster management and aid coordination between government relief agencies and international aid organisations, the 1996 document seems to be more concerned with the mitigation of the impact of food shortages. Not much attention has been paid to the issue of ability to abate the likely or predicted events. The document does not include abatement programmes and it does not adequately address the problem of drought-prone areas. This failure arises from the stubborn refusal to recognise that the threat of drought to Uganda, where it affects 50 percent of the population every four to five years and has done so for the last thirty years, is real. Statements like 'with the exception of Karamoja which is particularly susceptible to periodic drought, Uganda is not normally prone to severe climatic disorder' by government officials is evidence of that refusal.

Food shortages occurring every 4-5 years and observed for over thirty years cannot be considered an accident or a coincidence. They are a pattern. The pattern is evidence of both the threat of drought and Uganda's vulnerability. While response is the key issue, it should not be simply in terms of national budgetary provisions or foreign exchange reserves for food purchases (for famine victims) in the international market or merely in terms of food aid flow.

While strategic famine reserves at household level and the encouragement of 'famine crops' such as cassava, potatoes and millet, will help to abate a crisis (famine), and while improved infrastructure, logistical support and coordination will help improve food distribution and, therefore, help mitigate the impact of food deficit in particular areas, the need for a sustainable long-term strategy for drought-prone areas to combat transitional food insecurity requires the greatest attention possible. This points to a serious need to give high priority to the development of small-scale irrigation schemes. In my view, the early warning systems provide no effective preparedness when there are no abatement or mitigation programmes.

Responses to agricultural backwardness

Africa's agriculture, especially that in sub-Saharan countries, is still predominantly traditional or peasant agriculture characterised by a number of inadequacies or shortcomings. First, the purpose of production is mostly subsistence to meet the family's basic domestic necessities of life such as food, firewood/charcoal, fibre and hides, even though it is also true that the majority of producers have increasingly begun to produce for the market in addition to subsistence, albeit in varying degrees of commercialisation.[32] As a consequence both subsistence and transitional producers are part and percel of the rural poor just slightly above both the landless and unemployed who are the poorest of the rural poor. Many of the subsistence producers may be self-sufficient in food supply (and hence not suffering from food poverty), but they suffer from cash income and assets poverty.[33]

Second, both subsistence and transitional peasant agriculture heavily rely on nature than on science and technology. In both modes of agriculture, what is done, how it is done and with what it is done, are still simple and crude. The main tools are the hoe, axe and panga. More than 50 percent of what A.T. Mosher calls 'a progressive rural structure'- i.e. the knowledge, the skills, incentives, technology and purchased inputs - is missing.

Third, capital investment in peasant agriculture is very low.[34] This leads to low ratios of factors to land. Since both variable inputs and capital are less than are desired, productivity (i.e. output per hectare and per farmer) is very low or lower than if they were operating under a progressive rural structure. Low productivity is one of the most outstanding characteristics of African agriculture, Uganda's included. National yields are said to be between 17 and 50 percent of those attainable at research stations. A panellist in the Winrock Round Table Discussion in 1992 attributed the low African agricultural productivity to:[35]

a) failure to develop crop varieties that will adapt to a difficult environment (i.e. little irrigation) and eventually be disease resistant and yield moderately despite nutrient deficiencies.

b) lack of a seed base i.e. germ plasm and appropriate seeds which is a consequence of reliance on seeds grown by farmers themselves with no know-how.

c) reliance on rain-fed agriculture but with rainfall being the most unpredictable of all the inputs necessary for agricultural production.

d) inadequate soil fertility maintenance and improvement.

A field survey undertaken in 18 districts of Uganda (almost half the country) by the Export Policy Analysis Unit (EPAU) of the Ministry of Planning and Economic Development in 1995 shows that the low use of improved seeds and fertilisers and the use of poor production techniques, led to low production levels.

Fourth, yield vulnerability is very high. Because of its heavy dependence on nature, the yield or output of peasant agriculture is very vulnerable to episodic events like drought, floods, and occurrence of diseases and pests.

Fifth, peasant agriculture suffers from infrastructural poverty. The necessary supporting systems (inputs supply, transport, financing, research, extension advice, etc) are either non-existent or grossly inadequate.

It is the process of eliminating these shortcomings of peasant agriculture that is called modernisation of agriculture. Thus, the modernisation of agriculture means transforming traditional forms of farming by adopting modern scientific methods and techniques as well as new technologies to increase productivity and qualitatively improve the standards of living of rural agricultural communities.

In operational terms, agricultural modernisation calls for:

a) changing the purpose of farming: instead of producing just for domestic supply we must produce for the market. This means a good deal more than it sounds. It means that whether we are producing food or non-food agricultural products, we should produce for cash by producing more than what is necessary for our home or family consumption. It means that we should be aware that agricultural products are not of the same value. There are low-value and high-value products. It means our farmers must change viewing agriculture merely as a source of food or a way of life. They must start perceiving and regarding farming as business.[36] Farming as a business requires that farmers graduate from being operators who just 'grow things' and become farm managers that run farm business. It means an orientation focusing on satisfying the market or market requirements in terms of availability and delivery in particular place (hence transportation), at a particular time (hence transportation and storage) and in the right form (hence packaging and processing). In short, modern marketing in a modern agriculture means that farmers' produce must be stored, transported, processed and delivered in the form, and at the time and to the places that consumers desire. This comes straight from business life where the customer is the king.

b) transforming the simple agricultural technology used in peasant agriculture. By simple technology in agriculture we mean, on the equipment side, implements and tools which are operated by human physical energy such as hoes, cutlasses, saws, bushknives, axes, pangas (machetes) etc. On the skills side, it means the gamut of culturally inherited local knowledge concerning cultivation, forestry, fishing, and livestock rearing etc.

The technologies used in modern agriculture, can be grouped into seven broad categories:[37]

Group 1	Power-driven vehicles: tractors, combine harvesters, lorries, bulldozers, tractor shovels, cranes, motor mowers, motor tillers, motor boats, trawlers, etc.
Group 2	Stationary power-driven machinery: threshers, pumps, engines, mills, crushers, mixers, air-conditioners, refrigeration plants, power saws, etc.
Group 3	Implements used in conjunction with groups 1 and 2 above: Ploughs, harrows, rolls, smoothers, planters, seed-drills, nets, etc.
Group 4	Equipment for crop protection: sprayers, dusters, spreaders for manure and fertilizers, etc.
Group 5	Chemical fertilizers
Group 6	Chemical pesticides, insecticides, herbicides
Group 7	High-yield-varieties (HYV) of seeds, high-yielding livestock breeds: plant and animal genetics.

Technologies from these seven groups have been or are being tried in Uganda, but the number of farmers that have applied them have been too few to effect the transformation of farming in the country.

The skills associated with the use of these seven groups of technologies are those of operating, repairing and maintaining the machinery and equipment, applying the results of the science of agronomy, including the latest advances in genetics, production planning, farm management, to ensure the:

- use of deliberately selected crop varieties, improved seeds and livestock breeds i.e. those of crops and livestock with a higher genetic potential;
- Maintenance and improvement of soil fertility through crop rotation, mulching, organic manure or fertilisers;
- use of practices that will ensure that there will be no build up of weeds, pests, diseases and no increase in soil acidity or toxic elements;
- protection to both crops and livestock against pests and diseases;
- protection to both crops and livestock against adverse changes in weather;
- investing money or financial capital to create productive capacity. The saying that 'money is made by money' is relevant here. A major feature of modern agriculture is increased use of capital inputs particularly those purchased from outside the agricultural sector;
- transforming the productivity of our agriculture through improvement of genetic potential, quality of inputs and the environment by means of research, adoption and acquisition;
- increase in the number of production cycles within a season or producing all year round by managing the environment through control of the constraints of temperature, rainfall and soil conditions;
- the promotion of supporting systems in the form of credit, input supply, transportation, marketing, extension or advisory services, research and a willingness to innovate or adopt innovations; and
- promotion and development of sustainable farming systems, i.e. those that are stable in the sense that they do not disrupt the environment or over-exploit natural resources (e.g. overgrazing), and those that are resilient in the sense that they absorb or withstand shocks and retain capacity in the face of disturbances such as adverse weather conditions.

It is thus clear from the essentials of the agricultural transformation process that agricultural modernisation is deemed to have occurred when a substantial number of rural households, operate farms commercially (selling a substantial portion of the value of their output); have incomes exceeding the poverty level, invest more heavily on the farm, purchase commercial inputs, including hired labour, in significant quantities, specialise in production at the farm level and adopt technologies on a regular basis.

The issue of technological change needs to be emphasised because of its critical role not only in agriculture and manufacturing, but in the whole economy. Hayami and Ruttan[38] have estimated that half of the difference in labour productivity between the more developed and less developed countries is explained by the use of modern technical inputs from the industrial sector and by human capital. The government of Uganda appreciates the criticality of technological change and hence its pronouncement that 'in order to accelerate agricultural sector growth and transformation in Uganda it is necessary to introduce profound technological change in the sector'. With improved productivity, realised through technological change, it is stipulated that per unit costs of agricultural production will be lowered, food production will become increasingly a profitable commercial activity and the competitiveness of Uganda's agricultural exports on international markets will increase. Technical change is what agricultural modernisation, as a development strategy, is trying to promote in Uganda.

In Uganda, the ongoing and planned agricultural recovery and reconstruction programmes since 1987 have aimed at creating incentives through the liberation of marketing and pricing, as well as institutional reform. The programmes have also aimed at reducing mass poverty and food insecurity through enhanced productivity that would in turn boost farmers per capita incomes and living standards. To increase productivity the programmes have been mainly concerned with research, input supply and extension services systems in the agricultural sector. These concerns have been the focus of all major agricultural projects such as the Agricultural Development Project in the north and north east, the Farming Systems Support Programme, the South Western Agricultural Rehabilitation Project, the rehabilitation of the Soroti facility for manufacturing agricultural tools and equipment, the Uganda Seeds Project, the Uganda Root Crops Programme, the establishment of the NARO and the introduction of unified Agricultural Extension Programme.

Planned programmes, with 'modernisation' as their theme, are based on a sector-wide approach, thus shifting away from project approach, within the context of decentralisation but in response to challenges that have proved to be very resilient in the last one hundred years. These include the preponderance of subsistence agriculture, low agricultural productivity, poverty, food insecurity (seasonal and in particular disadvantaged areas), and reliance on public sector activities (services and investments). The new approach to the modernisation of agriculture in Uganda focuses on achieving the following:

- a technology-based agriculture, with adoption of appropriate improved husbandry and farming practices e.g. high yielding, disease and pest resistant planting materials, fertilizers and mechanical inputs - including labour-saving technology.
- a competitive agriculture, with lower costs per unit of production and marketing, to overcome the disadvantages of being a land-locked, high transport cost economy.
- a diversifying agriculture, with commodities of higher value and higher income elasticity of demand, especially fruits, vegetables, and livestock.

– an agricultural sector with intensified agro-processing for value addition to raw commodities.

– an exporting agriculture, with increased trade in traditional cereals (millet, sorghum) into the regional market and food aid contracts, increased traditional exports of coffee, tea and cotton, new exports in horticulture and spices, and quality, reliability of supply and standards for export.

- an agriculture in which all the total factor productivity is increased, for both land and labour.

To initiate the planned programmes which will constitute the modernisation process, government carried out wide consultations with various stakeholders - central government ministries and agencies, members of parliament, farmers' organisations and other NGOs, training institutions and district officials. The consultations held in 1996 and 1997 led to the writing of a document entitled 'Modernisation of Agriculture in Uganda – The Way Forward 1996-2000.' This modernisation of agriculture plan proposed the following investment programme in the prioritised areas of action.

Strengthening research, extension and farmer linkages	Ushs 129.70 billion/US$ 120.10 million
Development of production and marketing infrastructure	Ushs 105.43 billion/US$ 97.63 million
Targeting zonal production (renamed targeting commercial agriculture production)	Ushs 79.64 billion/US$ 73.74 million
Improved access and availability of credit in rural areas	Ushs 40.25 billion/US$ 37.27 million
Promotion of development of agro-based rural enterprises	Ushs 10.09 billion/US$ 9.34 million
Total Budget	Ushs 365.11 billion/US$ 338.08 million

Source: Draft Statement to the December 1998 Consultative Group Meeting

However, this plan may not be implemented as it is primarily because the planned expenditures therein are likely to be much more than the resources available both from donors and the government. This plan also needed to be reviewed again to:

• clarify the role of the central and local governments;
• clarify the role of the private sector; and
• identify those areas of investment that have highest returns to scarce public resources.

Consequently, another more in-depth consultative process, taking into account the additional concerns identified above, was initiated to:

- identify the resource envelop available for public investment in the agricultural sector;
- enable stakeholders develop a shared vision for the sector;
- work out a strategy and incentives for greater private investment in the sector;
- clearly identify and understand the appropriate roles of the private sector, central and local governments; and
- work out a strategy and incentives for greater private investment in the sector.

In the quest for the modernisation of agriculture, the 1998 consultative process which is a review of the earlier plan (1996-2000) has identified a number of priority areas which include improving research, extension and farmer linkages, investment in infrastructure (markets, roads, water, communication etc), promoting agricultural production for the market, agricultural education (formal and informal), improving access to and availability of credit in rural areas. (I would in addition, stress productive use of credit), promoting private sector role in the modernisation of agriculture, capacity building in central and local governments (regulatory services, data base establishment including production of agricultural statistics), promoting development of rural agro-based enterprises, environmental management, forestry development and management, good governance, and building social capital.

Before these areas could be subjected to another level of prioritisation that would be consistent with available resources and implementation capacity, a review of the relative roles of the expected actors - central government, local governments (i.e. the public sector) and the private sector - was undertaken. The framework within which the roles of the respective actors to be decided upon was that of decentralisation already introduced in the country by way of administrative reform. The salient features of Uganda's decentralisation exercise includes the transfer of political financial and planning authority from the central government to local government councils. Local governments are increasingly taking responsibility for the delivery of services, and the promotion of popular participation and empowerment of local people in decision making.

Accordingly, therefore, the role of central government in the modernisation of agriculture was identified as follows:

- Policy formulation: The government will provide a comprehensive agricultural policy, which shall elaborate a shared vision of the objectives and principles for the development of the agricultural sector;
- Funding of agricultural activities: Government will mobilise and allocate resources for implementation of agricultural activities. The Ministry of

Finance, Planning and Economic Development (MFPED) are responsible for determination and management of the resource allocation system;

• Capacity building: The central government can offer support to local governments through technical assistance. Technical assistance cane take the form of training, development of contextual guidance about procedures, and promotion of examples of good practices in the relevant area. The role of districts will require capacity building in planning, priority setting and designing extension delivery mechanisms that suit their circumstances while ensuring greater private sector participation.

• Performance monitoring: The MAAIF is mandated to carry out regular performance monitoring. Monitoring should inform the government to offer corrective advice where necessary;

• Promoting the role of the private sector: As a result of liberalisation and divestiture, the private sector will play an increasingly important role in the delivery of services. Government will formulate policies and strategy of promoting a stronger private sector involvement in agriculture sector development; and

• Personnel: The central government will assist local government to identify, recruit and deploy technically qualified personnel at the district and sub-county level in order to promote agricultural development[39].

In terms of actual activities, government has decided that in the next three to five years (i.e. 1999-2003) its main thrust for public action in the modernisation of agriculture will be to:

i) finance extension services for smallholders;
ii) finance agricultural research for smallholders;
iii) finance control of epidemic disease and pests;
iv) build capacity for production of foundation seed;
v) provide regulatory services;
vi) finance collection of agricultural statistical data and production and marketing information;
vii) finance the implementation of land reform;
viii) finance capacity building of agriculture and related institutions including private/NGO rural financial institutions;
ix) set policies and regulations to foster the expansion of the private sector supply of modern inputs and services (including establishment of rural financial services);
x) construct fish landing sites; and
xi) finance development of irrigation and capacity building of smallholders in water harvesting, soil and water conservation.

Although local governments are responsible for planning and implementing decentralised services and programmes including the modernisation of agriculture, there is no legislation, as yet, binding them to give priority to agricultural modernisation. In the 1997/98 financial year, only 3 out of the 39 districts analysed had budgeted more than 3 percent of their expenditure on agriculture, the majority having budgeted to spend only 1 percent on the sector. Government may have to use conditional grants to persuade districts to give priority to agricultural modernisation.

Despite the fact that the private sector leadership is the hall-mark of the liberalisation process in Uganda and other African economies, policy-strategies should not lose sight of the uniqueness of the farming business. No economy in the world – not even those of US and UK which are flag-bearers of free market systems – has left agriculture purely in the hands of the private sector.

In Uganda, given uniqueness of agriculture, government has always intervened in this sector of the economy, thereby entrenching public services as an essential and integral part of the agricultural industry. Besides, agriculture in comparison with other investment opportunities, is not attractive because the risks involved are too high to the private sector. Even the FAO has expressed reservations about private sector-driven agriculture on the ground it may also lack capacity to take up functions previously undertaken by government. This implies that in Uganda there can be no complete government withdrawal from the development and management of the agricultural sector.

Government policy formulation recognises a role for the private sector in agricultural modernisation, but this role has not yet been specified into actual activities. But, since government has already pronounced that it will not be involved in the direct supply or production of agricultural inputs or in the processing or marketing of outputs[40], it is reasonable to suppose that these are the areas in which the private sector is expected to play an effective role in the context of liberalisation and privatisation. One can also envisage a role for the private sector, farmers organisations, and other NGOs in agricultural extension. To enhance the capacity of the private sector the government has already indicated that it will form a private sector steering group to assist with designing measures to support private sector development and participation.

The government resolution and determination to modernise agriculture are important, but capacity (financial, organisational, technological and ethical) is critical. Projected total expenditure on agricultural modernisation is Shs 55 billion for 1998/99, shs. 53.0 billion for 1999/2000, shs. 41.0 billion for 2000/ 2001 and 34.5 billion for 2001/2002. But these projections and several other issues of policy and implementation are being continuously reviewed and refined. In a workshop preceding the December 1998 donors consultative group meeting at which the government of Uganda vision and strategy for agricultural modernisation was presented, it was indicated that DANIDA and DFID have agreed to jointly fund a 12 - 18 months project to support Uganda's efforts to establish an appropriate policy as well as institutional and financial framework for the modernisation of agriculture. The intended outputs are:

-   shared vision objectives and principles for the agriculture sector;
-   an agreed and affordable medium term expenditure for publicly funded activities in the sector;
-   examination of the role of government in agriculture to reflect the recent rationalisation of MAAIF responsibilities and on-going decentralisation process;
-   a strategy for promoting stronger private involvement in agricultural sector development;
-   strategies by which districts and sub-counties may be strengthened to perform their respective roles;
-   definition of the major programme areas requiring GoU and/or donor support.

In the final analysis, it needs to be emphasised that as agricultural modernisation, in the African context, means commercialisation and technological transformation, the main issue is improved profitability. Consequently, the relevant policy strategies and programmes are those that will:

(i)   enable producers increase incomes from sales,
(ii) .   make agricultural enterprises or agribusiness more productive; and
(iii)   help producers reduce costs of production and improve their competitiveness.

Responses to mass poverty

Poverty is an extremely complex issue. In its simplest sense, it means unsatisfied want (e.g. inadequate income) or deprivation (in terms of lacking, or insufficient access to, resources) or the inability to meet basic needs. In practice poverty may manifest itself in terms of low income, food shortages, lack of assets, lack of infrastructure, landlessness inadequately (in quantity and quality). Furthermore, poverty can be seen or perceived from a mental or cultural perspective as isolation, vulnerability, powerlessness, hopelessness or 'not having enough to live in human dignity'.[41] The complexity of the issue came out clearly in the definition of poverty given at the World Summit for Social Development in Copenhagen (March 1995):

Poverty has various manifestations, including lack of income and productive resources sufficient to ensure sustainable livelihoods; hunger and malnutrition; ill health; limited or lack of access to education and other basic services; increased morbidity and mortality from illness; homelessness and inadequate housing; unsafe environments; and social discrimination and exclusion. It is also characterized by lack of participation in decision-making and in civil, social and cultural life.[42]

The core of this all-encompassing statement is a structural definition of poverty in which poverty is regarded as a product of a social system and reflects differences in access of various groups to sources of economic and political power.

Seeking to eliminate poverty is necessary for a number of reasons. First of all, poverty inflicts harm (physical and psychological) upon individuals or communities. Secondly, the poor live under insecurity or constant economic worries such as loss of job, income, and home. Thirdly, poverty breeds inefficiency. Hungry children cannot study properly; malnourished adults cannot be fully productive as workers; and an economy where a large proportion of the population is very poor has a structure of demand that does not encourage the production and marketing of the goods that are most needed. Fourthly, poverty is associated with inequality which is a major source of social tension in human societies.

Both nationally and internationally rural poverty has become a central concern of development analysts and practitioners (international organisations, NGOs and independent scholars) especially after 1970 for a number of very important reasons. Rural poverty is a major component of world-wide poverty not only because the rural poor are numerically dominant but also because the incidence of poverty is disproportionately high among the rural population. According to the World Bank, 85 percent of the people who live in absolute poverty in the so-called Third World countries are in rural areas. In most African countries, rural dwellers are not only the largest (75- 95 percent) poorest group, but they are also the most disadvantaged occupational group. The severity of the problem and the special characteristics of rural areas and rural dwellers - especially the association between rural poverty and environmental degradation or between poverty generation and environmental decay make the problem a priority area for development, research and promotion of sustainable development in the post-modern times.

The causes of poverty are as complex as its nature. They are complex in the sense that they are integrated or interlocking. Both the primary sources of poverty (or the generating variables) such as assets, occupation, employment, wages and demographic factors; and characteristic variables such as income, health and status[43] interact to constitute the overall process of poverty-generation.[44] A simplified schematic representation of the key variables and

Figure 7.2: Relations in the generation of poverty

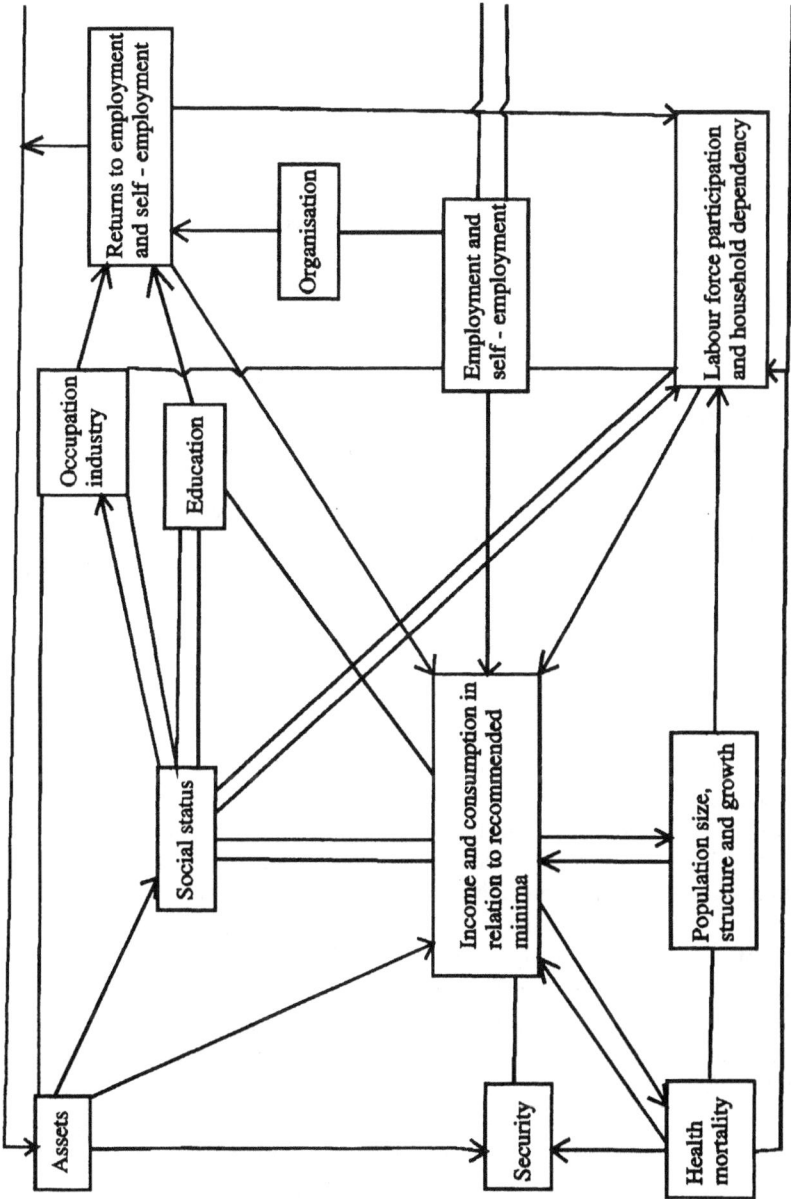

the main relationships in the generation of poverty is depicted in Figure 7:2. The major point demonstrated by the figure is not only the relationships in the generation of poverty but also the complexity of the phenomenon in that the process of poverty generation is a set of interlocking vicious circles which operate to perpetuate poverty. Whatever different analysts - World Bank,[45] EPRC,[46] CDRN[47] - may say or have said about the nature and causes of poverty in Uganda, the most essential point to note is that poverty has its main roots in the structures, processes and mechanisms which determine or govern the ownership, distribution and utilisation of productive assets as well as the distribution of roles, sanctions, and power in society.

From the viewpoint of causes, poverty can be categorised into three types.[48] The first of these types is basic or intrinsic poverty which is characterised by absence or insufficiency of significant possibilities (endowment) of enrichment.

The second is induced poverty resulting from the iniquitous economic order (e.g. predatory policies), and the exploitation of ignorance or weakness.

The third is emergent poverty brought about by more or less temporary circumstances, for instance, wars and civic strife or natural disasters such as drought, earthquakes, floods etc. These three categories of poverty exist or have existed in Uganda as the 1997 UNDP study of poverty in Uganda has shown (See A. Balihuta *et al*, 1997).

A review of prescriptive models - including industrialisation, rural development, redistribution with growth and the basic needs approach - formulated over the past several decades in response to the painful question of how to solve the problem of poverty in undeveloped countries is presented in J.R. Bibangambah, 'Approaches to the problem of Rural Poverty in Africa'. The approaches suggested in the 1970s and the 1980s were inadequate because they focused almost exclusively on economic factors (and hence they are reductionist). To be sure economic factors are significant, and in most situations they constitute the single most important dimension to be altered. However, while economic interventions are necessary, they are not sufficient, given a multiplicity of poverty generating factors. Since poverty has its roots in the structure, processes and mechanisms of social reproduction, a reshuffle in the order that governs ownership, distribution and utilisation of productive assets, the distribution of roles, sanctions and power in society becomes indispensable. This is what is called a structural approach. However, how to bring about structural change in a non-revolutionary manner is a problem that still remains to be answered.

While the structural approach is considered an ideal whose realisation is highly doubtful, the many dimensions of poverty and its interlocking causes still call for a multiple strategy attack, as no single strategy can be wholly effective. A multiple poverty reduction strategy should have the following elements or components;

i)   Economic transformation (i.e. both growth and structural change of the key economic sectors);
ii) Human resource development;
iii) Macro-economic policies; and
iv) Targeting the poor and widening their sources of livelihood.

The challenge of development is to improve the quality of people's lives. Although a better quality of life calls for several things, including higher standards of education, health, nutrition, a cleaner environment and equal opportunities, the most basic of these requirements is higher income or purchasing power.[49] Improved incomes are a product of improved economic structures and economic and technological processes. The 'economic miracle' in the once-admired and now crisis-racked Asian tigers - Hong Kong, Korea, Singapore, Taiwan, Indonesia, Malaysia and Thailand - is attributed to:

i)   More rapid output and productivity growth in agriculture;
ii) Higher rates of growth of manufactured exports;
iii) Higher growth rates of physical capital, exceeding 20 percent of GDP on average between 1960 and 1990, supported by higher rates of domestic savings;
iv) Higher initial levels and growth rates of human capital; and
v)   Generally higher rates of productivity growth.

It is held, after several studies, including those of the World Bank, that prior to the 1997/98 crisis, the East Asian economies thrived - sustained rapid growth, reduced poverty or raised standards of living - not only because they got the economic policy fundamentals right, but also because governments used a combination of fundamental and interventionist policies to accumulate physical and human capital; allocate this capital to highly productive investments; acquire and master technology and achieve rapid productivity growth.

Unlike the seven East Asian countries, most African countries including Uganda, are characterised by a preponderance of subsistence agriculture, primary exports, low rates of savings,[50] pre-industrial activities, extremely low levels of productivity, illiteracy and technological backwardness. Hence the need for transformation is real and urgent.

The historical experience of Europe and Japan suggests that the reduction or elimination of poverty is a protracted process that is accomplished through overall economic development of a national economy. It was after a long period of industrial growth that the majority of the people in these countries overcame poverty. This experience suggests that low income developing countries must also promote industrial growth, although in the case of Uganda there is a so-called big-push method' into service based sectors spearhead by the Uganda Investment Authority, as a new approach to development and intended to largely by-pass traditional-type manufacturing which relies on imported raw materials making a land-locked country like Uganda a high-cost production centre.

The key to alleviating mass poverty in rural areas must be found in agricultural transformation from subsistence to commercial agriculture, based on high-value products; and from low-level productivity to high-level productivity; and from non-profitable to profitable economic organisation. This is a pre-condition for the reduction of rural poverty. It is important that everyone able to work has an income-generating activity as his source of livelihood.

Industrial growth and agricultural transformation do not necessarily mean that aggregate growth of output or of income is a sufficient condition for eliminating poverty. The creation of wealth through the production process is a necessary condition and hence an element in a multiple strategy attack on poverty.

The notion that investing in people is the strongest foundation for lasting economic and social progress is part of the current 'consensus on development'.

Technical progress and widespread education have played key roles in poverty elimination in both Europe and Japan. The rapid rise of the newly industrialised countries of Asia was also largely due to the high quality and discipline of their labour. In the past, skills training, which is necessary both for capacity enhancement, and technological advancement was not given priority. Human resources development - through relevant education, appropriate skills-training and improved health – is one of the essentials for the development of 'social absorptive capacity' needed to introduce and spread new technologies. This needs to be complemented with the development of appropriate 'work ethics' - diligence and ingenuity -which, in turn, requires an institutional set-up that sanctions such work ethics.

Macro-economic policies can affect the levels of income and living conditions of the poor by changing any of the following:

- Access to productivity assets such as land, equipment, machinery, knowledge and information etc;
- Returns on productive assets;
- Employment opportunities;
- Access to social services such as education, health etc;
- Nature and magnitude of transfer payments such as social security, relief etc.

The macro-policies that are likely to have positive impact on poverty, especially rural poverty include policies:

– regarding ownership and operation of land (e.g. redistributive land reforms, tenancy and other institutional reforms, legal provisions) are important in providing access to the most important productive asset in agriculture to the poor.
– concerning the spread of knowledge and information about yield-raising techniques and practices in agriculture; determine the extent to which poorer farmers can have access to the most important non-tangible asset and raise their income by using it.
– providing incentives through pricing and other non-exploitative policies to improve the returns to the poor's labour.
– discouraging premature adoption of labour-saving devices in countries with large numbers of the unemployed or landless agricultural labourers.

This implies having explicit policies and programmes specifically directed at the poor. These include:

• delivery of key social services to the poor e.g. primary health care, protected water supplies, or safe water, good sanitation and primary education;
• policies promoting the availability of key inputs;
• expenditure on extension services to help poor artisans and other cottage industry entrepreneurs get access to knowledge of improved technologies and product designs;
• policies like saving schemes or grassroots development funds or 'seed money' to help the poor not only to acquire productive assets and working capital, but also to serve as buffers against contingencies, enabling the poor to meet sudden or major needs;
• widening of opportunities including employment, for individuals and social groups to assure command over flows of food and cash; and
• educating the poor about sustainable use of whatever assets they have and the environment.

In anticipation of shocks from structural adjustment programmes and with the inspiration of the 'Social Dimensions of Adjustment (SDA) Programme prepared by the World Bank, UNDP and the African Development Bank as well as 'Programme of Action to Mitigate the Social Costs of Adjustment (PAMSCAD) in Ghana, the government of Uganda launched the Programme for Alleviation of Poverty and Social Costs of Adjustment (PAPSCA) in October 1990 as a strategic way to address the needs of some of the more 'politically visible vulnerable groups in the Ugandan society' - war widows, orphans, retrenched civil servants, Kampala slum-dwellers and children from AIDS affected families. The major components of PAPSCA programme were a) the rehabilitation and improvement of primary education schools by constructing 4,212 classrooms in 520 primary schools in 12 of the poorest districts of Uganda, b) low-cost water sanitation, health, and education in Rubaga division of Kampala city through water quality improvement, the construction of ventilated improved pit (VIP) latrines and, surface water drainage; health and education programme; c) the provision of assistance to AIDS orphans; and incentives such as agricultural implements, credit facilities and skills training to foster families.

The programme also intended to provide assistance to 25,000 war widows and their dependents in Luwero district through the development and implementation of community based health care for widows and their households, the establishment of a medical clinic for treatment of widows and their dependants, training in agriculture, health, basic trade skills and income generating activities. As most of these social services were supported through grants the target groups could not sustain them after project life. Thus, the project had no significant impact.

A similar programme was the Community Action Programme (CAP) which was funded by the Netherlands government and implemented by the Office of the Prime Minister. The programme was envisioned to be a quick disbursing, accessible and flexible financial instrument established to fund micro-projects in the West Nile region of Uganda. The broad objective of the CAP was to facilitate the financing of socio-economic micro-projects identified and initiated by local communities. The latter were expected to participate in the implementation and management of micro-projects.

Another programme, the Veterans Assistance Programme, was designed to smooth the transition of the demobilised soldiers into civilian life. It, therefore, aimed at assisting the resettlement of about 50,000 demobilised soldiers and their dependants who were estimated at 150,000. The programme included the provision of settling-in packages inclusive of clothing, building materials, agricultural tools and seeds, school fees and medical provision for up to one year.

In northern Uganda, the government launched World Bank-funded Northern Uganda Rehabilitation Programme (NURP) worth US$ 93.6m whose intention was to rehabilitate both infrastructure and productive capacity in that part of the country. The programme covers agriculture (rural credit scheme, cassava and seed multiplication, teacher training and technical institutes), highways and feeder roads, water supply (both rural and urban) and urban development (streets and markets, maintenance of urban services, training and strategic town planning).

The programme for the Alleviation of Poverty (PAP) was introduced in 1994 as a rural credit and training programme to provide credit to the rural poor, both individuals as well as groups. The programme primarily aims at financing, on a sustainable basis, income and employment generating micro-projects identified and managed by the poor themselves in their rural setting. It vigorously encourages loans recovery in order to build a revolving fund. The credit is extended in the form of short-term loans recoverable over a maximum period of 12 months. It is implemented through non-governmental organisations (NGOs), community based organisations operating at district level as intermediary entities (IEs) and also directly through project staff. The IEs should be present and operating at village level and, above all, they must be acceptable to district authorities and the communities they are to serve.

The programme is funded by a loan from the African Development Bank amounting to US$13.5m, which is 90 percent of the total programme cost while the Government of Uganda tops up the balance of US$1.5m. By 1997, PAP had disbursed more than Shs 2.7bn, to 22 districts since its inception in 1994. Government now feels that the project can be extended to all parts of the country. On the ground, the impact of this project is not clear but repayment of credit is reported to be impressive i.e. over 75 percent.

In 1996 the Uganda government initiated and fully funded the *Entandikwa* credit scheme which provides 'seed money' to facilitate small entrepreneurs to undertake productive economic/commercial ventures. It targets those who cannot obtain credit under the traditional commercial lending especially the women and youth. It is intended to assist the poor (though not the poorest) both in rural and urban areas. The implementing agencies are: Intermediary agencies (IAs), county steering committees (CSCs) and district steering committees. Its inadequacies and ineffectiveness are the limited outcomes that can be expected from loan sizes or population coverage given an allocation of UShs 30m per county. The introduction of the scheme coincided with a presidential and general parliamentary elections and, consequently, some, if not most, of the loans were treated by beneficiaries as reward from the elected government.

Non-governmental organisations (NGOs) are part of what Graham Hancock, the author of *Lords of poverty*, has called the 'Development Industry'[51]. The non-national also known in Africa as 'Northern NGOs' in Africa like Oxfam, CARE, Action Aid etc, have become central to the administration of foreign aid especially during the last two decades. The NGO channel is supposed to be 'a new type of international social system which is framed by a particular relationship between internal socio-economic and political mechanisms and external donor interests'[52], and hence it is an international donor-driven system.

Even before the term poverty alleviation (or reduction) got popularised globally, NGOs were working around it from different perspectives, some of which do not easily fit into everyday definition of 'poverty' which concentrates on material deprivation, employment and generally the acquisition of money. However, as already indicated in our more comprehensive definition of poverty, while material deprivation is of immediate importance, poverty is ultimately about power and powerlessness. In short, people living in poverty are not only materially deprived, but are also socially and politically marginalised. It is because of this that NGOs in Uganda have projects relating to non-economic aspects of poverty such as health, education, water, nutrition, shelter, environmental protection, human rights, energy saving, corruption, information sharing, peace, increased opportunities for participation and gender relations. As the UN Social Summit pointed out, these are fundamentals to any serious poverty elimination programme.   They provide the real foundation for sustainable livelihood.

For any poverty programme to succeed, the poor themselves must be involved so that they can explain their own condition.   NGOs have a comparative advantage in that they are grassroots-oriented. They live and work with the people using participatory approaches.   Evidence of people participation in development projects facilitated by NGOs is abundant.   It is especially noteworthy that rural women previously regarded as passive have shown that under conducive circumstances, they can be very active.   These so-called 'non-economic' strategies have enhanced people's empowerment and made them aware that their condition is not God-given.   Besides, these programmes help reduce ignorance, disease, hunger and fatalism.   Evidence further suggests that such programmes have led to more receptivity of new ideas and the real economic initiatives introduced by NGOs, government and other stakeholders.   Such initiatives have enabled many NGOs to design integrated programmes.   They combine the social, political and economic goals.

In the economic fields, NGOs have particularly been involved in income-generating activities, rural credit schemes, trade and marketing, and acquisition of employment skills etc. Examples of income-generating activities include better quality agricultural produce practised by such network members as Environmental Alert and Buso Foundation in Mpigi district, Matilong Integrated Programme in Soroti district, Mirembe Self Help in Kayunga, Mukono district, and many CBOs under Kigulu Development Group in Iganga district.

Vocational and technical skills for employment are also widespread. Some of the members involved include Seeta Talents Calls Club Recycling Project in Mukono, URDT in Kagadi and Appropriate Technology Development Centre in Kasese. Examples of those involved in diary farming, piggery, bee-keeping, rabbit production are too many to quote. A non-governmental organisation particularly focusing on the economic empowerment of rural women and heavily involved in the promotion of improved agriculture and increased incomes is the National Strategy for the Advancement of Rural Women of Uganda (NSARWU) started by Mrs Janet Museveni.[53]

Information generated through NGO research has proved to be very useful. The NGOs involved include Gender Resource Centre, UWONET, FIDA, ACFODE, URDT, Mirembe Self Help, CDRN and DETREC. CDRN has recently been a pioneer in producing information on poverty in selected districts using an approach that gives the poor a chance to talk about their own conditions.[54]

One cannot talk about NGOs and poverty without referring to micro financing activities. To some people, this is considered the most immediate tangible need for the communities that NGOs work with. Organisations like Uganda Women Finance Credit Trust (UWFCT), VEDCO, PRIDE AFRICA, and FINCA are quite advanced in this field. Such funds have enabled the communities to set up successful small-scale micro-enterprises.

At the international level, NGOs (both Ugandan and foreign or international like Oxfam) have been in the forefront in advocating debt reduction so that the money saved may be re-channelled to the welfare of the poor.[55]

Measurable poverty reduction specifically attributable to NGOs is not easy to establish. However, they are doing a good job if their recent efforts in spreading new technologies and improved farming practices in the production of food crops previously neglected are anything to go by. These efforts are a step in the right direction in the struggle against food poverty.

Acknowledging that the country's central government lacks the capacity to fully deliver key social services to the poor, thereby adversely affecting their capacity to participate in the economic process, the Uganda government adopted and launched a decentralisation programme in October 1992. Its objective was to transfer the functions, powers and responsibilities from the central to local governments. Besides the empowerment of local governments, there was hope that decentralisation would offer an institutional framework for community-based organisations and NGOs to get effectively involved in delivering the most needed social services to the poor.

The government began implementing the decentralisation programme in the fiscal year 1993/94, starting with 13 districts. By the 1995/96 financial year all the districts (39 then) had been decentralised. In February 1996 a review workshop was held in Kampala with the aim of assessing the progress of the decentralisation programme, and making an agenda for the future. Among the challenges identified were the need to increase local democratic control; avoid inordinate centralisation of decision-making; increase local administrative effectiveness; increase local revenue mobilisation and self-reliance; and rationalise local structures.

In the light of the important elements raised by the aforementioned review workshop, and in order to align the local governments law (i.e. Decentralisation Statute 1993) with the 1995 Uganda constitution, the law has been re-enacted (into Local Government Act 1997) to effect the decentralisation of functions, powers and services at all levels to ensure good governance and democratic participation in, and control of, decision-making by the people. In the new law, the taxation, legislative, political and executive powers of local governments have been spelt out. Recruiting and employing is now done by the districts which receive unconditional grants from central government to implement their plans and priorities.

With the devolved political power, districts can now plan for their development and deliberately make such plans poverty-focused. Thus, decentralisation provides an excellent opportunity to deal effectively with the poverty of choices and opportunity. Through people-centred participatory district planning, priority choices and emergent opportunities can be captured by the private, voluntary and public sectors to improve the welfare of the people, provided the local leadership does not become self-serving and parasitic.

Decentralisation should lead to greater transparency and accountability in the use of public funds, since local authorities are much closer to their clients than officials in the central government. But lack of experience of local officials and a poorly informed citizenry can and are leading to mistakes and abuses. The financial decentralisation in terms of both the tax revenue retained by the lower levels of local administration and the grants sent to the districts by the central government are a welcome move. However, instead of promoting spatial equity, decentralisation can widen regional disparities if poor areas are not provided with external resources in the form of equalisation grants.

At the 1995 Paris Consultative Group meeting on Uganda, the paradox of sustained economic growth and widespread poverty was a matter of concern. A national dialogue which was recommended at the CG meeting culminated in a national conference on this subject in November 1995. Subsequently, a national task force was established to prepare a national strategy and plan of action. After a long consultative process with representatives from government, non-governmental organisations, the private sector as well as development partners, the Poverty Eradication Action Plan (PEAP) was formulated in early 1997,[56] to act as the policy framework for the eradication of poverty for the next two decades.

In this plan, it was decided that the best way to emancipate people from poverty is not to give them hand-outs but to enable households to earn decent incomes and facilitate the improvement of the quality of their lives. To achieve this national aspiration, the government has adopted the following poverty eradication strategies:

i)   maintaining and consolidating the existing macroeconomic policy in order to keep the economy on the growth path and also provide the requisite macroeconomic incentives to enable the poor participate in the growth process;
ii)   making economic growth sufficiently broad-based to encompass the poor by focusing public expenditure on increasing economic opportunities particularly in agriculture;
iii) provision of basic social services to the masses;
iv)   creation of a national capacity to facilitate adequate and quick response to economic problems and disasters;
v)   building a secure, democratic, just and tolerant political order that would promote transparency and accountability.

The main components of the plan are infrastructure development, especially the rehabilitation and maintenance of feeder roads and improving the efficiency of market infrastructure; human resources development, especially enhancing health, skills development, productivity and morale; governance, especially the issues of political and macro-economic stability and micro-economic incentives, consultation, participation, protection and promotion of fundamental human rights, administration of law and justice, and political and administrative transparency and accountability; rural development, especially agricultural and small enterprises development, particularly the issues of research-extension-producer linkages, credit and financial services, land, food security, environmental regeneration, water management and entrepreneurship development. The advantage with this PEAP is that for the first time, instead of relying on the 'trickle down process' of economic growth, Uganda has an explicit policy framework for the eradiction of poverty. This plan has a clearly stated objective namely to 'eradicate mass poverty from Uganda society through empowering households to earn decent incomes and facilitate the improvement of their quality of life.' Against this objective a systematic monitoring of progress is possible. If progress is found deficient, either the plan can be adjusted or a corrective action can be introduced.

In this connection the Uganda government has commissioned two major activities. First, a nationwide District Resource Endowment Profile Survey (DREPS), aimed at resource mapping the entire country and establishing comprehensive databases centrally and at each of the forty five (45) districts of Uganda, has begun. One of the major outputs of this activity will be the implementation of a District Resource Information System (DRIS) which will, amongst other things, provide detailed micro-socio-economic data on the characteristics of the poor and provide sufficient information for adequate planning at both local and central government levels as well as in all sectors in each of the districts in the country. Secondly, a participatory poverty assessment project (UPPAD) which is a three year research and advocacy project that seeks to bring the voice and perspective of the poor into national and district planning for poverty reduction in Uganda by enhancing knowledge about the nature and causes of poverty and strategies to combat it,.has also been launched.

The PEAP is also charged with building district capacity to plan for poverty eradication; developing a national system for integrating qualitative poverty monitoring; and establishing the capacity for participatory policy research in Uganda.   To ensure that the government's PEAP is fully implemented and also to provide accountability for HIPC debt relief, Poverty Action Fund (PAF) was established as part of the 1998/99 national budget. Essentially, the PAF comprises the savings in external debt service following the HIPC Debt Initiative and donor contributions to the fund. In the 1998/99 financial year, the PAF resources, which are additional funds for the poverty eradication programme, are planned as follows:

Government of Uganda (UShs. billions)		
HIPC debt Initiative cashflow savings	(US$ 37.2)	44.64
Additional Donor Funding		
UK PRISFAC Classroom Construction Support		4.72
Other donors		7.39
Total Poverty Action Fund Resources		56.75

Additional expenditures, made possible by these additional resources are directed into activities consistent with the Poverty Eradication Action Plan as follows:

Table 7.1: Funds earmarked for the PEAP (UShs in billions)

Additional expenditures	GoU budget 1997/98	Additional resources from Poverty Action Fund 1998/99	GOU budget 1998/99	% Increase
Donor supported				
Primary school construction				
(new district (grants)	–	6.22	6.22	
Primary health care	1.70	4.60	6.30	270
Monitoring by districts, line ministries and central ministries		1.29	1.29	
Subsector Total	**1.70**	**12.11**	**13.89**	**712**
GOU/HIPC supported				
Primary education grant	21.99	8.01	30.00	36
Primary education · development budget	4.52	2.35	6.88	52
Rural Roads conditional grant for maintenance	4.99	7.00	11.99	140
Rural roads development budget	7.04	6.71	13.75	95
Agriculture extension (new expenditure)	–	4.00	4.00	–
District water supply and sanitation budget	5.26	8.17	13.43	155
NGO primary health care (new conditional grant)	–	2.00	2.00	–
Lunch allowance-district health units (conditional grants)	2.77	3.88	6.65	140

Table 7.1: continued

Primary health care development budget	2.77	3.88	6.65	140
Inspector General of Government	1.00	0.82	1.82	82
Provision for enhanced monitoring of expenditure	1.58	2.23	3.81	141
Sub-total GOU/HIPC	**49.65**	**49.91**	**99.56**	**101**
Total gross expenditure	**51.35**	**62.02**	**113.37**	**121**
Less contingency for possible delays in project implementation				
Total net expenditure		**56.75**		

Source: Government of Uganda: Budget Day Brief on the Poverty Action
Fund, June 1998.

Government has initiated what have come to be known as 'Poverty Action Fund Quarterly Meetings ' (formally donor meetings) at which a quarterly funds utilisation report is presented. Participants in these meetings include donors, the Ministry of Finance, Planning and Economic Development, representatives of relevant line ministries - Education, Health, Agriculture, Water and Natural Resources, Works, Local Government - and representatives of NGOs and the media. The deliberate involvement of NGOs and the media is intended to provide a forum for government to share information with them and to enhance transparency. More importantly, government acknowledges the key role NGOs play in fighting poverty. Besides receiving accountability for resources made expended for poverty eradication, these meetings are expected to explore ways of establishing closer collaboration between the government, the donor community and NGOs or civil society.

The Land Act, uses an incrementalist approach to accommodate the necessary 'political balancing', but recognises some of the structural causes of poverty by seeking to protect and spread citizens' access to land, and by protecting family property against deprivation by unreasonable spouses. By curtailing the eviction of people from *mailo*, public and customary lands, and by curtailing fraudulent alienation of land from peasant customary owners, the Act will slow down the growth of landlessness and hence reduce one of the major causes of rural poverty in Uganda. If the relatively increased security of land tenure and somewhat liberalised land market can cause land to be used more productively,[57] this will be a positive contribution towards the reduction of both food and income poverty.

However, as already indicated in Chapter Four, the legal means of spreading citizens' access to land have been overloaded onto one instrument - the Land Fund - which overloading makes the job of the fund a 'mission impossible'. Besides, the benefits that may be realised are, given the impediments discussed in Chapter Six, long-term whereas mass poverty calls for both immediate as well as medium-term and long-term remedies.

As already indicated in our assessment of the impact of the reform process, government statistician's claims of poverty decline from 56 percent in 1992 to 46 percent in 1996 have failed to match people's perceived and actual needs. There are many people in the country who are too poor to meet their basic needs. As the UNDP has pointed out in the Uganda Human Development Report, poverty remains pervasive especially in rural areas, and 55 percent of Uganda's population live on less than US $1 per day.

Responses to constraints on rural financial services

The availability of financial services has a crucial role to play in agricultural and rural development. Firstly, the application of modern inputs is essential for increasing productivity in agriculture and enabling farmers to diversify away from subsistence production, where productivity is low, into higher-value agricultural activities. But modern inputs are expensive for farmers and entail cost outlays which precede the earning of revenue from the sale of crops. Given the low level cash incomes and liquid savings in rural areas, some form of credit is required in order to enable farmers to purchase modern inputs. If lack of credit is not a major obstacle to rural development, its availability is an accelerator. Secondly, credit is needed to finance the fixed and working capital requirements of non-farm, small-scale enterprises such as retailing, crop storage and food processing. Thirdly, savings create capacity for investment and also help to smooth consumption expenditures in the face of unstable incomes.

However, lack of access to financial services, particularly formal sector services, is a widespread characteristic of the rural economy in African countries, as well as in many other developing countries.

A variety of policy approaches to tackle the problem of farmers' lack of access to financial services have been applied over the last three decades as shown in our presentation in Chapter Four. Until the late 1980s, the premises underlying rural financial policies were that farmers' demand for formal sector credit existed, but that commercial banks would not meet this demand voluntarily (their lending policies being too risk-averse). In the words of one commentator, the 'constraints arise from the lack of adequate information for lenders and the absence of credible contract enforcement mechanisms .... The risk-reduction behaviour of lenders leads to fragmented markets, ineffective credit allocation, and a wide credit gap.'[58]

Government intervention was, therefore, needed in order to improve farmers' access to credit and to reduce its cost. Many of the policy initiatives, however, were not very successful as we have shown in Chapter Four. Beneficiaries were limited in number (often limited to the larger farmers), and/or rural credit schemes (development finance institutions and special rural lending schemes) were financially unsustainable because of very high rates of loan losses. As a result, there has been a shift in policy approaches to rural finance in recent years, with much greater emphasis now placed on the financial sustainability of rural finance institutions, the use of market criteria in allocating and pricing credit, and savings mobilisation.

The general thrust of recent policy reforms is to remove direct government controls over credit allocation and interest rates, and instead, focus on the institutional reforms needed to create financially sustainable rural financial institutions. The changes are part of broader policy reforms in the financial sector entailing financial liberalisation and institutional strengthening.

The main elements of these financial sector reforms are the removal of most of government allocative credit directives, such as the minimum percentage of loans to be allocated to agriculture; the removal of interest rate controls (including preferential lending rates for agriculture), the abolition of the requirement that banks open rural branches, the restructuring of financially distressed public sector banks, development finance institutions and co-operative banks so that they operate according to commercial principles.

Although some elements of subsidised lending remain, largely in special lending schemes, the public sector finance institutions now place more emphasis on commercial evaluation of the loan applications, loan recovery and charging lending rates which cover their costs. Restructuring has often entailed the retrenchment of unprofitable rural branch networks. In Uganda, the UCB has closed more than 100 branches, mostly in rural areas.

While financial market liberalisation has stimulated some new entry by private sector banks, the experience of Uganda is that the majority of the new private sector banks have not established branches in rural areas, but instead, they focus predominantly on servicing urban banking markets.

Some analysts have contended that financial markets liberalisation, which is a macroeconomic policy reform, has not been effective in improving credit delivery in Africa as the obstacles to financial markets development are not simply policy-induced but have structural and institutional origins.[59] Means should be devised to strengthen links between formal credit institutions (with surplus resources) and semi-formal institutions that lack such resources but have a comparative advantage in reaching the poor. Accordingly, incentives should be devised for formal institutions to allocate credit through informal agents.

Innovations are defined as new ideas, behaviours or services that are qualitatively new or substantially different from existing ones. As innovation in the sense of technical progress embodies the development of new products (services) or changes in processes, institutions, and market systems, a recent IFPRI Food Policy Review[60] has categorised financial innovations as:

i)   Financial system innovations which relate to changes in the finance system as a whole and affect all participants in the intermediation process e.g. establishment of new finance organisations and changes in legal and regulatory framework.

ii) Financial institution innovations which refer to changes in the structure, organisation and legal form of an institution. They often seek to overcome legal and economic constraints on the extension of financial services to market segments such as the rural poor.

iii) Processing innovations which focus on improving the organisation and the supply of products and services of a financial institution. They are often based on technical progress such as computerisation, and are introduced to increase efficiency and expand market shares.

iv) Financial product innovations which are defined as new or modified financial services that did not exist in the market before or differ substantially from existing services.

All the four categories of innovations have a role to play in poverty reduction efforts. System innovations can improve financial markets integration and expand customer-coverage; institutional innovations can improve service accessibility for the poor; process innovations are cost-reducing and increase institutional efficiency; product innovations ameliorate the banking institutions orientation towards customers' demands.

As an alternative to the banks and development finance institutions, innovative rural finance institutions which utilise social links with the rural population have been or are being established in several developing countries with donor support. Most of these RFIs were or are started by NGOs and many of them have been inspired by the success of the Grameen Bank established in 1976 by a Bangladesh economist, Professor Mohammud Yunus, in Bangladesh. The RFIs provide micro-credit (i.e. very small loans), often together with savings facilities, to small farmers and the rural poor. They utilise group lending schemes to facilitate the allocation and recovery of credit.

Very small deposits and loans are referred to together as micro-finance.[61] During the 1990s, the provision of micro-finance and particularly the provision of micro-credit has increasingly been acclaimed as an effective means of poverty reduction.

The enthusiasm that has been generated and the need to help the idea take mainstream, as women issues have done, culminated in a micro-credit summit in February 1997 in Washington, co-chaired by Hillary Clinton and attended by several heads of state and the leaders of the World Bank /UNDP.

As already indicated, micro-financing activities constitute one of the main contributions of NGOs to poverty reduction efforts. Convinced that it would not be economically viable and prudent for government to establish an agricultural bank for the sole purpose of providing financial services to farmers in rural areas, government has adopted the following policies for the development of micro/rural financial system in the medium to long-term perspectives. First of all, government is withdrawing (though slowly) from direct provision of micro/rural finance services and is restricting its functions to policy-making in order provide a conducive and enabling environment for effective private sector participation in the micro-finance industry while taking supporting actions to reduce risks in agriculture. Government will participate in the development of institutions which can guarantee the transformation of short-term money into long-term loans as this is currently a major bottleneck. Secondly, government is shifting its focus on micro-rural finance from project approach to development of micro-rural financial services approach. It is also providing financial support for capacity building of institutions and agencies involved in provision of micro-rural finance.

Given the fact that the commercial banks cannot provide micro-finance services on viable basis, the promotion and development of micro-finance industry is being based on grassroots institutions or micro/rural financial Intermediaries (MRFIs) such as co-operative societies, farmers/women groups, NGOs, etc. Such institutions have a comparative advantage to provide financial services at grassroots level for two reasons. First, local knowledge of the client at the grassroots reduces the need for collateral/security particularly when the clients form groups to provide 'joint and multiple liability' for loan acquisition. Secondly, the proximity to the clients, minimises operational and overhead costs and provides an effective way of reducing interest rates for agricultural production.

Rural finance institutions in the form of full-fledged village banks owned by village committees and able to raise equity, mobilise savings and deliver credit have already been started in the country with funding from USAID and UNDP through the Private Sector Development Programme. Institutions that are currently involved in the micro-finance industry in Uganda may be grouped into six main categories below:

Formal finance institutions: Currently two commercial banks i.e. The Co-operative Bank and Centenary Rural Development Bank (CERUDEB) are involved in delivery of micro finance services. The Uganda Post Office Savings Bank (UPOSB) is being revitalised to exploit its great potential for mobilisation of savings from rural areas. It is envisaged that the capacity building programmes for the formal financial institutions would focus mainly on developing their effective linkages with micro finance institutions.

NGOs: There are numerous local and foreign NGOs involved in micro finance industry in Uganda. Some of these NGOs have been contracted to deliver credit under government funded programmes. Other NGOs are specialised in the provision of micro-finance services. The specialised NGOs are largely foreign-based and include FINCA, PRIDE AFRICA, FAULU-UGANDA, FOCCAS, MED-VET, etc. The local NGOs are largely multi-sectoral with finance components in their programmes. Such NGOs include URDT, ACFODE, UWESO, VEDCO, etc. There are also a few local NGOs that are now operating as specialised micro-finance institutions and these include UWFT, UGAFODE, PACT, etc. These local micro finance institutions still have a limited outreach. In general, the NGOs have exhibited a great potential by acting as second tier institutions for the mobilisation, promotion and development of grassroots-based financial institutions.

Community based micro finance institutions: These institutions comprise mainly such institutions as primary co-operative societies, farmer groups, women groups, etc. The major objective of a capacity building programme for such institutions would be to transform them into viable financial institutions at the grassroots level in all parts of the country. Some of them could be transformed into full-fledged village banks.

Special institutions: There are several institutions and projects like UCA, PRESTO, PSDP, etc whose activities are focused on building the capacity of micro-finance institutions. They offer training, technical assistance and grants for capacity building of micro finance institutions. Some institutions are currently being utilized as promoters for capacity building of rural institutions under the Cotton Sub-sector Development Project (CSDP).

Micro/rural financial institutions: two important micro finance associations have recently been formed by the stakeholders involved in the micro/rural finance business. These are the Association of Micro/Rural Finance Intermediaries in Uganda (ARMFI) at the grassroots level and the Association of Micro Finance Institutions of Uganda (AMFIU) at the second tier level mainly for coordination, mobilisation and sensitisation of industry participants, and in general, promoting activities related to micro/rural finance. Both associations have noble objectives but they are currently severely resource constrained.

At the time of writing (July 1998) all the necessary data about the number of micro-finance institutions and beneficiaries is not available. However, information published by USAID-funded PRESTO Project's Centre for Micro-Finance indicates that there are about 45 micro-finance institutions with a total loan portfolio of USh. 9.8 billion and savings mobilised equivalent to USh. 12.2 billion. These savings have been mobilised from over 47,000 individual clients throughout Uganda. This represents an average loan outstanding per individual of about Shs.207,000/= and an average savings of USh 258,000/=. But the present coverage represents about 5.9 percent of the estimated potential clientele for micro enterprise financial services[62].

The world's first global micro-credit summit in Washington, which brought together more than 2,000 people representing NGOs, multilateral agencies and beneficiaries of the schemes, was intended to launch a global campaign to reach and access 100 million of the world's poorest families with credit for self-employment and other financial and business services by the year 2005. The cost of the initiative is put at an estimated $21.6 billion expected from bilateral agencies, banks, savings and interest payments.

Responses to inequities in gender relations

In Uganda, as in many other developing countries, the need to remove inequities in gender[63] relations in both household and the community has become a key objective of social change and development. This need has received recognition in national and international fora as an aspect of social integration, social justice and sustainable development. In current development terminology ,what is needed has come to be known as women's empowerment.

The call for women's empowerment is a response to:

- Disparities in access to education as shown by school enrolment ratios for boys and girls and a high rate of illiteracy standing at 60 percent for women. Illiteracy implies limited capacity for acquiring marketable skills and for discharging multiple responsibilities;

- Disparities in access to economic opportunities as shown by lack of meaningful control over productive resources or economic decisions, restricted access to economically productive resources; performance of less lucrative economic roles as compared to those played by men; special problems of rural women; special problems of single-parent families especially those headed by females as widows or unmarried mothers;

- Disparities in access to health;

- Heavy workloads and longer working hours for women in the absence of drudgery-saving or labour-saving technology in the performance of both household and farming tasks; and

• Failure by women to benefit from their numerous tasks in the household and farm.

In effect, therefore, the call for women's empowerment is a call for mobility, economic security, ability to make both small and large purchases (i.e. economic power), involvement in major household decisions, relative freedom from domination by the family (i.e. equal relationship within marriage and parenthood), political and legal awareness and participation in political and other public activities.

Women's position in Uganda is directly connected to poverty which is especially concentrated in rural areas. Their roles in the household include child care and the welfare of the family, including securing food. The persistent inadequate, or even lack of, food storage facilities in rural areas undermine household food security and augments women's burden. The agricultural sector is also largely dependent on women's labour in terms of production and sale of food crops. Though cash crop production may, to a limited extent, be undertaken by women, trends indicate that marketing of these crops falls within the male domain. As pertains to land ownership, patrilineal societies exclude women. A widow is often denied the right to inherit her deceased husband's land, which automatically is taken over by either the clan or the deceased husband's male kin. Land ownership guarantees access to credit since land acts as collateral. However, the present land ownership regime generally marginalises women by denying them access to credit despite their large contribution to food production.

The 1995 constitution underlines women rights and gender equality in Uganda. Special attention is given to gender balance on all constitutional aspects with firm recognition of the significant role women play in society. Government responded to the needs and problems of women by establishing a Ministry of Gender and Community Development (now the Ministry of Gender, Labour and Social Development) This ministry has, since 1990, been implementing a programme of Women in Development (WID) with projects designed to emancipate women legally and economically.

Projects focusing on economic emancipation include those providing training in the management of income-generating activities and those providing informal credit and extension services. Projects focusing on legal emancipation include those concerned with reforming inappropriate laws, promoting the awareness of legal rights among women, and the training of grassroots para-legal personnel to act as base-foot legal advisers for rural women. Only pilot efforts in this area have so far been made, but they have been found to be particularly effective in reducing the incidence of domestic violence in the project areas.

Since 1991 a DANIDA-funded project concentrates on integrating gender aspects into selected ministries' sector policies; in addition it has a long-term component of legislative reform whose aim is to improve women's status, particularly in rural areas, by giving information on and training in the existing legislation.

Overall, the Ministry of Gender and Community Development is spearheading national efforts to 'mainstream' gender issues in all sectors of life. Workshops have been conducted for top officials in all government ministries for training in gender analysis and gender-oriented policy development.

In addition to these governmental efforts, a large number of women NGOs (ACFODE, FIDA, NAOWU, UWFCT etc) have been set up, working both singly and collectively, to liberate women economically and legally. They include those that operate legal aid clinics for women and those that provide financial and technical support (including skills training) for community-based women's organisations.

Increased numbers of women in the national legislature, local government councils, local political structures, achieved through affirmative action, has given them the strength to articulate women's issues and to participate in policy decision making. This, together with their current status in economic and commercial institutions and activities, is an indication of the empowerment they have received in the last decade. Unfortunately, such a degree of empowerment has not spread to the majority of women.

Responses to environmental degradation

Environmental issues have achieved prominence only in the last decade. The Brundtland Report[64] focused the attention of the international community on the links between poverty and environmental degradation. While many of the arguments in the report have been criticised,[65] the central thesis that poverty and environmental degradation are linked has not been seriously challenged.[66]

In their *Rural Development and the Environment,* S. Barraclough et al state that one cannot use deviation from the 'natural' environment as a measure of degradation because the natural environment in the sense that it has been undisturbed by human activities no longer exists.[67] They, therefore, define environmental degradation as *'natural environment's diminished capacity to satisfy human needs or its increased propensity to cause harm'.*

A particularly critical aspect of environmental degradation, especially in sub-Saharan Africa, is land degradation. This occurs in three main forms: desertification in dryland areas, deforestation and soil erosion in hillside areas and loss of soil fertility through overcultivation or soil exhaustion in many cropped areas. In Uganda overgrazing which destroys vegetation cover and thereby leaving the soils bare is a very conspicuous cause of land degradation. In a country like Uganda where an estimated 90 percent of the population exclusively depend on wood fuel for the energy needs, deforestation is accentuated by the preponderant use of fuelwood as the main source of energy for cooking.

Environmental degradation processes are frequently associated with local level proximate causes such as careless natural resource use, inappropriate technologies, poverty, demographic changes, local power structures, social conflicts and natural processes or calamities. They are also linked with policies and institutions that may be national or global in scope and origin. Examples include market forces, national economic policies, land tenure and political institutions as well as internal social conflicts, international wars and changes in regional or global climates.

Some analysts argue that environmental degradation is primarily associated with poverty. While this is true in the case of soil erosion and deforestation which are known to be worse in poor countries in comparison with rich ones, it has been recorded that three quarters of greenhouse gas emission and hazardous industrial wastes are generated in rich industrialised countries. What needs to be underscored is that poverty is both an important exacerbating cause, and an effect, of environmental degradation in the poor countries.

In the colonial era, environmental protection policies in Uganda, as elsewhere in sub-Saharan Africa, were limited to establishing protected areas such as game and forest reserves and national parks, and the introduction of soil and water conservation practices as part of government agricultural policy. This approach continued for the first two decades of the post-independence period. It was not until 1986 that a full-fledged Ministry of Environmental Protection was established and charged with the responsibility of coordinating natural resources so as to ensure their availability for sustainable development and the preservation of the human environment.

The upgrading of environment to a sectoral status led to the incorporation of environmental protection projects in the national Rehabilitation and Development Plan that started in the financial year 1986/87. The objectives of the environmental plan spelt out in the Rehabilitation and Development Plan were as follows:

- Protection of life supporting systems (vegetation, air, water, animals) and ecological processes and cycles which maintain human life;
- Prevention of degradation, misuse, destruction and depopulation of the entire environment and especially the natural resources;
- Promotion of sound environmental development by incorporating environmental considerations in the planning processes; and

- Incorporation of environmental considerations in the education system.

With the assistance of the World Bank and other donors,[68] the Uganda government initiated a National Environmental Action Plan (NEAP) for the purpose of providing a framework for integrating environmental considerations into the overall national economic and social development plan.

A National Environment Statute has been in place since 1995 and under this the National Environment Authority (NEMA) has been established to coordinate and implement environmental concerns in national planning via government policy in conformity with the law, and to initiate legislative proposals, standards and guidelines on the environment. NEMA has already embarked on priority programmes such as capacity building for environmental management, enhancement of legislative/regulatory frameworks, development of procedures and regulations for environmental impact assessment, development of environmental standards, public awareness, education and training as well as strengthening of the environmental information system.

Although environmental policies and programmes in Uganda are relatively new, they are already being felt as in the case of prevention of encroachment on wetlands and requiring prospective industrialists and other investors to undertake environmental pre-audits in order to ensure that the intended industrial establishments will not adversely affect any given environmental resource.

Response to long-term challenges

Economic development implies increasing technological and organisational capacity to produce goods and services. The acquisition of ability to sustain and enhance this capacity to meet long-term needs and demands is the greatest challenge beyond the current macro-economic reforms. An appropriate response to this challenge requires a long-term vision and strategic planning to guide short-term and medium-term actions. To face up to the challenge of promoting the emergence of a shared vision and national aspirations around which the population can be mobilised for the country's development, the Uganda government has instituted the UNDP-funded National Long-Term Perspective Studies (NLTPS) as a process of national reflection about the future, and for the purpose of designing long-term development strategies critical for sustainable development and national transformation. Through a process code-named Uganda Vision 2025 various stakeholders have been consulted on the kind of country they would like to see by the year 2025. They have reviewed the country's strengths and weaknesses, opportunities and threats, and possible strategies for attaining national goals. A national agreement on all these issues is now emerging. Beyond its study phase, the implementation of the Uganda Vision 2025 will entail reviewing all development plans, national, local, sectoral and non-governmental, and reformulating priorities and strategies to bring them into conformity with the new demands imposed on the country by the development needs.

Conclusion

The responses that have been analysed in this Chapter are a manifestation of: firstly, an appreciation, by those in leadership, of the imperative to pull Africa out of the crisis of perpetual poverty and backwardness, secondly, a recognition of the criticality of certain aspects of the development task or mission, thirdly, evidence of the reform and reconstruction efforts and new initiatives that have taken or are taking place.

The policies and programmes being implemented are based on normative thinking and in-depth diagnosis of the challenges facing Uganda both now and in the next century. The economic reshaping in Uganda and indeed of the rest of sub-Saharan Africa, is not just a response to needs but also possibilities. Thus considerations of both endogenous and exogenous factors have influenced the feasibility and viability rating of the policies that have been adopted. However, good policies and programmes alone cannot guarantee success. A lot is yet to be done by way of implementation.

Notes

1. Food Security is highlighted in the 1995 Uganda constitution as No 22 of the National Objectives and Principles of State Policy.
2. A food system is defined as a 'socially and ecologically determined system of food production and exchange, of food consumption and of reproduction' *(Cannon, 1991, Bohle* 1993).
3. Swift J. (1990). *Major Issues in African Pastoral Rehabilitation and Development,* IDS, University of Sussex.
4. White, M. (1990). 'The process of survival in South Eastern Uganda', In M. Bovin and Manger, *Adaptive Strategies in African Arid Lands,* SIAs; Uppsala, Sweden.
5. Gariyo Z. (1992). 'Appropriate technology, Productivity and employment in Agriculture in . Uganda: a case study of the Kibimba and Doho Rice Schemes', FAO.
6. This is not to deny widespread food shortage (and shortage of other goods) in other parts of the country and associated with the ravages of the mismanagement of the 1970's and the civil war.
7. USAID, (1992). *Definition of Food Security:,* Policy Determination PNAAV468, Washington.
8. The International Food Policy Research Institute has interpreted food security to be synonymous with *nutrition security.* Accordingly, it maintains that food security has three main components: Food availability, food access, and food utilisation. (See, 'A conceptual Framework of food security and generic indicator categories", in K.Chung *et al* (1971) : *Identifying the food insecure:* IFPRI.

9. World Bank, *Poverty and Hunger: Issues and options for Food Security in Developing Countries,* Washington DC: World Bank.

10. Anderson J.R. and Candizzo P.L. , (1984). 'Food Risk and the Poor' in *Food Policy,* vol 9, No 1.

11. Ellis F. (1992). *Agricultural Policies in developing countries,* Cambridge University Press.

12. World Bank *op.cit.*

13. UNICEF, (1990). *Strategy for improved Nutrition of children and women in Developing countries* New York, Hahn H. and Behlin F., (1993). *'Regional Food Security or nutrition security* - what difference does it make? in H.U Thimm *et al* (eds), *Regional food security and rural infrastructure,* International symposium Giessen/Raluscholzhausen.

14. Tweeten L., (1992). *Food security Discussion paper PN—ABK - 833.*

15. UNICEF, *op.cit.*

16. Government of Uganda, (1984) *Towards a National food Strategy,* vol I and II, the Royal Tropical Institute, Amsterdam, Netherlands.

17. FAO, (1985). Report of the WCARRD Follow up UN Inter-Agency Mission to Uganda, WCARRD Mission, No 16.

18. The WCARRD mission made a serious mis-specification of a food security strategy by failing to include means to combat poverty and hence means to enhance access to food.

19. Lofchie M. (1972). 'Political and economic origins of African hunger' *Journal of Modern African Studies* vol 13, No 4.

20. Nsibambi A. 1988) 'Solving Uganda's food problem', in H.B. Hansen and M. Twaddle, *Uganda Now: Between Decay and Development*; Oxford: James Currey.

21. Most economists object to the use of food reserve stocks as being costly to maintain.

22. The 1990 report makes no reference to the 1984 report though both of them were prepared at the invitation of and for the same country, Uganda. It is true political regimes had changed but the ministry of Agriculture, whose technocrats have a duty to collate information for policy formulation was still in existence.

23. Measures to increase food supply included provision of agricultural inputs by projects such as the Agricultural Development Project, the farming systems support programmes, the South Western Agricultural rehabilitation Project, rehabilitation of the Soroti facility for manufacturing agricultural tools and equipment, the Kasese legume seed Project and the Uganda Root Crops Programme.

24. To prevent or reduce food losses and to stabilise food supply between harvest season and to counteract the impact of drought, the Ministry of Agriculture undertook measures to improve storage at house hold, regional and national levels through the food losses project and a food storage Project.

25. The consultants subscribe to the view that Uganda has no need for a national food reserve for the following reasons:
    i) Uganda has a national food surplus and will most probably continue to produce a surplus for export. Local deficits can be met from this surplus.
    ii) rainfall is relatively reliable and most areas have two crops in a yea.
    iii) Plantains /bananas/Matooke and Cassava are the main food crops. Cassava can be "stored" in the field and plantains can be harvested through out the year.
    iv) the majority of households own or have access to land and farm householders keep a significant stock till the next harvest.

26. Maxwell S. (1996). 'Food Security: A post modern Perspective,' *Food Policy,* vol 21, No 2.

27. Sen. A.K. (1981). *Poverty and Famines: An Essay on entitlement and deprivation,* Oxford: Clarendon Press.

28. FAO points out, however, that, especially in LDC's the issue of food supplies is still important because most of those people who are food-insecure live in rural areas and obtain some of their nutritional requirements directly from their own food production. Hence FAO

argues that the essence of food security is that all people at all times have access to safe and nutritious food to maintain a healthy and active life". This definition incorporates three elements of food security: Availability of food supplies, access to food by households and individuals and inter-temporal stability of food supplies.

29. Tweeten L. et al, (1992). *Food Security discussion Paper (PN-ABK-833).*
30. T.A. Nguyen, the Policy Advisor, who was the principal author of the document claims that the 'Balanced Policy Approach' is a USAID approach.
31. Desai B.M. and Mellor J.W. (1993). *Institutional finance for Agricultural Development: An analytical survey of critical issues IFPRI Food Policy Review No 1,* Zeller M. *et al,* (1997) 'Rural finance for food security for the poor;' *IFPRI Food Policy Review,* No 4.
32. The basically subsistence production is estimated to constitute 30% of Uganda's agriculture, while transitional agriculture (i.e partly for subsistence and partly for the market) constitutes 50-60 percent.
33. Poverty means unsatisfied want or deprivation.
34. I have estimated that for a five acre peasant family farm, growing one acre of coffee, one acre of bananas, 0.5 beans, cassava, Maize, Millet and groundnuts and rearing one indigenous cow, two goats and four chicken, the money capital investment is about UShs. 500,000 or US$ 500.
35. Seckler D. , *Agricultural Transformation in Africa, Winrock International* Institute for Agricultural Development.
36. Under this same value orientation, modernisation, especially commercialisation of Agriculture, calls for farm operators to know the difference between I) Farm Investment and external facilitation of public service. II) Operators decision and external advice. The farmer himself must be responsible for the investment, operations and business decisions while the responsibility of advisors or extension personnel is only technical advice/guidance.
37. Bhagavan M.R., (1990). *The technological transformation of the Third world;* London and New Jersey: Zed Books Ltd.
38. Hayami Y. and Ruttan V.W. (1985). *Agricultural development:* An international perspective, John Hopkins University Press.
39. Draft statement to the December 1998 Donors consultative Group meeting.
40. Government of Uganda: Draft statement to the December 1998 consultative meeting.
41. Current theory also makes a distinction between 'relative poverty' and 'absolute poverty'. See Bibangambah J.R., (1985). 'Approaches to the problems of rural poverty in Africa', In Kiros F.G. (ed), *Challenging rural poverty,* African world Press.
42. United Nations Report of the World Summit for Social Development in Copenhagen, April 1995.
43. A more detailed treatment of each of the poverty generating variables and each of the characteristic variables is found in Bibangambah J.R., (1985) 'Approaches to the problem of Rural poverty in Africa' in F.G. Kiros, *Challenging Rural Poverty.* Also, A. Balihuta et al, 'Development of an analytical framework for the study of poverty in Uganda' cited in UNDP, (1997). *Uganda Human Development Report,* submitted that poverty in Uganda is ultimately and jointly caused by low level of endowment, ignorance, mismanagement, inadequate technology, inefficient and unfair social institutions and shocks of various nature.
44. Rogers G.B. (1976). 'A conceptualisation of poverty in Rural India', *World Development Vol* 4 No 4.
45. World Bank, (1993) *Uganda: Growing out of Poverty* , Washington DC; World Bank (1995) Uganda *The challenge of growth and Poverty reduction,* Washington D.C.
46. Balihuta A. et al (1995/96). 'The development of an analytical Framework for the study of Poverty in Uganda,' Economic Policy Research Centre.

47. Community development resource Network (1995) (CDRN), (1995) 'Poverty in Uganda, situation, Trends and Process'.

48. Bakhit I. *et al:* (1996). *Attacking the Roots of Poverty*, Marburg consult.

49. The only sure cure for poverty is for every household to have a regular income and this, in turn, requires that every household be with something to sell on a regular basis or be with investments that are able to generate income regularly.

50. The estimated annual saving in Uganda stands at 3% GDP and this has forced the country to rely on external borrowing to meet its developmental and Investment needs.

51. Hancock G., (1989). *Lords of Poverty*, New York: The Antlantic Monthly Press.

52. Terje Tvedt, (1998). *Angels of Mercy or Development Diplomats?: NGOs and Foreign Aid,* Trenton Africa: World Press and Oxford: James Currey.

53. The author is on the Board of Directors for NSARWU.

54. Community Development Resource Network (CDRN), op.cit!

55. In Uganda, Government spends $ 3 per person on health compared to $ 8 per person on debt servicing. See Oxfam 'Debt Relief and Poverty reduction: New Hope for Uganda', by Oxfam.

56. The final plan document was published in June 1997. See Government of Uganda (1997). Poverty Eradication Action Plan, Ministry of Planning and Economic Development.

57. I am myself not convinced that a certificate of occupancy will enable the holder to get access to productive credit.

58. Earnest Eryeetey (1996) 'Rural Finance in Africa: Institutional Developments and Access for the Poor', *Annual World Bank Conference on Development Economics.*

59. Earnest Eryeetey (1996) *Ibid.*

60 Zeller .M. *et al, 'Rural Finance for Food Security for the Poor,' Food Policy Review* No. 4, International food Policy Research Institute.

61. Johnson S. and Rogally B. , (1997). *Micro finance & Poverty reduction,* Oxfam and Action AID.

62. MCcord M. (1998). 'The role of Micro Finance Institutions in reducing poverty in Uganda', *The Ugandan Banker, vol 6, No 1.*

63. Gender is said to be 'a social construct of sex roles' or a definition of the prerogatives of male & female (see Hope Mwesigye, 'Gender and Constitutionalism in Uganda'). It may also be defined as 'the state of being male or female' or as 'social relations between men and women'.

64. World commission on Environment and Development (WCED) 1987 our Common future New York, Oxford University Press The Brundtland report led among other things to the earth summit in Rio.

65. Leach M. and Mearns R. (eds) (1996). *The lie of the land: Challenging Received wisdom on the African continent*, Oxford: International Africa Institute.

66. UNCTD, (1997). *The Least Developed countries 1997 report UN*, New York and Geneva.

67. Even before early agriculture and cities emerged over 10,000 years ago, many eco systems had already been altered by hunting or human induced burning of vegetation.

68. Other assistance came from the United Nations Environmental Programme, the International union for Conservation of Nature (IUCN) and World Wildlife Fund.

8

Lessons for the future

The analytical survey shows that Africa has been searching for the material prosperity and quality of life (or standard of living) that other peoples and other continents have already attained. The study has shown that inappropriate policies distorted or dampened incentives for production, undermined prospects for higher incomes, produced and shielded inefficiency and mismanagement, failed to promote productivity, led to underperformance and failed to create capacity for long-term economic growth or sustainable economic development. In the words of UN Secretary General Kofi Annan, 'Not enough was done to create conditions for sustainable development. This is the reality of Africa's recent past. This reality must be confronted honestly and constructively by all concerned if the people of Africa are to enjoy the security and economic opportunities they seek and deserve.'[1]

According to Schultz 'a country wishing to achieve economic growth of major importance in developing countries should or must allocate effort and capital to increase the quantity of reproducible goods, improve the quality of the people as productive agents and raise the level of the productive arts'[2]. This is very pertinent to the African situation. Of particular importance is the investment in education and technical training, which are critical to the advancement of knowledge and skills and enhancement of creativeness, innovativeness and capacity building.

Talking about the importance of education, F. Herbison has stated that 'a country which is unable to develop the skills and knowledge of its people and to utilize them effectively in the national economy will be unable to develop anything else'.[3] Galbraith has articulated education's profound influence even more perceptively and concretely in the following words:

> Poverty is man's powerful and massive affliction. It is the progenitor of much further pain - from hunger and disease on to civil conflict and war .... There are two broad lines of action ... The first is to combat accommodation. It is by universal education - literacy and its employment - that individuals gain access to the world outside the culture of poverty and its controlling equilibrium. The second is to facilitate that escape ... Economic development consists in enlarging the opportunity ... to escape the equilibrium and culture of poverty.[4]

Malaysian Prime Minister Mohathir Mohammed supported this view with evidence from Asia when he submitted to the TICAD 11, in October 1998, that 'East Asia's so-called economic miracle was because the region put its development emphasis on education and worker skills rather than looking to international aid.'

Most sub-Saharan African countries are yet to attain the three essentials needed to create the necessary technological and organisational capacity for development. Firstly, the rates of domestic savings and investment (estimated at 3 percent and 10 percent of GDP respectively) are very low.[5] The South East Asian countries (the Asian tigers) have rates of investment that are over 30 percent. Secondly, illiteracy rates in Africa are very high, especially for women. Adult illiteracy in Uganda is estimated at 52 percent for the total population and 65 percent for women.[6] Thirdly, insufficient technical education has led to shortages of technicians and artisans and the continued use of rudimentary implements. Given these conditions, it is clear that two of the most important tasks facing sub-Saharan African countries in their efforts to achieve economic progress are the eradication of illiteracy and the raising of the rate of capital formation. Since advanced technologies often require large amounts of capital, the rate of investment will typically place a limit on the degree of technological progress that a country can achieve.

As one way of mobilising additional investment, African countries often turn to external borrowing. Presently, sub-Saharan Africa's external debt is estimated at US$ 235 billion while that of Uganda is estimated at US$3.6 billion.[7] In the case of Uganda, except for the infrustructual developments of the 1960s and the recovery programmes of the 1990s, there is very little to show for these external credit resources. The same is true of the domestically funded credit. Thus, although the limited availability of resources for development is an issue, what is even more critical is the failure to utilise available investment resources productively. This is clearly demonstrated by the alarming stock of non-performing loans in both commercial and development banks, and the disappointing performance of public sector enterprises.

Africa's development efforts are not only constrained by the inadequacy of investment resources but also by lack of competent and efficient management to use the resources productively. The crisis in the banks of the East African countries illuminate the same danger. This crisis is a product of governance characterised by insider lending, poor monitoring of loan accounts, under-qualified staff, little or no cashflow appraisal of loan projects, huge stocks of non-performing loans, graft and cronyism and the failure to enforce the necessary rules and regulations.

Given that, in African countries including Uganda, there are massive increases (annual growth rate 3.4 percent) in the labour force, employment creation must become an independent goal of national policy[8]. Experience shows that even if the most labour-intensive production technologies are employed, it is unlikely that agriculture will provide the rates of growth necessary to absorb all the growing labour force. Thus, in a predominantly agricultural country like Uganda, the ultimate goal of rural development strategy has to be not only agriculture-oriented, but must at the same time foster non-agricultural growth. This is what is known as agriculture-led industrialisation strategy. The promotion of industrial growth calls for, among other requirements, market expansion which can only be achieved through the creation of regional or sub-regional markets.

Coping with the effects of rising population is constrained not only by the labour absorptive capacity of the various enterprises and sectors and hence the inability to create enough jobs to match job seekers but also by a conflict of objectives or substitution effect in that the goals of employment creation and economic growth/technological progress do not invariably coincide.

The other approach to the problem of population growth is concerned with the attempt to lower the rate of population increase, usually through various family planning campaigns which are designed to reduce the birth rate. However, available knowledge suggests that birth control programmes take a long time to contain population growth to desired levels. The problems of lack of education, of expense, of inadequate or unsuitable methods and, more importantly, the social reluctance to have fewer children suggest that even for countries with full-fledged birth control programmes, the results will come slowly.

The case for industrialisation has recently been brought to the forefront again by the resurrection of the old issue of vulnerability to the world economic environment. The Asian financial crisis and political unrest have forced some opinion leaders and analysts to revisit the issue of vulnerability associated with economic openness. The crisis has been blamed on currency trading and speculation. The roots of this seem to have been a mess originating from the devaluation of currencies and share prices propelled by dollar pegs i.e. the fact that the various countries had exchange rates linked to the US dollar. Essentially, therefore, critics are blaming globalisation and what they see as evils of global markets. In the words of the Malaysian prime minister, at the Tokyo International Conference on African Development (TICAD II): 'Along with the collapsing economy have gone the political stability and social well being of the peoples of these countries. Where before there was wealth and plenty, where before there was political and social stability, we see today extreme deprivation and turmoil.'

Africa's vulnerability has roots not just in openness but in excessive dependence on primary exports. It has been observed, for instance, that although most of Africa's financial markets have escaped the turmoil caused in stock exchanges around the globe - largely because they did not have large amounts of portfolio investments from foreign investors - Asia's economic crisis will affect Africa's growth in 1998/99 by reducing the demand and hence the price of the region's key commodity exports - rubber, palm oil and timber (from Ghana) gold, diamonds (from South Africa), crude oil (from Angola, Nigeria and Gabon), copper (from Zambia), etc.

In recent years it was fashionable, especially on the part of commentators from outside Africa, to evaluate African economic performance on the basis of growth rates, without giving any consideration to the source, content, equity and sustainability of that growth. However, consensus is emerging that accelerated growth is not enough. A new view is that poverty reduction requires pro-poor growth. In the case of Africa whose population is predominantly rural and poor, pro-poor growth is that pattern of growth that would favour rural development, enhanced incomes and productivity in agriculture and the growth of labour intensive small and medium scale enterprises, ensuring the poor's participation in the production process.

Besides deficiencies in physical and technological capacities, shortcomings in organisational capacities are also prevalent. Many institutions are run with external funding, and the quality and work ethic of our human resources have been weighed and found wanting. The effectiveness of our institutions is very low because of organisational deficiencies and indiscipline.[9] The experience with the outcome of the 1981/86 stabilisation and adjustment programmes also suggests that it is capacity (technological and organisational) that is the real indicator of economic strength. GDP growth rates were positive for the period 1981-1983. But in June 1984 the economy collapsed when the flow of foreign aid ceased.

In search of development and poverty eradication, an increasing number of African countries, Uganda inclusive, are adopting a development paradigm that is based on the philosophy that productivity, competitiveness and efficiency are the keys to economic success. The words of the new Botswana president, Festus Mogae, that 'we cannot go very far unless productivity is improved throughout the economy at policy, management and operational levels' are representative of the new realisation and orientation. The improvement of productivity requires that the quality of production technologies and the quality of the environment (especially in the case of biologically-based production systems or processes) are significantly raised.[10]

To be competitive and effective contestants[11] in regional and international trade, African countries must improve the quality of their products and become cost effective producers. They must also increase their capabilities to satisfy customers' needs i.e. ensuring that goods are produced, stored, transported, delivered on time and where required[12]. There is ample evidence that Ugandan exporters have often failed to meet delivery schedules to European markets. Presently, only a limited number of African countries - Mauritius, Tunisia, Botswana, Namibia, Morocco, Egypt, South Africa and Swaziland - have a positive competitiveness index. Uganda has a negative competitiveness index of -0.16. This calls for significant improvement in labour productivity (and other inputs), infrastructural capacity – especially the progressive reduction, if not elimination of transport (road, air, rail) and utility (electricity, water) bottlenecks.

With the experiences of the World Bank and IMF- sponsored economic reforms in underdeveloped countries, I concur with Gerald Meir that:

> The criteria of efficiency still dominate the notion of an economic improvement. Distributional issues are side-stepped by the condition that a policy that leads to an improvement would allow the gainers from the policy to compensate the losers".[13]

The paradox is that Uganda has combined impressive economic growth (an average rate of 6.5 percent per annum since 1986) with poverty afflicting over 50 percent of the population. This is clear evidence that the real world aggregate growth rates do not necessarily lead to the reduction of poverty for ordinary households. This suggests that economic rationality does not absolve economic development policy makers of the responsibility to be 'trustees for the poor'. As African countries continue their search for development it needs to be stressed that besides the other required capacities, they need a capacity for lasting peace, security and stability if the search is to remain on course and end successfully.

Notes

1.   Remarks by U.N. Secretary General, Kofi Annan, before he went on his tour of a number of African countries in May 1998. They were quoted in the May 4th 1998 issue of Uganda's daily News paper - the New Vision.
2.   Schultz T.W. , (1980) "The economics of being poor", *Journal of Political economy*; vol. 88, No.4.
3.   Herbison F.H. (1973). *Human Resources as the Wealth of Nations*, Princeton University Press.
4.   Galbraith J.K. , (1979). *The Nature of Mass Poverty*, Cambridge MA: Havard University Press.
5.   Low rates of saving imply that Uganda is characterised by values and attitudes that do not favour thrift and saving. The creation of a special institution known as Uganda Investment Authority in 1991 for purposes of attracting and facilitating both foreign and local private investment is an important policy initiative in efforts to foster investment-led economic growth. The same applies to the establishment of the Private Sector Foundation in 1996 to facilitate private sector development.

6.   Uganda's newly introduced universal primary education (UPE) is responding to the need to transform the country into a more literate nation.

7.   It is reported that Uganda which in 1997 became the first candidate to the debt relief under the heavily indebted poor countries initiative (HIPC) received, in April 1998, a final approval from the IMF and World Bank to receive US$ 650 million of debt relief and U.K cancelled all Ugandan debt in December 1999.

8.   A 1997 ILO/UNDP report "Jobs for Africa: A policy framework for an Employment - intensive growth strategy" Projected that some 7.4 million New Job seekers would enter Africa's labour market in 1998 and that the numbers of unemployed would have risen to 10.4 million in 2008.

9.   We need to note here that low productivity is tied to poverty in a mutual relationship' each being both cause and effect of the other. Workers in Africa are part of the large mass of people who suffer from under nutrition, malnutrition and other serious defects in their levels of living, in particular lack of elementary health and educational standards, extremely bad housing conditions and sanitation all of which impair their willingness and ability to work and work intensively; thus holding down productivity. This implies that investment in health and education to enhance population quality and welfare would raise productivity.

10. According to World Economic Forum's Africa Competitiveness report, not only are Ugandans low productivity workers but Uganda also has, together with Zambia, the worst banks.

11. Unfortunately, the disciples of free trade do not fully practice what they preach. On one hand they are the greatest exponents of liberalisation but on the other, they are trustees for the bad rules of the game or what has been called 'unjust world economic order'. Poor nations are made to supply their raw materials cheaply where-as developed countries sell their manufactured products expensively. The US which is claimed to be the leading free market economy in the world is presenting to Africa a trade agenda expecting total compliance. A senior US official is quoted to have been puzzled over Nelson Mandela's objection to an agenda titled "African Growth and Opportunity bill" which contains a conditionality that restricts the freedom of African countries to trade with countries other than those acceptable to the US! What is puzzling about an objection to curtailment of one's freedom to trade wherever one wants? Congressman Jesse Jackson Jr has depicted it as contempt for Africa's economic self-determination.

12. The needs and wants that require to be satisfied by the marketing process are known as marketing utilities of form, time and place.

13. Meier G. 1984. *Emerging from Poverty: The economics that really matters*, Oxford University Press.

Bibliography

Abbot, J.C. and Creupeland H. C., 1966, *Agricultural Marketing Boards: Their Establishment and Operation,* Rome: FAO.

Adams, D.W., 1996, 'Rural finance in Uganda: Questions and New Options', Mimeo.

Agricultural Secretariat, Bank of Uganda, 1985, *Agricultural Price Policy - Methodologies and Issues in Price Determination,* Kampala.

Anderson, J. R. and P. L. Scandizzo, 1984, 'Food Risk and the Poor', *Food Policy,* Vol. No. 9.

Argyris, C., 1970, *Intervention Theory and Method: A behavioural Science View,* Cambridge Mass: Addison-Weley Publishing Company, Mass.

Bakhit, I. et al, 1996, *Attacking Roots of Poverty,* Marburg: Marburg Consult.

Bhaganvan, M. R, 1990, *The Technological Transformation of the Third World,* London: Zed Books Ltd.

Banugire, F.R., 1987, 'The Impact of the Economic Crisis on Fixed Income Earners.' in: Weibe, P. D. and Dodge, C. P. *Beyond Crisis: Development Issues in Uganda,* Kampala: MISR

Banugire, F.R., 1989, 'Uneven and unbalanced development: Development Strategies and Conflict', in K. Rupesinghe, *Conflict Resolution in Uganda,* London: James Currey.

Barraclough, S. et al , 1997, *Rural Development and the Environment,* Geneva: UNRISD.

Bauer, P.T., 1952, 'Fluctuations in Incomes of Primary Producers', *Economic Journal.*

Bauer, P.T., 1952, *West African Trade,* Cambridge University Press.

Bates, R.H., 1981, *Essays on the Political Economy of Rural Africa,* Cambridge University Press.

Bates, R.H., 1981, *Markets and States in Tropical Africa.* University of California Press.

Bates, R.H., 1990, 'The Political Framework for Agricultural Policy Decisions'. In C. K. Eicher and John M. Staaz: *Agricultural Development in the Third World, ,* Baltimore: John Hopkins University Press.

Bates, R.H., 1991, 'Agricultural Policy & the Study of Politics in Post-Independence Africa', In D. Rimmer (ed.) *Africa 30 Years On,* Oxford: James Currey.

Belshaw, D.G.R., 1963, 'The Level of Incentives: A Factor Limiting Agricultural Production in Uganda', *A paper presented at the Annual Conference of the Uganda Agricultural Association.*

Belshaw, D.G.R., 1968, 'Price and Marketing Policy for Uganda's export crops', East African *Journal of Rural Development ,* Vol. 1, No.2.

Belshaw, D.G.R., 1988, 'Agriculture-led recovery in post-Amin Uganda: the causes of failure and the bases for success.' in H.B. Hansen and M. Twaddle: *Uganda Now: Between Decay and Development*, Oxford: James Currey

Belshaw, D.G.R., 1996, 'Sectoral and Institutional Pitfalls for the Unwarry Macroeconomist: Agricultural and Economic Under-performance in Uganda', University of East Anglia, UK.

Bernstein, H. et al, 1992; *Rural Livelihoods: Crises and Response*, Oxford University Press.

Besley, T., 1996, 'Political Economy of Alleviating Poverty: Theory and Institutions', *World Bank Conference on Development Economics.*

Bibangambah, J.R., 1983, 'A Mischievous Attitude to African Agriculture,' *Food Policy* Vol. 8 No. 4.

Bibangambah, J.R, 1985, *'Approaches to the Problem of Rural Poverty in Africa'*, in F.G. Kiros (Ed.), *Challenging Rural Poverty*, New Jersey: Africa World Press.

Bibangambah, J.R. and Jansson B. E, 1988, 'Foundations of Agricultural Price Policy with special reference to Producer prices'. *UCA Development Paper No.3*, Kampala.

Bibangambah, J.R,, 1989, *'Agricultural Market Intervention and Pricing Policies in Africa:* The Case of Uganda', FAO Economic and Social Development Paper No 88, Rome: FAO.

Bibangambah, J.R., 1990, 'The Basic Needs Approach to the Problem of African Rural Poverty', *Eastern Africa Journal of Rural Development*, Vol. 16.

Bibangambah, J.R., 1993, 'Macro-economic constraints and the growth of the Informal Sector', in Baker J. and Pedersen P. (eds.) The *Rural-Urban Interface in Africa.* Scandinavian Institute of African Studies, Uppsala, Sweden.

Bibangambah, J.R., 1993, 'Impact of Structural Adjustment on Agricultural Producers', in J. C. Munene (ed), *Empowerment, Poverty and Structural Adjustment in Uganda*, Kampala: FES.

Bibangambah J.R., 1995, 'Towards Optimum Utilization of Credit in Uganda', *Ugandan Banker,* Vol.3 No 1.

Bibangambah, J.R., 1996, *The Marketing of Smallholder Crops in Uganda*, Kampala: Fountain Publishers.

Biggs, S. and Farrington J, 1991, *Agricultural Research and the Rural Poor: A Review of Social Science Analysis.* International Development Research Centre (IDRC), Ottawa.

Bohle, H.G., 1993, 'The Geography of Vulnerable Food Systems', in H. G. Bohle et al (eds): *Coping with Vulnerability and Criticality*, Verlag Breitenbach Publishers, Germany.

Bohman, M. and Jarvish, L.1990, 'The International Coffee Agreement: Economics of the Non-member Market,' *European Review of Agricultural Economics,* Vol. 17, N0 1.

Borlang, N. E. and Dowswell, C. R, 1995, 'Mobilizing Science and Technology to get Agriculture Moving in Africa', *Development Policy Review,* Vol 13, No.1.

Carr, S., 1982, 'The Impact of Government Intervention on Smallholder Development in North and East Uganda', ADO Occasional Paper No 5, London: Wye College.

Cleaver, M. K. and Donovan, W.G., 1995, 'Agriculture, Poverty and Policy Reform in sub-saharan Africa', *World Bank Discussion Paper* No 280, Washington D.C.

Collier, P., 1991, 'Africa's External Economic Relations, 1960-90', in D. R. Rimmer (ed), *Africa 30 Year On,* London: The Royal African Society.

Commonwealth Secretariat 1979, *The Rehabilitation of the Economy of Uganda.* London.

Desai, B. M. and Mellor, J. W., 1993, *'Institutional Finance for Agricultural Development:* An Analytical Survey of Critical Issues, *IFPRI Food Policy Review* No 1.

East African Royal Commission, 1955, Report, London: HMSO.

Eicher, C. K. and Baker D.C., 1982, *Research on Agricultural Development in sub-Saharan Africa: A Critical Survey. MSU International Development Paper No.1.*

Eicher, C. K., 1982, 'Facing Up to Africa's Food Crisis', *Foreign Affairs ,* No. 61.

Eicher, C. K. and Staaz, J.M., 1990,' *Agricultural Development in the Third World.* Baltimore: John Hopkins University Press.

Eicher, C.K., 1986, 'Transforming African Agriculture', *The Hunger Project Paper ,* No 14.

Ellis, F., 1988, 'Evolution of Price and Marketing Policy in Tanzania.' in C. Harvey (ed) *Agricultural Pricing Policy in Africa,* London: Macmillan Publishers.

Ellis, F., 1992, *Agricultural Policies in Developing Countries,* Cambridge University Press.

Eryeetey, E., 1996, 'Rural Finance in Africa: Institutional Developments and Access for the Poor', *World Bank Conference on Development Economics.*

Eshetu, C., 1990, *Food Crisis in Africa: Policy Management Issues,* New Delhi: Vikas Publishing House Pvt. Ltd.

Essang S.M., 1978 'On the Relevance of Growth Models to Rural Development'. In: J.R. Bibangambah and B. Wanji (eds): *Contemporary Problems and Issues in Rural Development,* Nkanga 10, MISR.

Eturu, L., 1986, 'Role of Central Banks in the Promotion of Investment and Financing of Agriculture, Industry and Exports', Agricultural Secretariat, Bank of Uganda.

FitzGerald, E.V.K., 1991, 'Nicaragua: Economic Crisis and Transition of the Periphery', in Dharam Ghai (ed). *The IMF and the South: The Social Impact of Crisis and Adjustment, London: Zed Books Ltd.*

Friedman, M. and Friedman R. 1980, *Free to Choose*, Harcourt Bracee Publishers.

Gariyo, Z., 1992, Appropriate Technology, productivity and employment in Agriculture in Uganda: A Case Study of Kibimba and Doho Irrigation Schemes, Rome: FAO.

Galbraith, J.K., 1979, *The Nature of Mass Poverty*, Cambridge MA: Havard University Press.

Gallup, J.L. and Jeffrey D. Sachs, 1998, '*Geography and Economic Development*', *Annual World Bank Conference on Development Economics* The World Bank, Washington DC.

Geer, T., 1971, *An Oligopoly, The World Economy and Stabilisation Schemes*, New York, Dunellan Press.

Goldsmith, A., 1995, 'The State, the Market and Economic Development: A Second Look at Adam Smith in Theory and Practice', *Development and Change,* Vol 26, No 4.

Gilbert, C.L., 1996, 'International Commodity Agreement : An Obituary', *World Development*, Vol 24 No.1.

Government of Uganda 1967, Report of the Committee of Inquiry into the Coffee Industry. Entebbe: Government Printer.

Government of Uganda 1967, *Report of the Committee of Inquiry into the Cotton Industry*, Entebbe: government Printer.

Government of Uganda 1984, *Towards a National Food Strategy Vol 1 and II Report by the Royal Tropical Institute, Amsterdam, Netherlands.*

Government of Uganda 1987, *Report of World Bank Agricultural Task Force,* Kampala: MPED.

Government of Uganda 1992, *The Way Forward II: Medium Term Sectoral Strategy 1991 - 1995*, Kampala: MPED.

Government of Uganda 1996, *National Food Strategy*, Kampala: MPED.

Government of Uganda 1997, *Poverty Eradication Action Plan*, Kampala: MPED.

Gwyer, G.D., 1973, 'East Africa and Three International Commodity Agreements: The Lesson of Experience', in V. F. Amann (ed): *Agricultural Policy Issues in East Africa,* Kampala: Makerere University.

Hansen, H. B. and Twaddle, M., (eds), 1998, *Developing Uganda*, Kampala: Fountain Publishers and Oxford: James Currey.

Haring, J. E. et al, 1969: 'Marketing Boards and Price Funds in Uganda 1950-1960', *Journal of Agricultural Economics.*, Vol. 20, No. 3.

Hayami, Y. and Ruttan, V.W., 1972, 'Strategies for Agricultural Development', *Food Research Institute Studies*, No II.

Hayami, Y. and Ruttan, V.W., 1985, *Agricultural Development: An International Perspective*, Baltimore: Johns Hopkins University Press.

Helleiner, G. K., 1964, 'The Fiscal Role of Marketing Boards in Nigeria's Economic Development'. *Economic Journal*, Vol. 7.

Herbison, F.H., 1973, *Human Resources as the Wealth of Nations*, Princeton University Press.

Hinderink, J. and Sterkenburg, 1987, *Agricultural Commercialization and Government Policy in Africa.*, London: KPI Limited.

Idachaba F.S., 1973, 'Marketing Board Crop Taxation and Input Subsidies: A second-best Approach'. *Nigerian Journal of Economic and Social Studies* Vol. 15.

Jamal, V., 1987, 'Ugandan Economic Crisis: Dimensions and Cure.' In: P.D. Wiebe and C.P. Dodge: *Beyond Crisis: Development Issues in Uganda,* Kampala: MISR.

Jamal, V., 1991, 'The Agrarian Context of the Ugandan Crisis.' in H.B. Hansen and M. Twaddle (eds.): *Changing Uganda*: London: James Currey and Kampala: Fountain Publishers.

Johnson, S. and Rogally, B., 1997, *Micro-finance and Poverty Reduction*, Oxfam and Action Aid.

Jones, S., 1991, 'The Road to Privatization', *Finance and Development*, Vol. 28 No.1.

Kaberuka, W., *1990, The Political Economy of Uganda 1890 - 1971, New York, Vintage Press.*

Kyamuresire, A., 1988, *A History of the Uganda Co-operative Movement 1913 - 1988*, Kampala: UCA.

Kox, H.L.M, 1991, 'Integration of Environmental Externalities in International Commodity Agreements', *World Development,* Vol.19, No.8.

Kox, H.L.M., 1993, 'International Agreements to deal with Environmental Externalities of Primary Commodity Exports'. Paper prepared for the *International Conference on striking a Green Deal: Europe's Role in Environment and South-North Trade Relations,* Brussels: The European Parliament.

Laker-Ojok, R., 1996, 'Managing Input Supplies for Small Farmers in Uganda in P. L. Langseth et al (eds.): *Uganda Landmarks in Rebuilding a Nation*, Kampala: Fountain Publishers.

Lele, Uma and Christiansen R.E. 1989, 'Markets, Marketing Boards and Co-operatives in Africa; Issues in Adjustment Policy', *MADIA Discussion Paper II*, Washington DC: The World Bank.

Mkandawire, T., 1985, 'Agricultural Economics Training and Research in Africa: A Perspective from ZIDS', A paper presented at a *conference on Agricultural Economics, Training and Research in Africa*, Harare, Zimbabwe.

Mamdani, M., 1982, '*Karamoja:* Colonial Roots of Famine', *Review of African Political Economy*, No. 25.

Maxwell, S., 1996, 'Food Security: A Post-modern Perspective', *Food Policy,* Vol. 21, No. 2.

Meier, G. M 1984, *Emerging from Poverty: The Economics that Really Matters.* Oxford University Press.

Migot-Adhola, S.E. and Bruce, J. W., 1994, *Searching for Land Tenure Security in Africa,* Iowa: Kendall Publishing Co.

Monke, E. A. and Pearson S.R., 1989, *The Policy Analysis Matrix for Agricultural Development.*, Cornell University Press.

Morris, H. F. and Read, J. S, 1966, Uganda: *The Development of its Laws and Constitution,* London: Stevens and Sons.

Mugaju, J. B., 1990, Development Planning versus Economic Performance in Uganda, 1961-1971, *TransAfrican Journal of History,* vol. 19.

Mukwaya, A B., 1953, *Land Tenure in Buganda*, Eagle Press.

Myrdal, G., 1970, *The Challenge of World Poverty:* A World Anti-poverty Programme, Penguin Press.

Nguyen, T.A., 1996, Food Security and Exports, EPAU Policy Paper No. 4.

Nsereko, J., 1995, 'Problems of Non-performing Advances', *The Ugandan Banker,* Vol. 3 No. 1.

Nsibambi, A., 1988, 'Solving Uganda's Food Problem', in H. B. Hansen and M. Twaddle, *Uganda Now: Between Decay and Development,* London: James Currey.

Nsibambi, A. (ed) 1998, *Decentralisation and Civil Society in Uganda: The Quest for Good Governance,* Kampala: Fountain Publishers.

Obol-Ochola, J., 1969, *Land Reform in East Africa*, Kampala: MOF.

Ochieng, E. O. 1997, *Economic Stabilization and Adjustment Programmes in Uganda* 1981 - 1995, Kampala: FES.

Odwongo, W., 1961, 'Problems of Developing Rural Financial Markets in Uganda', *The Ugandan Banker,* Vol 4. No.1.

Opio-Odongo, J., 1988, 'Uganda's Co-operative Movement at Seventy-Five'. *UCA Development Paper No. 5.*

Opio-Odongo, J., 1992, *Designs on the Land*, Nairobi: Acts Press.

Opio-Odongo, J., 1987, 'Facing the Food Crisis in Sub-Saharan Africa', *Journal of Agricultural Administration,* No. 27.

Radke, D., 1979, 'Existing and Possible Multilateral Commodity Agreements: A Survey', *In Economics* Vol. 19.

Ranis, G., 1995, 'Another Look at the East Asian Miracle', *The World Bank Economic Review*, Vol. 9 No.3.

Rodgers, G. B., 1976, 'A Conceptualization of Poverty in Rural India', *World Development* Vol. 4, No. 4.

Sapru, R.K., 1994, *Public Policy: Formulation, Implementation and Evaluation*, New Delhi: Sterling Publishers.

Seckler, D., 1993, *Agricultural Transformation in Africa*, Winrock Institute for Agricultural Development.

Sen, A. K., 1981, *Poverty and Famines: An Essay on entitlement and Deprivation*, Oxford: Clarendon Press.

Shultze, T.W., 1980, 'The Economics of Being Poor', *Journal of Political Economy*, vol/ 88, No. 4.

Streeten, P., 1987, *'What Price Food?': Agricultural Price Policies in Developing Countries*, London: Macmillan Press.

Swift, J., 1990, *Major Issues in African Pastoral Rehabilitation and Development*, IDS, University of Sussex.

Timmer, C. P., 1986, *Getting the Prices Right: The Scope and Limits of Agricultural Price Policy*. Cornell University Press.

Tweeten, L., 1992, 'Food Security': *Discussion Paper PN-ABK-833*.

Thim, H. U et al (eds.), 1993, *Regional Food Security and Rural Infrastructure*, International Symposium, Giessen, Germany.

UNCTAD, 1997, *The Least Developed Countries Report*, New York and Geneva: UN.

UNDP 1997: *Uganda Human Development Report*, Kampala.

UNDP 1998: *Uganda Human Development Report*, Kampala.

Van der Laan, H. L. and W. T. M. Vvan Haaren, 1990, *African Marketing Boards under Structural Adjustment: The Experience of Sub-Saharan Africa during the 1980s*, Working Paper No.13 (African Studies Center, Leiden.

Wade, R., 1990, *Governing the Market: Economic Theory and the Role of Government in East Asian Industrialization*, Princeton University Press.

Werhane, P., 1991, *Adam Smith and his Legacy for Modern Capitalism*, Oxford University, Press.

White, M., 1990, 'The Process of Survival in South-Eastern Uganda', in M. Bovin: *Adaptive Strategies in African Arid Lands*, SIAS, Uppsala, Sweden.

World Bank, 1986, *Poverty and Hunger: Issues and Options for Food Security in Developing Countries*, Washington DC: World Bank.

World Bank, 1993, *The East Asian Miracle: Economic Growth ad Public Policy*, Oxford University Press.

World Bank, 1993, *Uganda: Growing out of Poverty: A Country Study*, Washington DC.

World Bank, 1995, *Uganda: The Challenge of Growth and Poverty Reduction,* Washington DC.

World Commission on Environment and Development (WCED) 1987, *Our Common Future,* New York: Oxford University Press.

Yoshida, M., 1984, *Agricultural Marketing Intervention in East Africa,* Institute of Developing Economies, Tokyo, Japan.

Zeller, M. et al, 1997, 'Rural Finance for Food Security for the Poor,' IFPRI, *Food Policy Review* No 4.

Index

1975 Land Reform Decree 101

Action Fund (PAF) 170
Advisory and promotion board 12
Agricultural
    market prices 43–63
    co-operatives 20
    commodity markets 10, 21
    commodity pricing 60
    economy 111
    exports 16, 36, 44, 57, 108,
        139, 145, 152
    extension programme 152
    implements 64, 71, 164
    inputs 50, 63, 65, 66, 67, 68,
        69, 70, 71, 73, 75, 92,
        112, 131, 141, 156, 184
    market prices 43
    marketing boards 10, 18, 22,
        39, 193 *See also* parastals
    modernisation 37, 149, 151,
        152, 156, 157
    output 77, 146
    policies 61, 105, 184, 195
    policy committee (APC) 122
    prices 6, 43
    research 4, 5, 8, 70, 122, 134, 146,
        155, 194
    sector 6, 18, 41, 43, 44, 50, 75,
        122, 132, 151, 152, 153,
        154, 156, 157, 179
    technology 115, 146, 150
Agro-chemicals 63, 74

Bank of Uganda (BOU) 72, 79
British American Tobacco Company
    (BAT) 73
Buganda Agreement of 1900 99
Capitalist 7, 17, 111
Co-operative
    Bank 82, 91, 177
    credit scheme 82, 86, 164, 165
    unions 65, 73, 79, 80, 81,
        122, 123, 126, 134

Coffee
    agreement 28, 29, 30, 31, 34,
        41, 195
    exports 20, 31, 130
    marketing board 11, 15, 19, 20, 47
    markets 30, 31
colonial
    era 108, 181
    policy 116
commodity markets 5, 10, 21, 27,
        34, 35, 40, 41, 50, 91, 99
Cotton Development Organisation
    (CDO) 126
Credit
    institutions 5, 80, 175
crown land 93, 95, 99
Crown Lands Ordinance 99

Dairy Corporation 21, 128
Decentralisation 152, 154, 167, 168,
        198
Domestic economy 22, 23

Economic
    development 1, 3, 4, 7, 9,
        18, 37, 75, 139, 144, 149, 155,
        161, 172, 182, 186, 187, 191, 196
    growth 7, 39, 81, 108, 122, 128,
        129, 144, 168, 169, 187,
        189, 191, 199
    planning 3
    policy 8, 101, 161, 185
    recovery 92, 121, 129
    recovery programme 121
    reforms 10, 27, 88, 91, 121,
        128, 182, 191
Entandikwa 165
Environmental
    degradation 35, 158, 180, 181
    issues 35, 180
    protection 34, 144, 166, 181
ex-colonial 1
Export
    Policy Analysis Unit (EPAU) 149
    Traditional crops 51, 111

Farm demonstration 141
Finance
    institutions 79, 87, 155, 174, 175,
        176, 177, 178, 186
    markets 76, 108, 109, 174, 175,
        189, 198
    system 83, 107, 175, 176
Fiscal policy 4, 92
Food crop 17, 141, 146
    marketing 17
    production 146
Food
    insecurity 131, 133, 135, 136,
        144, 145, 146, 148, 152
    policy 137, 139, 143, 146, 145,
        175, 183, 184, 185, 186,
        193, 194, 195, 198, 200
    production 43, 63, 113, 135,
        136, 137, 139, 141, 145,
        152, 179, 183, 184
    reserves 144
    security 6, 7, 134, 135, 136, 137,
        139, 142, 143, 145, 146, 169,
        179, 183, 184, 185, 186,
        198, 199, 200
Food strategy report 142.
foreign exchange 4, 13, 29, 50,
        60, 61, 65, 91, 111, 112,
        116, 120, 121, 122, 127,
        128, 129, 130, 141, 147
    markets 91
    rate 60, 121, 129
free market system 19, 44, 144
freehold tenure 94, 103, 104

Gross Domestic Product (GDP) 37,
        38, 76, 77, 81, 107, 116,
        129, 130, 161, 186, 188, 190
Government Intervention
    factor markets 63
    foreign exchange 91
Gross National Product (GNP) 37

IMF/World Bank 120, 121
Import substitution 42, 111
incentive policy package 139
Income
    distribution 6, 18
    inequalities 7

Industrial
    economies 1
    production 37, 130
    revolution 1, 37
industrialisation policy 106
inflation 43, 83, 84, 86, 89, 92,
        113, 116, 119, 120, 129, 130
institutional reform 122, 152
International Coffee Organisation 31
International Commodity Agreement
        (ICA) 196

labour
    market 3, 192
    supply 3
Land
    boards 97, 99, 103
    fund 103, 104, 173
    ownership 93, 109, 179
    reform 7, 99, 100, 101, 102, 103,
        104, 109, 110, 155, 198
    registration 100, 101, 103, 104,
        109
    tenure 90, 93, 94, 96, 97, 98,
        99, 101, 102, 103, 104,
        109, 173, 181, 198
    use 105
leasehold 99, 100-104
Liberalisation 11, 23, 24, 35, 67, 68,
        92, 103, 121, 122, 123, 124,
        126-128, 130, 133, 134, 145,
        155, 156, 174, 192
Lint Marketing Board 11, 15, 20, 134
Loan
    appraisal 87, 109
    recovery 81, 83, 87, 89, 90, 174

Mailo land 94, 99, 102, 103, 109
Market
    controls 7
    economy 22, 192
    information 8, 74, 141
    prices 6, 32, 35, 43,
        44, 57, 59, 126
    marketing boards 10-21, 23, 24, 26,
        34, 36, 37, 39, 40, 47, 80,
        81, 108, 111, 112, 122 134,
        193, 197, 199. *See also*
        marketing boards

Modernisation of Agriculture 149, 152-157. *See also* agricultural modernisation

National Agricultural Research Organisation (NARO) 146
National Food Strategy 134, 137, 139, 140, 143, 145, 184, 196. *See also* food security
Nationalisation 113
Non-Performing Assets Recovery Trust (NPART) 91

OAU 117
Ox-ploughing 64

parastatal
    bodies 4
    marketing boards 10, 122
Peasant agriculture 148, 149, 150
Per capita
    consumption 1
    income 136, 140
Poverty
    Action Fund (PAF) 170
    alleviation 145, 166
    eradication Action Plan (PEAP) 168
    reduction 134, 144, 145, 160, 167, 170, 175, 176, 185, 186, 197, 190, 200
Price
    interventions 19
    management 53
    policy 43, 44, 61, 193, 194, 199
    stabilisation boards 12, 13
Pricing policies 8, 40, 47, 61, 53, 194
Private enterprise 7, 19, 20, 116, 144
Privatisation 67, 79, 81, 122, 128, 156
Produce Marketing Board (PMB) 21
Producer prices 6, 13, 18, 44, 46, 47, 50, 51, 53, 57-60, 113, 119, 126
Public
    Land 99, 100
    Lands Act 99
    Sector 5, 6, 8, 10, 22, 116, 152, 154, 174, 188

Quota allocation 31, 32

Regulatory boards 12
Rural agricultural communities 149
Rural
    banks 5
    development 9, 39, 139, 160, 169, 174, 177, 180, 189, 190, 193, 194, 195
    economy 173
    financial institutions 155, 174, 177
    poverty 18, 133, 140, 158, 160, 162, 163, 173, 185, 194
Rural Farmers Scheme 71, 86. *See also* UCB

sectoral policies 43
small farmer production 140
stabilisation
    fund 22
Statutory marketing boards 21. *See also* marketing boards
structural
    adjustment 22-24, 27, 39, 81, 92, 106, 116, 121, 122, 129, 130, 133-134, 163, 194, 199
    approach 160
Structuralist view 19
subsidy policies 5
subsistence
    agriculture 48, 50, 115, 152, 161
    economies 22
    producers 148

taxation policy 86
technological revolution 1
technologies 5, 35, 63, 90, 108, 118, 132, 145, 146, 149, 150, 151, 162-163, 167, 181, 188, 189, 190
terms of trade 35, 43, 44, 62, 106, 107, 112, 121
Tractor Hire Service (THS) 41, 64
trade agreements 36

UCB 71, 72, 75, 77, 79, 80,
    82, 85, 86, 91, 174
Uganda Central Co-operative Union
    (UCCU) 65
Uganda Coffee Development Authority
    (UCDA) 134
Uganda Development Bank (UDB) 81
Uganda National Farmers Association
    (UNFA) 146
Uganda National Plan of Action for
    Nutrition (UNPAN) 143

Uganda Seed Project 66
Uganda Tea Authority 11, 21, 127
Uganda Tea Growers Cooperation 11
UNICEF 38, 106, 107, 110, 184
Urbanisation 106

World Bank/IMF
    Conditionalities 120
    structural adjustment 22, 135 *See also*
        Structural Adjustment

www.ingramcontent.com/pod-product-compliance
Lightning Source LLC
Chambersburg PA
CBHW072123020426
42334CB00018B/1687